D0025278

THE AWNTYRS OFF ARTHURE

AT THE TERNE WATHELYNE

In the tyme of Arthur an aunter by'tydde
By þe turne Wathelau as þe boke telles
Whan he to Carlele was comen and conqueror kydde
With Dukes and duſſiperes þat w· þe dere dwelles
To hunte at þe herdes þat longe had ben hydde
In a day þei hem dight to þe depe delles
To fall of þe femailes in foreſt and frydde
Fayre by þe firmyſthamis in frithes and felles
Thus to ride arn þei went þe wlonkeſt in wedes
  Bothe þe kyng and þe quene
  And al þe doughti by dene ——— Dame Gaynuõ he ledes
  By Galwayn gayeſt on grene
¶ Thus ſ Galwayn þe may Gaynuõ he ledes
In a gleterand gide þat gleiued full gay
With riche ribaynes ridſſet· ho ſo ƺ ight redes
Rayled with rybees of ƺ iaſſ aray
her hode of a heƺde hulve· þˢ herˢ hede hedes
Of pillõ of paltwejſ of peire to pay
Schurde in a ſhort cloke þat þe rapne ſkedes
Set ouey with ſaffꝭes ſepely to ſay
With ſaffres ſ̃ ſeladpues· ſet by þe ſides———
hete ſadel ſette of þat ilke ———
Eande with ſambutes of ſilke——— Faili·ſhe glides——
In a mule as þe mylke———
¶ Al in gleterand golde gayly ho glides
þe gattes with ſ Galwayn bi þe grene welle
And þat biƺ ne on his blouke with þe quene bides
þat borne was in Bortopiue by boke and by belle
he ladde þat lady ſo longe by þe ſalbe ſides
Vnder a lorꝛe þer light leƺe by a felle

The Awntyrs off Arthure
at the Terne Wathelyne

A Critical Edition

ROBERT J. GATES

UNIVERSITY OF PENNSYLVANIA PRESS
PHILADELPHIA

Publication of this book has been made possible by a grant from the Haney Foundation of the University of Pennsylvania

Library of Congress Catalog Card Number: 69–16539

Acknowledgments. I am grateful to the following for permission to quote copyrighted material: The University of California Press, for permission to quote from William Matthews' *The Tragedy of Arthur,* 1960; Wayne State University Press, for permission to quote from Thomas C. Rumble's edition of *The Breton Lays in Middle English,* 1965; The Athlone Press of the University of London, for permission to quote from George Kane's edition of *Piers Plowman: The A Version,* 1960; the Council of the Early English Text Society, for permission to quote from L. F. Casson's edition of *The Romance of Sir Degrevant,* 1949. Thanks are also due to the Dean and Chapter of Lincoln, and to the Bodleian, Lambeth, and Bodmer libraries for permission to use manuscripts in their collections.

SBN: 8122–7587–X
Printed in the United States of America

PREFACE

The last published edition of *The Awntyrs off Arthure* appeared in the late nineteenth century, before the discovery of the Lambeth MS. My purpose in preparing this edition has been to collate all four MSS of the poem and to present for the first time a text which makes full use of the information obtained from such a study. The results are presented in the form of a copy-text edition of the Douce MS emended with readings from the Thornton, Ireland, and Lambeth MSS, with a record of all variant readings.

The exposition of editorial methods and the citing of variants are somewhat fuller than that of most recent editions of medieval texts. This is necessary, in part, to prove the validity of conflation, properly used, as a method of editing, and also to show how the MSS of *The Awntyrs* bear out completely the conclusions about scribal practices which George Kane adduces from his study of the MSS of *Piers Plowman*. My aim throughout has been to provide an accurate and useful text of the poem, and the supplementary material is oriented, as far as possible, to this end.

I owe a great debt to all previous editors and students of the poem, beyond what could be acknowledged in the notes. I am very thankful for more immediate help and encouragement to Professor John McLaughlin, who directed the preparation of the edition in its original form as a dissertation; to the other members of my committee, Professors John McGalliard, Robert Howren, Donald Sutherland, and Stavros Deligiorgis; to the Graduate College of the University of Iowa for a fellowship which allowed me to devote a year to this work; to Professor Paul Burtness, who was kind enough to lend me his copies of the Thornton and Ireland MSS and whose study of the language of the poem has been very useful; and finally and most importantly to my wife and children for alternately putting up with and encouraging me as the need arose.

R. J. G.

CONTENTS

LIST OF ABBREVIATIONS

BROWN AND
ROBBINS: *Carleton Brown and Rossell Hope Robbins,*
                 The Index of Middle English Verse, *New*
                 York, 1943.

D: *Douce MS.*

EETS(ES):   *Early English Text Society (Extra Series).*

I: *Ireland MS.*

L: *Lambeth MS.*

LSE: Leeds Studies in English and Kindred Lan-
                 guages.

ME: *Middle English.*

MED: *Hans Kurath, Sherman F. Kuhn et al., eds.,*
                 Middle English Dictionary, *Ann Arbor,*
                 1952–.

MP: Modern Philology.

OE: *Old English.*

OED: *James H. Murray et al., eds.,* The Oxford
                 English Dictionary, *Oxford, 1933.*

PMLA: Publications of The Modern Language As-
                 sociation.

RES: The Review of English Studies.

STS: *Scottish Text Society.*

T: *Thornton MS.*

WELLS: *J. E. Wells,* A Manual of the Writings in
                 Middle English 1050–1400, *New Haven,*
                 Conn., 1916 (with nine supplements to
                 1945).

INTRODUCTION

✤✤✤✤

INTRODUCTION

PART I

The Awntyrs off Arthure at the Terne Wathelyne is an anonymous ME poem of the late fourteenth century which survives in four MSS. A product of the alliterative "revival" of the North and the West Midlands, it shares a unique combination of alliteration, rhyme, and thirteen-line stanza form with a small group of poems, mainly from the North. The stanza consists of nine long alliterative lines rhyming abababababc and a "wheel" of four shorter lines (two or three main stresses) rhyming dddc. *The Awntyrs, Golagros and Gawane, The Buke of the Howlat,* and *Rauf Coilʒear* have this form, while *The Pistill of Susan* and *The Quatrefoil of Love* differ only in having a "bob" of two syllables for the ninth line. The "bob and wheel" also appears in *Sir Gawain and the Green Knight,* marking, as J. P. Oakden says, "the most interesting point of contact between the two 'revivals,' " that of the North and that of the West Midlands.[1]

Two features which add to the formal complexity of *The Awntyrs* are consecutive alliteration and stanza-linking. Over half of the fifty-five stanzas in the poem begin with two lines which alliterate on the same sound, and there are many instances within the stanza of groups

[1] *Alliterative Poetry in Middle English:* I. *The Dialectal and Metrical Survey,* Manchester, 1930, p. 218. Oakden also lists other alliterative poems which share some of these features, pp. 217–219.

of two, three, and four lines with the same alliteration. The linking of one stanza to another by repetition of a word or phrase (also called enchaining, *concatenatio,* iteration, or *anadiplosis*) is not an unknown device in Middle English, occurring in five other romances.[2] However, *The Awntyrs* is unique in also having interior linking between the eighth and ninth lines of each stanza. Linking is sometimes absent between stanzas, and, more frequently, within the stanza, particularly in the second half of the poem.[3] However, some of the links which are not present in one MS or another can be restored by collating all four MSS. *The Awntyrs* has one further formal characteristic—it begins and ends with the same words. A. C. L. Brown has suggested that both this feature and linking are due to "a possible influence of Irish and Welsh verse upon English alliterative poetry of the Welsh marches." [4]

The Awntyrs off Arthure, in spite of its title (which is found only in T and was probably taken from the first two lines by a scribe), contains two episodes in which Gawain plays an important role. In the first episode, while Arthur

---

[2] *Sir Perceval of Galles, Sir Degrevant, The Avowynge of Arthur, Sir Tristrem,* and *Thomas of Erceldoune.* Margaret P. Medary, "Stanza-Linking in Middle English Verse," *Romanic Review,* VII (1916), 251.

[3] The number of times linking occurs depends to some extent on what departures we will accept from the normal use of a repeated word or phrase. Miss Medary, in her article noted above, attempts to show by a study of *Sir Perceval* that linking "by thought" (p. 249), by partial similarities between distinct words ("hare" with "Hardely," p. 252), or by pronouns and prepositions was felt to be adequate. Her examples in most cases are unconvincing.

[4] "On the Origin of Stanza-Linking in English Alliterative Verse," *Romanic Review,* VII (1916), 275. See also J. S. P. Tatlock, "Dante's Terza Rima," *PMLA,* LI (1936), 895–903.

and his court are out hunting deer, Gawain and Queen Guenevere go off by themselves under a laurel tree. Accompanied by a sudden storm, the ghost of Guenevere's mother appears, black from the torments of hell, and warns her daughter about pride and the sins of the flesh. She asks Guenevere to have a "trental" of thirty masses said for her soul, and prophesies to Gawain the future victory of Arthur over the Romans and the eventual destruction of the Round Table by Modred. After the ghost departs, the court goes to "Rondoles halle" for supper, where the second episode takes place.

In the midst of the feast a lovely lady enters, leading a knight. The knight, Sir Galeron of Galloway, claims that Arthur has unjustly taken his lands and given them to Gawain. Gawain offers to defend the honor of the Round Table and a combat is set for the next day. During the battle both knights fight fiercely until Galeron receives a severe wound. His lady screams at the sight of his blood and, at her request, Guenevere has Arthur stop the fight. Galeron, realizing that he has been defeated, yields his claim, but the king restores his lands and gives Gawain other properties in place of them. Galeron returns with Arthur to Carlisle where he marries the lady and is made a knight of the Round Table. The poem ends with Guenevere sending word throughout England to have masses said for her mother's soul.

The two moral dilemmas raised in the first part of the poem, the soul in torment and the injustices of Arthur and his knights, are resolved in the conclusion. Guenevere undertakes to lessen her mother's suffering by prayer and devotion, and the honor of the Round Table is upheld by the generous treatment of Sir Galeron.

1. MANUSCRIPTS

D MS Douce 324   Bodleian Library[5]

This is a short folio manuscript in paper, containing only *The Awntyrs*. It consists of twelve leaves, ruled with a plummet, which measure approximately 11⅝ by 8 inches. There are thirty lines to a page and "at the bottom of each leaf is a series of signatures in red, beginning with a.i., and ending with b.iii." [6]

The Awntyrs begins without a title on f.1a and ends on f.11b, the last leaf being ruled but blank. It is in a clear fifteenth-century book hand and the only punctuation is an infrequent full stop in the middle of the line. The beginning of each stanza is marked by a paragraph symbol (¶), and there are large ornamented capitals at ll. 1 (stanza 1), 339 (stanza 27), and 508 (stanza 40). At the bottom of f.8b appears the catchword *he folowed*. D is the most complete of the four MSS, lacking only six lines.[7]

In his edition of the poem, Madden dates the MS in the latter half of the fifteenth century: "The age of the [Douce] MS is assigned by Pinkerton and Laing to the reign of Henry the Sixth, but I do not think it can claim a higher antiquity than the period of his successor, or about the years 1460–1480" (p. 327). The *MED* gives

[5] See *Catalogue of the Printed Books and Manuscripts bequethed by Francis Douce, Esq. to the Bodleian Library,* Oxford, 1840, II, 57; also Falconer Madan, *A Summary Catalogue of Western Manuscripts in the Bodleian Library at Oxford,* Oxford, 1897, IV, 595; Sir Frederic Madden, *Syr Gawayne,* London, 1839, p. lviii.

[6] Madden, p. lviii. These are not all apparent in my microfilm copy of the manuscript. Perhaps it has been cut.

[7] In all references to missing lines I have included l. 48, which is lacking in all four MSS.

the date as "a. 1450." This MS was bequeathed to the Bodleian by Francis Douce at his death in 1834.[8]

The dialect of D is predominantly North Midland, though it shares with the other three manuscripts many Northern features, especially in the rhymes. Both S. O. Andrew[9] and A. G. Hooper[10] call D a West Midland copy, but, as can be seen below, the evidence is ambiguous (see especially the form of the 3rd person plural pronoun). The significant features of spelling and morphology which supply evidence for determining the dialect of D are the following:[11]

a) OE ā is spelled *o* except in rhymes and in words appearing elsewhere in rhyme:

grones	632
holy	177, 254
home	412
stone	580
lorde	36, 272, etc.
rose (v.)	317

b) OE ă before a nasal is usually spelled *o* (West Midland):

nome	416
honde	235

---

[8] Douce has appended a note to the manuscript mentioning a few earlier owners (see Madan, p. 595). He also made a copy of the manuscript, which is No. 21883 in Madan, p. 589.

[9] "Huchoun's Works," *RES,* V (1929), 12–21.

[10] " 'The Awntyrs off Arthure': Dialect and Authorship," *LSE,* IV (1935), 62–74.

[11] The characteristics and examples are representative only; counter-examples are numerous due to scribal mixture. For a thorough study of all four manuscripts, on which this summary is partly based, see Paul Burtness, *A Language Study of "The Awntyrs off Arthure at the Terne Wathelyn,"* Unpub. dissertation, University of Chicago, 1953.

bronde 122, 528, etc.
longe (adv.) 5, 31
mone 348, 352 (cf. mane, 206, 266, 643)

c) OE y̆ and e̯o almost exclusively have spellings which indicate unrounding:

(y̆)	syne	134
	hilles	420
	kyne	139
	king	62, 77, etc.
	fille (n.)	411, 574
(ȳ)	hide (n.)	108
	pride	239
	whi	136
(e̯o)	worthi	159
	world	189, 215, etc.
(ēo)	depe	6
	fendes	186
	prestes	705

d) OE ō has the (non-Northern) spelling o:
rode (n.) 317 (T rude)
good 93, 458, etc. (T gude)
hode 18 (T hude)
boke 2, 30 (T buke)

e) OE hw is spelled wh:
while 266
whele (n.) 266
whene 175

f) Forms of the verb 'shall' are always spelled with sh (11, 73, 102, 135, etc.).

g) Unstressed vowels in inflexional suffixes are spelled with *e,* occasionally *i* or *y* (cf. MS I below, with West Midland *u*):

(genitives)	Arthures	309
	kinges	262
	lyues	702
	erlis	482
(plurals)	dukes	4
	saffres	21
	erles	33
	holtes	43
(comparatives)	lenger	314
	gretter	147
	radder	161
(weak preterites)	greued	515
	serued	452
	fondred	542
	iusted	502
(weak past participles)	warned	194
	browed	385
	stuffed	391
(3rd pers. sing.)	telles	2
	dwelles	4
	ledes	14
	glides	27

h) Weak preterites and past participles end in a voiced stop (see above for examples).

i) The 3rd person singular of the present indicative ends in a sibilant (see above for examples).

j) The plural present indicative ends in *-e* or *-ene:*

dare	52
lighte	32
semble	66
folowene	47
durkene	52
suwene	67

k) The present participle always ends in *-and:*

sneterand	82
gleterand	15, 27, 496
ledand	344

l) The third person plural pronoun is *hem* (objective, ll. 6, 34, 35, etc.) and *here* (possessive, ll. 44, 45, 240, etc.) or *hour* (458, 488).

m) The usual form of the feminine personal pronoun is *ho* (ll. 27, 70, 118, etc.) but *she* also occurs (ll. 26, 333).

T Thornton MS [12]   Lincoln Cathedral Library 91

This is a large folio volume in paper of 314 leaves measuring approximately 11½ by 8¼ inches. It is imperfect at the beginning and end, leaves are missing in other places, and many leaves are damaged. *The Awntyrs* begins with the title "Here By gynnes The Awn*e*tyrs off Arthure at The Terne Wathelyn*e*" on f.154a and ends on f.161a. It is written 35–41 lines to the page in a "small and occasionally negligent hand." [13] There are large illu-

---

[12] See James O. Halliwell, *The Thornton Romances,* London, 1844, pp. xxv–xxxvi; also Madden, pp. l–lviii. The manuscript also contains the alliterative *Morte Arthure,* the romances of *Octavyane, Syr Ysambrace,* and *Syr Degrevante,* and various tales, legends and prayers in English and Latin.

[13] Madden, p. 1. It is a cursive rather than book hand.

minated capitals at ll. 1 (stanza 1) and 378 (stanza 30).
The four short lines which make up the wheel are written
as two through stanza 14 and separately thereafter. T is
the least complete of the four manuscripts, lacking some
107 lines and parts of at least 18 others. (A leaf is missing
between ff.159 and 160.)

The Thornton manuscript has been dated by Madden
and others around 1430–1440. Margaret S. Ogden, in
her study of one of the prose pieces of the manuscript,
says: "The Lincoln MS. seems to have been written some
time after 1422, the date assigned to a holy woman's
visions of purgatory in one of the prose pieces, and before 1453–1454, the date given in the note recording the
birth of Robert Thornton at Ryedale." [14] The manuscript
was probably in the possession of the Thornton family
until it was given to Lincoln Cathedral Library, perhaps
as late as the nineteenth century (Ogden, p. x).

T is a Northern copy with some Midland features. The
significant dialect characteristics which differ from those
of D are:

a) OE ā is usually spelled *a,* but there are some instances, even in rhyme, of *o:*

stane	109
daa	54 ('doe')
sare	633
mare	199, 256 (cf. more 100)
halye	177 (cf. holy 254)
hame	412 (cf. home 292)

---

[14] *The "Liber de Diversis Medicinis,"* EETS 207, London, 1938, pp.
x–xi. Miss Ogden identifies the scribe as "Robert Thornton, who
became the lord of East Newton on the death of his father in 1418"
(p. xi).

b) OE ă before a nasal is spelled *a:*
    hande(s)   235, 663, etc.
    lange (adv.)   5, 31
    lande   279, 676
    mane   266, 348

c) OE ō is usually spelled *u* (see [d] above under MS D).

d) Forms of the verb 'shall' are always spelled with Northern *s* (ll. 101, 135, 169, 711, etc.).

e) Present indicative plural ends in a sibilant, except when immediately preceded by a personal pronoun subject (ll. 6, 40, 42, 52, etc.).

f) The third person plural pronoun is the Northern *þaym, þam* (objective) and *þaire* (possessive).

g) The form of the feminine personal pronoun is *scho.*

I Ireland MS [15]   Bibliotheca Bodmeriana, Coligny,
                     Geneva, f.5a

This is a parchment manuscript of 100 folios measuring approximately 10⅘ by 7½ inches. The current binding is apparently not the original and contains two sets of gatherings separately paged. The first of these, which contains *The Awntyrs, Sir Amadace,* and *The Avowing of Arthur,* consists of five gatherings of six sheets with signatures at the beginning and end of each gathering.

The Awntyrs begins without title on f.1a and ends at

---

[15] See Bruce Dickens, "The Date of the Ireland Manuscript," *LSE,* II (1933), 62–66; also John Robson, *Three Early English Metrical Romances,* London, 1842, pp. xxxviii–xlv.

the bottom of f.15b. There are 21–26 lines to the page. The beginnings of three stanzas have been indented for later illumination, which was never supplied (ll. 1–3, stanza 1; ll. 261–2, stanza 21; ll. 508–9, stanza 40). Before stanzas 21 and 40 there is a space left in the manuscript and *a fitte* is written marginally. For the first few stanzas the line-divisions are frequently wrong (see notes to ll. 27–28 and 31–32) and the four lines of the wheel are written as two until stanza 7. I lacks 17 lines, including all of stanza 39.

The manuscript was formerly thought to date from around 1400–1413 on the evidence of the second set of gatherings, which is a record of the manor of Hale.[16] However, Dickens has shown that the romances were originally separate and dates them on paleographic evidence c. 1450–1460.[17] The manuscript remained in the Ireland family until 1945 when it was sold at auction by Major Ireland Blackburne, and is now in the Bodmer library in Switzerland.[18]

I is written in the West Midland dialect with an admixture of Northern features. It differs from D in the following characteristics:

a) It has rounded forms of OE ĕŏ in *hor, hom,* and *ho.*

---

[16] "The earliest of these records appear to have been entered in the year 1413; the romances were presumably copied into the MS before this date." Mary Serjeantson, "The Dialects of the West Midland," *RES,* III (1927), 328. For a description of these records see Robson, pp. xxxvii–xliii.

[17] Dickens, pp. 63–65. He suggests that "the romances may have been copied at Hale itself, perhaps for John de Ireland who held the manor from 1435–1462" (p. 65).

[18] See A. I. Doyle, "Note 105. Date of a MS in Bibliotheca Bodmeriana," *The Book Collector,* VIII (1959), 69.

b) OE *hw* is spelled *qu*. I is the only manuscript to have this usually Northern feature:

quen	266, 339
quat	93, 204
quere	644, 476
quele (n.)	266

c) Unstressed vowels in inflectional endings are often *u* (West Midland):

(genitive)	goddus	242
	kingus	262
(plurals)	delus	6
	herdus	42
(comparative)	grattur	147
	raddur	161
(weak preterites)	dubbut	695
	greuut	515
	musut	110
(weak past participles)	seruut	339
	grauntut	140
(3rd person singular)	telus	2
	dwellus	4
	ledus	14
	glidus	27

d) Weak preterites and past participles end in a voiceless stop (see above, c).

e) The third person plural pronouns are *hom* (objective) and *hor, þayre* (both frequent, possessive).

f) *Scho* occurs as a variant of *ho* for the feminine personal pronoun.

g) Northern *at* with the infinitive once (1. 635).

L Lambeth Palace Library MS 491 [19]

This is a large miscellaneous collection in paper and vellum containing 329 leaves measuring 8⅞ by 5¾ inches. The first 290 folios, in vellum, which include *The Awntyrs, Brut in English, The Sege of Jerusalem, A tretys of the kynges of Cologne* and a poem on hunting, are separated from 35 leaves of paper in a later hand by four leaves of modern paper.

The Awntyrs begins without title on f.275a and ends at the bottom of f.286b, with 30–39 lines to a page. There is one illuminated capital at 1. 1. Twelve lines and portions of 8 others are lacking.

The manuscript is dated in the first half of the fifteenth century by Hooper [20] and Bülbring (p. 383). It has been in the Lambeth collection since the seventeenth century and its earlier history is unknown.

L is the southernmost copy of *The Awntyrs*. It has been classified as Southern by Andrew and Hooper, mostly on the basis of the interdental suffix in the present indicative plural. Burtness argues for an origin in the East Midlands, perhaps London, but, as he points out, the evidence is scanty and often ambiguous. L differs from D in the following ways:

[19] See M. R. James and C. Jenkins, *A Descriptive Catalogue of the Manuscripts in the Library of Lambeth Palace,* London, 1932, p. 681; also K. Bülbring, "Über die Hs. Nr. 491 der Lambeth Bibliothek," *Herrig's Archiv,* LXXXVI (1891), 383–7.

[20] "The Lambeth Palace MS. of 'The Awntyrs off Arthure,'" *LSE,* III (1934), 38.

a) There are no instances in L of the rounding of OE ĕŏ which occur occasionally in D and I.

b) In the third person singular sibilant suffixes predominate but -*iþ* and -*yth* also occur (ll. 15, 31, 238, 242, 310, etc.).

c) The forms for the weak plural vary greatly, -*e*, -*is*, -*ys*, -*yn*, -*in*, -*es*, -*ith*, -*iþ* and *ø*. Note that in l. 4 the plural verb ends in -*ith* where the rhyme demands -*s*.

d) The present participle ends in -*ing*.

e) The forms of the third person plural pronoun are *hem* (objective) and *her* (possessive).

f) *She* occurs consistently for the feminine pronoun.

g) L is the only manuscript which consistently retains the past participle prefix:

y-born	227
y-wonne	274
y-dighte	454
y-lost	462

2. PREVIOUS EDITIONS

The Awntyrs was first printed by J. Pinkerton in his *Scotish Poems,* London, 1792. He used the Douce MS and entitled the poem "Sir Gawan and Sir Galaron of Galloway." [21] According to Madden it is a poor job:

He divided it into two parts, and prefixed an argument to each, but his text is extremely incorrect,

---

[21] For a history of the dispute over whether Pinkerton came by the text honestly see Clayton P. Christianson, *"The Awntyrs of Arthure": An Edition,* Unpub. dissertation, Washington University, 1964, pp. v–vi.

and, as he was confessedly ignorant of the language, his Glossary exhibits many errors. From this edition, bad as it is, the first twenty-six stanzas were transferred to Sibbald's *Chronicle of Scottish Poetry,* 8vo, vol. i, p. xvii. (p. 326)

The Thornton MS was first printed by David Laing in his *Select Remains of the Ancient and Popular Poetry of Scotland,* London, 1822 (Rev. John Small 1885, W. C. Hazlitt 1895). He gives some variants from the Douce MS. The first edition which can claim scholarly accuracy is that by Sir Frederic Madden in *Syr Gawayne,* London, 1839. He printed a diplomatic text of the Thornton MS and collated it closely with the Douce, recording all substantive variants. His notes and glossary are quite full and the edition, now rare, is still useful.

The Ireland MS was first edited by John Robson in *Three Early English Metrical Romances,* London, 1842. Although he expands suspensions and contractions without notice and regularizes some of the orthography, the text is accurate. The last published edition of *The Awntyrs* is in F. J. Amours' edition of *Scottish Alliterative Poems in Riming Stanzas* for the Scottish Text Society, Edinburgh and London, 1892, 1897. He prints the Thornton and Douce MSS on facing pages and gives many variant lines from Robson's edition of I in the footnotes. In the introduction, Amours attempts to construct a stemma for the MSS, but he was unaware of the existence of the Lambeth MS. His notes are very full and the glossary is complete for T. This is the best edition for a comparative study of T and D.

There have recently been two editions of *The Awntyrs* produced as doctoral dissertations. *A Critical Edition of* the *"Aunturs of Arthur,"* by Florence Ann Paton (University of Colorado, 1963) is the only edition of the Lambeth MS. It includes variants from the other three MSS but no emendations. The notes to the text are explanatory rather than textual, and the glossary is very selective. Clayton P. Christianson (see fn. 21) prints all four MSS, but does not collate or emend the text. His Introduction contains the fullest attempt so far to assess the poem from a literary point of view. There are many mistakes in transcribing the MSS, and the notes and glossary are selective.[22]

A modern rendering of *The Awntyrs* is included in Jessie L. Weston's *Romance, Vision and Satire,* Boston, 1912.

3. SOURCES AND ANALOGUES

The Awntyrs off Arthure consists of two episodes, quite different in character though connected by their moral intent, and there is no known source for the poem in this form. The second episode is a fairly conventional story of challenge and battle of the sort common in Arthurian romance. The lovely lady leading a knight into the hall, Gawain's acceptance of the challenge, and the induction of the defeated knight into the Round Table are all familiar. Gawain's opponent, Sir Galeron, does not have a major role in any other poem.[23] He appears in Malory ("Sir Galleron off Galowey") where he is de-

---

[22] Since this was written another dissertation has appeared: Ralph Hanna III, *"The Awntyrs off Arthure at the Terne Wathelyne": An Edition Based on Bodleian Library MS. Douce 324* (New Haven, 1967).

[23] For occurrences of the name in English see Robert W. Ackerman, *An Index of the Arthurian Names in Middle English,* Stanford, 1952, pp. 96–97.

feated by Sir Palomydes. He lends his armor to Sir Tristram, who overcomes Palomydes, and then Galeron and
Tristram become Palomydes' godfathers when he is baptized.[24] Galeron is also mentioned in the alliterative
Morte Arthure, Sir Gawain and the Carl of Carlisle and
a few French romances.[25] Finally, the story in *The
Awntyrs* has been so well assimilated to the local geography of Scotland that specific resemblances to a possible
source would probably not be very exact.

The first episode of *The Awntyrs* is related to two
themes which appear with many variations throughout
medieval literature. The theme of a mortal who is visited
by a fairy under a tree or by a stream (both of which are
present in our poem) is combined with a vision of a soul
in torment who admonishes the sinful. The variations of
these themes which appear together in two other Middle
English romances suggest that the first is an adumbration
of the "wish-child" theme [26] and the second a version of

[24] Eugène Vinaver, ed., *The Works of Sir Thomas Malory*, Oxford,
1947, II, 840–45.

[25] "The name is derived from the French *Galeran*, which occurs
frequently in *chansons de geste* (cf. Langlois, *Tables des noms pro-
pres de toute nature compris dans chansons de geste imprimées*, pp.
248–9) and elsewhere. In French Arthurian romances the name is
found in *Perceval le Gallois* 16, 314–16 (ed. by Potvin):

> Et Galerans dis li Galois
> Fu cil ki onques ne fu las,
> O le roi Caradot bris-bras.

In *Perlesvaus* (ed. by Nitze and Jenkins, I, p. 51) *Galerians de la
Blanche Tor* is mentioned as a paternal uncle of Perceval. It seems
that the French Arthurian romances connect the name with Wales,
the English with Scotland." Auvo Kurvinen, *Sir Gawain and the
Carl of Carlisle*, Helsinki, 1961, p. 164.

[26] For a discussion of and further references to the "Wish-Child or
Wonder-Child folk-tales" see Laura A. Hibbard, *Mediæval Romance
in England*, New York, 1924, pp. 52ff. All of these motifs can be
traced further into Romance (*Tale of Beryn, The Lay of Tydorel*),
saint's legends (St. Cuthbert, the Oedipus and Judas stories), and

the recognition between mother and child by means of a token. In *Sir Gowther*,[27] a lady who wants a child goes into an orchard where she meets a devil under a chestnut tree and conceives a son (ll. 67ff.). While he is growing up, Sir Gowther is very wicked until he learns the secret of his birth from his mother, after which he turns to good works to defeat the devil. In *Sir Degare*,[28] the daughter of a king goes into the forest and becomes lost; her maidens then go to sleep under a chestnut tree (ll. 61–74).[29] A richly dressed knight comes and lies with the lady, after which he prophesies that she will bear him a son. He also leaves her a pointless sword, the token by which Sir Degare and his father later recognize each other. These resemblances are naturally very general, since the combinations and permutations of themes and motifs are very complicated.[30] There is one story, however, that of the mother of Pope Gregory, in which these themes are clearer, and which is the closest analogue to *The Awntyrs*.

The story of Gregory's mother appears in two quite different versions in the Middle Ages, each of which is

---

folklore through such works as Gerald Bordman's *Motif-Index to the English Metrical Romances,* Helsinki, 1963 (Folklore Fellows Communications No. 190).

[27] Thomas C. Rumble, ed. *The Breton Lays in Middle English,* Detroit, 1965, pp. 178–204.

[28] Walter H. French and Charles B. Hale, *Middle English Metrical Romances,* New York, 1930, pp. 287–320.

[29] M. B. Ogle, "The Orchard Scene in *Tydorel* and *Sir Gowther*," *Romanic Review,* XIII (1922), 38. The chestnut tree is the usual locale of these stories (cf. *Sir Launfal,* 1. 220) but the laurel tree of *The Awntyrs* appears in the *Pseudo-Matthew,* in which Ann, the mother of Mary, after praying for a child, meets an angel of the lord in an orchard under a laurel tree.

[30] For an attempt to generalize about the different combinations see G. V. Smithers, "Story-Patterns in Some Breton Lays," *Medium Ævum,* XXII (1953), 61–92.

the source for certain motifs in our poem.[31] The first is a prose tale recorded in the Latin *Gesta Romanorum.*[32] Gregory is the child of an incestuous relationship between the son and daughter of the Emperor Marcus. (As Miss Hibbard points out [p. 302], the episode in *Sir Degare* is a rationalized form of an incestuous relationship.) Before his birth Gregory's father departs for the Holy Land, where he soon dies. His mother, now the empress, places the baby in a cask with gold and silver to provide for his upbringing. She encloses two tablets instructing whoever finds him to baptize him, and throws the cask into the sea. When he is grown, Gregory learns the secret of his birth and sets out for the Holy Land. However, he is blown by a storm to his mother's country where she is defending her castle against a rejected suitor. They do not recognize each other, and when Gregory defeats the attackers, he is rewarded with his mother's hand in marriage. One day she finds the tablets, and when she confronts her son with their evil fate, he exclaims, "Behold how the devil hems me in." [33] Gregory then goes away to become a religious hermit and is later made pope. At the

---

[31] George Neilson argued that *The Pearl* and *The Awntyrs* are derived from different parts of the Middle English *Trental of St. Gregory,* but the reference to the "token" which only appears in the Latin story (see below) shows the weakness of his argument. "Crosslinks between *The Pearl* and *The Awntyrs of Arthur,*" *The Scottish Antiquary* or *Northern Notes and Queries,* XVI (1902), 67–78.

[32] "De mirabili divina dispensatione et ortu beati Gregorii pape," Cap. 81 in *Gesta Romanorum,* ed. Hermann Oesterley, Berlin, 1872, pp. 399–409. The Middle English version of the story appears under the title "Eufemius a Riche Emperour" in *The Early English Versions of the Gesta Romanorum,* ed. Sidney Herrtage, EETSES 33, London, 1897, pp. 250–263, and varies slightly from the Latin. For other versions of the original Latin story see Herrtage, p. 489.

[33] "Ecce sic diabolus conclusit me." Oesterley, p. 406.

end of the poem his mother travels to Rome, where Gregory endows a monastery and makes her the abbess.

In *Sir Gowther*, as in this story, the defeat of the devil and rejection of the original sinful relationship is accompanied by the establishment of an abbey:

> There he did make another abbay,
> And put theryn monkes gray,
> That mykill cowde of lore—
> To syng and rede to the worldeys ende.
> ll. 655–658

In *The Awntyrs* Guenevere's mother is in the clutches of Lucifer (ll. 164–5), and at the end of the poem:

> Waynour gared wisely write into þe west
> To al þe religious to rede and to sing.
> ll. 703–704

The incident of the tablets, the token by which Gregory's mother recognizes him, is not necessary in *The Awntyrs* since the themes of incest and separation are no longer explicit. However, it explains the reference to a token in ll. 205ff.: [34]

> I brake a solempne a-vowe
> And no mane wist hit but þowe;
> By þat tokene þou trowe
> Þat soþely I sayne.

The second version of the Gregory story is a Middle English metrical romance, derived from Old French,

---

[34] In *Sir Degare,* in which the token is a pointless sword, the gold and silver of the Gregory story also appear (Hibbard, p. 303). The "solempne a-vowe" in this passage may refer to the incest or to the traditional vow of silence which a fairy places on a mortal (cf. *Sir Launfal*). Notice further the reference to "no *man* knew."

called *The Trental of St. Gregory*.[35] In this poem the incest and wish-child themes have been curtailed, and the moral warning becomes predominant. The appearance to Gregory of the ghost of his mother has the same dramatic character as the appearance of the ghost in *The Awntyrs*. Gregory's mother had been led into sin by the devil and borne a child which she secretely killed and buried. She died without being shriven, but, since she had lived an apparently holy life, everyone assumed she had gone to heaven. One day while Gregory is at mass his mother appears to him, surrounded by a dark cloud. The passage has many similarities to the appearance of Guenevere's mother (cf. ll. 82ff.):

And sodenly, yn myddes his masse,
Þer þrowȝ to hym such a derkenesse
Þat he lakkede ner þe dayes lyȝt,
For hit was derke as mydnyȝt;
In þat derkenes was myste among.
    All a-stonyed he stode, so hit stongke;
Be-syde he loked vnþur hys lere;
In þat derknes a þyng þrew hym nere,
A wonþurfull grysely creature,
Aftur a fend fyred with all her feture,
All ragged & rente, boþe elenge & euell,
As orrybull to be-holde as any deuell:
Mowthe, face, eres & yes,
Brennede all full of brennyng lyes.

---

[35] There are at least ten MSS of the poem (see Brown and Robbins Nos. 83, 1653, 3184, and Wells, p. 789 for bibliography) which have been classified into two versions by Albert Kaufmann in his critical edition of the poem "Trentalle Sancti Gregorii," *Erlanger Beiträge*, Vol. III, Erlangen and Leipzig, 1889. For the source of the poem see J. R. Hulbert, "The Sources of *St. Erkenwald* and *The Trental of Gregory*," *Modern Philology*, XVI (1919), 485–493.

> He was so agast of þat grysyly goste,
> That yn a swonyng he was almoste;
> He halsed hit, þorow goddes myȝte,
> That þe fende he putte to flyȝte,
> And be þe vertu of hys blode
> That for mankynde dyed on Rode,
> "Sey me sykerly þe soþe soone
> What þou hast yn þis place to done:
> What ys þy cause þou cursed wreche,
> Thus at masse me for to drecche?"
>
> Þe gost answered with drury chere
> "I am þy modur þat þe beere,
> Þat for vnschryuen dedes so derne
> In byttyr paynes þus y brenne."
>
> ll. 47–74 [36]

When asked why she is in such pain the ghost replies that she "lyuede in lustes wykkydly" (l. 89). The pope begins to cry and says:

> "Telle me now, modur, for loue of mary flour,
> If any þyng may þe help or sokour?
> Bedes, or masse, þy penaunce to bye,
> Or ony fastyng þy sorowe to aleye;
> What crafte, or caste, or any oþur þyng
> The may help, or be þy Releuyng."
>
> ll. 95–100

She replies that he should say a trental of masses for her soul, which he promises to do. When she returns a year later she is so beautiful that he takes her for the Virgin Mary, and then she is carried off to heaven by angels.

[36] All passages from *The Trental* are quoted from Frederick J. Furnivall, ed. *Political, Religious, and Love Poems*, EETS 15, London, 1886, pp. 114–122. Suspensions are not expanded.

A large part of the effect of the moral warning of this episode in *The Awntyrs* is due to the contrast between the beautiful and richly clad queen and her black and naked mother, disfigured through lust. This contrast also appears in *Thomas of Erceldoune*.[37] This poem, which also uses stanza linking, has some minor resemblances to *The Awntyrs*. As the narrator, Thomas, is walking in the country, he sees a lovely lady on a hunt with grey-hounds.[38] She is riding a palfrey with a saddle "sett with precyous stones" (1. 51), including "Berelle" and "jrale fyne." (The only known occurrences of "iral" in ME are in this poem and *The Awntyrs*.) She shines so brightly that Thomas thinks she is "marye moste of myghte, / þat bore þat chylde þat dyede for mee" (ll. 75–76). Thomas meets her *under a tree* and wants to lie with her. At first she refuses, saying "þat synne will for-doo all my beaute" (1. 104), but then she consents. As a result she changes into a horrible creature:

Thomas stode vpe in þat stede,
And he by-hclde þat lady gaye;
Hir hare it hange all ouer hir hede,
Hir eghne semede owte, þat are were graye.
And all þe riche clothynge was a-waye,
Þat he by-fore sawe in þat stede;
Hir a schanke blake, hir oþer graye,
And all hir body lyke the lede.

ll. 129–136

---

[37] Ed. James A. H. Murray, EETS 61, London, 1875. All quotations are from the Thornton MS.

[38] See Lucy Allen Paton, *Studies in the Fairy Mythology of Arthurian Romance,* Boston, 1903, pp. 15ff. The hunt as an induction to fairyland is a common motif and also appears in *The Avowing of Arthur* and *Sir Gawain and the Carl of Carlisle*.

The lady then takes Thomas into fairyland for three years.

When they return, the lady blows a horn to recall the greyhounds and goes to her castle. She tells Thomas he must return home, but he asks her for a "ferly" (l. 324) and she replies with a long historical and allegorical prophecy about the kings and wars of Scotland and England. In *The Awntyrs* Gawain asks the ghost how those knights shall fare who "Wynnene worshippe in werre þorghe wightnesse of hondes" (l. 264). She prophesies Arthur's future victory over the Romans (he has already conquered France), his betrayal and defeat by Modred, and the death of Gawain himself.

The general outline of this prophecy in *The Awntyrs* is the familiar story of Arthur's fall, but there are certain details which are only found elsewhere in the alliterative *Morte Arthure*. Many of these correspondences have been cited by Amours, George Neilson and others in attempts to prove the common authorship of these poems by "Huchown of the Awle Ryale." [39] William Matthews, in his study of *Morte Arthure* summarizes the most important similarities:

Some uncommon resemblances occur in the heraldic devices used in the two poems. The device borne by Gawain is usually described in romances as a double-headed eagle or a lion—*Sir Gawain and the Green Knight* is unique in making it a pentangle. In both *Morte Arthure* and *Awntyrs of Arthure,* however, this device is slightly different from normal —one or more 'griffones of golde.' More striking is

---

[39] Amours, pp. li–lxxxii; George Neilson, *Huchown of the Awle Ryale,* Glasgow, 1902. For a discussion of this point see below, "Authorship."

their agreement about Mordred's device. Descriptions of the traitor's arms are rare in the romances, but heraldic authorities say that they were very similar to Gawain's: '. . . de pourpre à un aigle à deux testes d'or, membrées de mesme, à un chef d'argent.' It is persuasive evidence of the connection of *Morte Arthure* and *Awntyrs of Arthure,* therefore, that they agree in describing his arms as a saltire engrailed, the former mentioning 'þe sawturoure engrelede' (l. 4182), the latter 'a sawtire engrelede of siluer fulle schene' (l. 307).

Equally curious correspondences occur in topographical and personal names. The campaign in Italy that forms an unusual part of *Morte Arthure* is briefly alluded to in one line of *Awntyrs:* 'Ther salle in tuskayne be tallde of that tresone' (l. 291); and a similar passing reference is made to Fortune's wheel: 'Maye no mane stere hym [Arthur] of strenghe whilles þe whele standis' (l. 266). The ghost of Guenevere's mother, prophesying the death of Gawain, tells him that 'in a slake þou salle be slayne' (l. 298); in *Morte Arthure,* the uncommon Norse loanword 'slake,' meaning a depression between hills, is used just before Gawain lands for his final battle: 'Thane was it slyke a slowde in slakkes full hugge' (l. 3719). This prophecy contains further topographical details that make it fairly sure what was the source:

> And ther salle the Rownde Tabille losse the re-
> nowne
> Be-syde ramessaye, fulle ryghte at a rydynge,
> And at Dorsett salle dy the doghetyeste of alle.
>
> (ll. 293–295)

The riding beside Romsey (seven miles from Southampton and still nearer to Winchester) corre-
sponds to the battle between Southampton and Winchester in *Morte Arthure,* and although Dorset is
incorrect (Romsey is just inside the Hampshire
border), the name must derive from a line in *Morte
Arthure* in which the king's movements to Cornwall
for the final battle are mentioned: 'Thane drawes he
to Dorsett, and dreches no langere' (l. 4052). As
symbols for the slaughter that Arthur has committed
in his conquest of France, the ghost names 'The
Frollo and þe Farnaghe' (1. 275) (the other manuscripts have 'Frol and his Farnet' and the rationaliz-
ing 'Freol and his folke'). These names are clearly
corruptions of names mentioned in the interpretation
of Arthur's dream in *Morte Arthure.* In that interpretation, the philosopher cites Frollo and Feraunt
as knights whom Arthur has slain in France and for
whom he should make expiation (l. 3404). Frollo
appears in all accounts of Arthur's conquest of
France, but Feraunt seems to be the invention of
the *Morte Arthure* poet.[40]

Matthews also points out some thematic resemblances
between the poems, and concludes with a suggestion
about their relationship:

It is also of interest that the ghost's prophecy in
AA is imagined as occurring after the conquest of
France and before the campaign against Lucius:
this timing and the association of the events with
Carlisle and its social pleasures might mean that *AA*
was conceived as a prologue to *MA,* the events tak-

[40] *The Tragedy of Arthur.* Berkeley, 1960, pp. 157–158.

ing place some time before Lucius' challenge. (p. 209)

It is the ghost's prophecy which affects the moral link between the two parts of the poem. She says that Arthur's fall will be caused by his covetousness (1. 265) and Gawain himself admits that they take people's lands "without any right" (1. 263). When Galeron comes to claim the lands which Arthur has given to Gawain, he demands only "reason and right" (1. 362). Further, it is Guenevere who, at the pleading of Galeron's lady, asks Arthur to stop the fight, perhaps as a result of her mother's warnings. As Matthews points out:

> Imperial conquests, won with wrong, are canceled out in a display of Christian charity, so that one might believe that the troubled ghost could have taken almost as much comfort from the effect of her moral advice as from the masses with which the poem ends. (p. 161)

4. DIALECT

Because of the variation which exists among the four MSS of *The Awntyrs* it is very difficult to determine the original dialect of the poem. First, each MS is in a different, but mixed, dialect. Second, whatever features are shared by all the MSS can only indicate the dialect of their archetype, which may have differed from that of the original poem because of the process of copying. Finally, the dialect of the original may have been mixed because of the use of traditional or formulaic phrases which preserve features not common in the dialect of the author.

That *The Awntyrs* was probably written in the North of England can be inferred from the knowledge which the poet displays of the area around Carlisle in which the poem is set. As A. G. Hooper says, in his study of the poem: [41]

> Tarn Wadling, Inglewood Forest and Plumpton all seem well known to the author, who may therefore have been a native of Cumberland or Westmoreland. He also shows a knowledge of Southwestern Scotland whilst, on the other hand, his idea of the South of England is vague.

This is supported by the fact that the southernmost copy, L, omits the references to Tarn Wadling (1. 2) and Inglewood Forest (1. 709). A further indication of Northern provenance is the stanza form, which occurs almost exclusively in poems written in the North and Scotland.[42]

When we turn to the dialect features of the MSS we find instances of Northern forms within the line in the non-Northern MSS D, I and L. Of course these features only prove that the poem was at one time copied in the Northern dialect, not that the original was Northern, but they are at least suggestive. Hooper lists the "appearance in MSS. other than T (in which the Northern dialect is best preserved) of typically Northern forms especially within the line (a) in I and D, and (b) especially in the Southern [sic., see "Manuscripts," above for the dialect features of L] copy L where D and I have Midland forms."

    (a)   I. vv. 4 dukys; 8 fermesones
            (beside the common -*us*).

---

[41] " 'The Awntyrs off Arthure': Dialect and Authorship," p. 62.
[42] Oakden, *The Dialectal and Metrical Survey,* pp. 217–218, and *A Survey of the Traditions,* p. 87.

32 scho; 538, 575, 661 þayre.
653 þay lepe; 592 bannes (3rd pl.).
122 brand; 107 woman.

D. vv. 4 dukes and dussiperes (-es usual in D).
26 she; 575 þaire.
129 þei skryke; 57 þei halowe.
463 kestes (imper. pl.).

(b) L. vv. 187 They hurle; þay hurlun (in I).
61 They go; þei gone (in D).
124 hyes (3rd pl.); hiȝene (in D).
129 shrikys (3rd pl.); þay scryken (in I).
136 þou walkes; walkest (in D).
41 bankis; bonkes (in I and D).
205 takyn; token (in D and I).

(pp. 62–63)

The only evidence for the dialect of the original which
is completely reliable is that based on the preservation
of certain features in rhyme.[43] This evidence has been
studied by Amours and Oakden,[44] both of whom con-
clude that the poem was originally composed in the
Northern dialect. However, they based their studies on T,
a Northern MS, and did not take into account the scribal
variants of D, I, and L which could invalidate some of

[43] Paul Burtness has examined the evidence of the alliteration, but,
as he points out, it is very meager, and the question of which alliterations may separate Northern from West Midland is not completely
clear. His conclusion is that "the limited and somewhat problematical
evidence in alliteration seems to indicate that the poem was written
in some form of Northern, i.e., in the area where *salle/solde* alliterates with the alveolar sibilant, where *hw-/cw-* and *hw-/w-* alliteration may both have been feasible, and where *give/gave/gift/get* had
an initial stop" (p. 160).

[44] Amours, pp. xlii and lxx; Oakden, *The Dialectal and Metrical
Survey,* pp. 113–114.

their evidence. S. O. Andrew [45] has shown that there are certain West Midland forms in rhyme, most notably words from OE ā rhyming with *gold* and certain infinitives in *n*. However, he allows this evidence to overbalance the Northern features in his attempt to prove the common authorship of *The Awntyrs, Morte Arthure,* and *The Pistill of Susan*. There are two possible explanations for the occurrence of the Midland forms. One is that the poet lived in an area of mixed dialect characteristics. A more probable explanation is provided by Hooper, whose article is an attempt to refute Andrew's claims about the dialect and authorship of the poem:

> It seems very reasonable to suppose . . . that the poets of this northwestern section of the country, in which alliterative poetry flourished, knew many other works in the same tradition, as our author must have known [*Morte Arthure*], and did not hesitate to use commonly recurring words, phrases and rhymes which have become the common stock of this particular tradition. . . .
>
> Of the rhymes mentioned by Andrew the 'gold' rhymes, the tags 'to sayne' v. 208, and 'to sene' v. 65 are phrases of this kind which the poet might well know from other alliterative works, and use to help out in his intricate system. (pp. 64–65)

Paul Burtness, in his study of the language of *The Awntyrs,* has examined all the evidence and taken into account the textual problem of manuscript variation. He agrees with Hooper that the original must have been Northern and that the Midland features are probably due to the alliterative tradition. The following outline of the

[45] "Huchoun's Works," *RES,* V (1929), 12–21.

significant dialect features in rhyme is condensed from
his study, pp. 138–148:

a) Evidence indicating Northern provenance:
OE ā occurs in a set of rhymes requiring [a:]
in stanzas 4 (ll. 41, 43, 45, 47), 7 (ll. 88, 89,
90), 8 (ll. 100, 104), 16 (ll. 197, 199, 201,
203), 19 (ll. 244, 245, 246), 20 (ll. 248, 250,
252, 254), 31 (ll. 399, 403), 41 (ll. 522, 524,
526, 528), 44 (ll. 561, 563, 565, 567), and 47
(ll. 608, 609, 610).
Present indicative plural of verbs occurs in a set
of rhymes requiring a sibilant in ll. 4, 124, 211,
321, 328, and 497.

b) Evidence necessary, but not sufficient, to prove
Northern provenance:
OE ȳ occurs in a set of rhymes requiring [i:,i]
in ll. 3, 5, 124, 328, 711.
The present plural form of the verb occurs without ending, when adjacent to a personal pronoun
subject, in ll. 60, 245, 505, 572, 575, 656, and
689.

c) Evidence conflicting with the assumption of
Northern provenance:
OE ā (<ald) occurs in lines where *gold* indicates an [o:/ɔ:] rhyme in stanzas 12, 29, 30,
and 52.
The infinitive with *-ne* occurs in rhyme in ll. 65,
204, 208.

There are also a few instances of contradictory dialect
evidence where the variation among MSS makes the
determination of the original rhyme difficult. The most

significant example is in stanza 46 (ll. 586, 588, 590, 592) where both Northern and Midland forms of the third person plural and past participle are found (see the note to these lines). On the whole, the assumption of Northern provenance made by most students of the poem seems to be correct.

5. AUTHORSHIP

As with most of the other ME alliterative poems, the author of *The Awntyrs* remains unknown. There have been various attempts to prove that a poet called Huchown of the Awle Ryale (or Auld Ryall), otherwise unidentified, wrote *The Awntyrs,* along with *Morte Arthure, The Pistill of Susan,* and any number of other alliterative works. The only basis for this claim is a passage in Andrew of Wyntoun's *Cronykil,* in which he says of Huchown:

> He made a gret Gest of Arthure,
> And þe Awntyr of Gawane,
> Þe Pistil als of Suet Susane.[46]

The argument over who Huchown may have been and what he wrote has had a long history.[47] Two names often connected with him are Sir Hugh of Eglinton and Clerk of Tranent, on the basis of some lines in William Dunbar's "Lament for the Makaris" ("he" refers to Death):

> The gude Syr Hew of Eglintoun,
> Et eik, Heryot, et Wyntoun,
> He has tane out of this cuntre;

· · · · · · · ·

[46] Book V, Chapter XIII, ll. 4310–11 (Cotton MS.) in *The Original Chronicle of Andrew of Wyntoun,* ed. F. J. Amours, STS 54, Edinburgh and London, 1906, Vol. IV, p. 23.
[47] For a bibliography see Wells, p. 826.

> Clerk of Tranent eik he hes tane,
> That maid the anteris of Gawane.[48]

Throughout the nineteenth century various combinations of these three names with most of the anonymous alliterative poems were suggested. The climax of this activity was the publication in 1902 of George Neilson's *Huchown of the Awle Ryale*,[49] in which he identified Huchown with Hugh of Eglinton and ascribed to him *The Wars of Alexander, The Destruction of Troy, Morte Arthure, The Pearl, Cleanness, Patience, Sir Gawain and the Green Knight, Erkenwald, Wynnere and Wastoure, The Parlement of the Thre Ages,* and *The Awntyrs off Arthure.* As Henry N. MacCracken points out, "We have here 40,000 lines of the very meat of Middle English literature identified as the work of a Scotchman." [50]

In 1910 MacCracken wrote a long article outlining in full the history of the dispute and carefully re-examining all the evidence. His conclusions, which have been accepted by most scholars, are that one Huchown of the Aule Ryall, who cannot be further identified, probably wrote *The Pistill of Susan,* but that the other two poems mentioned by Wyntoun must be presumed lost since no poems with the same titles now exist.

The arguments for common authorship of some of the alliterative poems had usually been made on the basis of similarities in style and diction, and shared phrases or lines. Those who argued against common authorship, such as MacCracken, pointed out that most of the similarities were the common stock of a poetic tradition and

---

[48] L1. 53–55, 65–66. *The Poems of William Dunbar,* ed. John Small STS 2, Edinburgh and London, 1893, p. 50.

[49] Glasgow, 1902.

[50] "Concerning Huchown," *PMLA,* XXV (1910), 516.

the rest could most plausibly be explained as borrowings. However, it was not until J. P. Oakden catalogued the formulas in the alliterative poems that the extent of such similarities was realized.

Recently, Ronald A. Waldron, following the lead of F. P. Magoun and others in their investigations of Old English poetry,[51] has suggested that the Middle English alliterative poems are formulaic because "there lies behind them a tradition—that is to say, a special Middle English tradition—of oral composition." [52] He gives examples of the patterns, or systems behind the specific formulas, and examines the first 25 lines of *Morte Arthure,* showing that it is overwhelmingly formulaic. Waldron, however, only considers poems in the alliterative long line without rhyme and we might ask how far an unquestionably literary poem such as *The Awntyrs* (since the rhyme and elaborate stanza form argue conclusively against oral composition in the sense of Lord [53]) may be formulaic. The answer will have a direct bearing on the possibility of determining the common authorship of *The Awntyrs* and other poems.

That *The Awntyrs* contains many of the familiar formulaic phrases of the alliterative tradition (such as

[51] F. P. Magoun, Jr., "The Oral-Formulaic Character of Anglo-Saxon Narrative Poetry," *Speculum,* XXVIII (1953), 446–67; reprinted in Lewis E. Nicholson, ed. *An Anthology of Beowulf Criticism* (Notre Dame, Ind., 1963), pp. 189–221. The development of the theory of oral composition by Milman Parry and Albert B. Lord is described in the basic text for the study of oral poetry, Lord's *The Singer of Tales,* Cambridge, Mass., 1960 (reprinted as an Atheneum paperback, New York, 1965).

[52] Ronald A. Waldron, "Oral Formulaic Technique and Middle English Alliterative Poetry," *Speculum,* XXXII (1957), 794.

[53] This is obvious throughout Lord's discussion of oral composition, but see especially his comment on the Oxford manuscript of the *Digenis Akritas:* "Both the rhyme and the enjambement point here to a 'literary' text." A. B. Lord, *The Singer of Tales,* New York, 1965, p. 216.

"by cross and by creed," "danger and dole," "cayser or king," "kyndils my care," "boun to battle," "cristened and crisomed," "proudest in palle," "wealth of the world" and many others) has been demonstrated by Oakden [54] and requires no further comment. There are also many lines and phrases which have been used by Amours, Neilson, Andrew and Matthews to indicate a relationship, either of common authorship or borrowing, between *The Awntyrs, Morte Arthure, The Pistill of Susan* and other alliterative poems. Many of these lines, especially when they bear on problems of the text, will be cited in the notes. However, there is a third group of similarities, not adequately studied, between *The Awntyrs* and the non-alliterative metrical romances. Again many of these are the "common alliterative formulas," but almost every line in the poem can be paralleled by a line in one of these romances. Some of these similarities will be found in the notes, but I will point out here, as an example, the parallels I have found between *The Awntyrs* and one of these romances, *Sir Degrevant*.[55]

The following phrases, most of them unexceptional, are found in both poems:

> gamen and gle, hardy and wight, known for kene, hound and horn, sooth to say, went on his way, mende (someone's) mis, I can right rede, worthely wight, fersely they fight, wathely wounded, to death he them dightes, slayne in a slakke, thanked God of his grace, truth I thee plight, that frely to fold, comely clad, armed ful clene, beryns full bold, what bote is (it) to lie, wlonkest in wedis, royally arrayed,

---

[54] *A Survey of the Traditions,* pp. 350–361.
[55] Ed. L. F. Casson, EETS 221, London, 1949. Lines are quoted from the Lincoln MS, unless marked C for the Cambridge MS. In the citing of formulas the spellings have been normalized.

knight kneled (him/her) tille, if it be thy will, seen
with sight, busked him ȝare, leap full light, to my
death day, (that) cruel and kene, that solas to sene,
graithed on grene, both king and queen, wele nor
wo, saw I never are, of all that were there, sighed
full sore, stonayed in that stounde, schawe schene,
til his lyves ende.

There are also many similiarities which extend over
a larger unit than the phrase:

> For-thi þay named [him] þat stownde
> Knyghte of þe Table Rownde.
>> *Deg.* 29–30
> Þei made Sir Galerone þat stonde
> A kniȝte of þe table ronde.
>> *AA.* 700–701

> Stedis stabillede in stallis.
>> *Deg.* 75
> His stede was stabled and led to þe stalle.
>> *AA.* 447

> Schyr scheldus they schrede,
> Many dowghty was dede,
> Ryche maylus wexen rede.
>> *Deg.* 309–311 (MS C)
> Shene sheldes were shred,
> Well ryche mayles wexun rede; (MS I)
> Many douȝti were a-dred.
>> *AA.* 569–571

> Syr Degreuuant gat a sted
> Þat was gode in ilk a ned.
>> *Deg.* 353–354 (MS C)

Als he stode by his stede,
Þat was so goode at nede.
AA. 556–557

Sir, God hase sent þe þat grace.
Deg. 425
God hase sent me this grace.
AA. 140 (MS T)

Hir courchefs were curious.
Deg. 669
Here kercheues were curiouse.
AA. 372

With wongus ful wete.
Deg. 840
. . . with wonges ful wete.
AA. 87

Þe lady louȝh hyr to scorn.
Deg. 954
And iche lede opone lyue wold laghe me to
scorne.
AA. 433

He beris a schelde of asure
Engrelyde with a sawtour.
Deg. 1045–1046
Suppriset with a suget þat beris of sable
A sauter engreled of siluer fulle shene.
AA. 306–307

With shuldrys shamly shent.
Deg. 1114 (MS C)
. . . and shildurs schomfully shent.
AA. 631 (MS I)

Þe gatus ful gayn.

Deg. 1692 (MS C)

. . . the gatis fulle gayne.

AA. 85 (MS T)

And scho suld make swylke accorde
By-twyx hym and hir lorde
Þat it solde be comforde
To all þat þam knewe.

Deg. 1801–1804

Woldest þou, leve lorde,
Make þes knightes accorde,
Hit were a grete conforde
For alle þat here ware.

AA. 634–637

With-outyn mor rehersyng
Made was þe sauȝthlyng.

Deg. 1821–1822 (MS C)

Wiþout more rehercynge
Made was here sawghtlynge.

AA. 661–662 (MS L)

The evidence, all of which cannot be quoted here,
indicates that a written poem such as *The Awntyrs* may
be completely formulaic. F. P. Magoun's statement that
"oral poetry is composed entirely of formulas . . . while
lettered poetry is never formulaic" has recently been
disproved for Old English poetry by Larry D. Benson.[56]

---

[56] "The Literary Character of Anglo-Saxon Formulaic Poetry,"
PMLA, LXXXI (1966), 334–341. The quotation from Magoun
(p. 180 in his article) is taken from Benson, p. 335. For some recent
views, which bear out these conclusions, see A. C. Baugh, "The
Middle English Romance: Some Questions of Creation, Presentation,
and Preservation," *Speculum,* XLII (1967), 1–31; Michael Curschmann, "Oral Poetry in Mediæval English, French, and German

The only conclusion we can draw is the negative one that similarities between *The Awntyrs* and any other poem cannot be used to prove common authorship. Whether parallels such as those quoted above are due to borrowing, or rather to the existence within the lettered formulaic tradition of units longer than the alliterative half-line (they are not really thematic) will have to await further comparative study of the poems involved.

6. DATE

The Awntyrs cannot be dated more exactly than the latter half of the fourteenth century. The latest date for the poem would be that of the Thornton MS, c. 1430. However, the amount of variation among the MSS and their wide separation argue for a relatively long period of transmission between them and the archetype. There are no allusions to contemporary events, and the only other evidence useful in dating the poem is the descriptions of the armor, hunting practices and ladies' clothing. Clayton Christianson has studied these features of the poem and concludes: "Such corroborating evidence from the contents of the poem, e.g., from descriptions of the ritual of hunting, of local geography, and of armor and costume—would strongly suggest, then, a more precise date for *The Awntyrs,* perhaps toward the end of Edward III's reign, or early in Richard II's" (p. xxv). Such conclusions are based on the unproven assumption that the references are topical and contemporary, and thus we must be satisfied with only a general dating of the poem.

Literature: Some Notes on Recent Research," *Speculum,* XLII (1967), 36–52; Donald Fry, "Old English Formulas and Systems," *English Studies,* XLVII. 3 (June, 1967), 1–12.

INTRODUCTION

PART II

1. THE EDITORIAL PROBLEM [57]

The minimum requirement for collating two or more MSS is that they be different "states" of the same "text," that is, that they be descended by a process of copying from a common original. The best evidence for such an assumption is the presence in all extant MSS of readings which, because they are not likely to have arisen independently, are called common errors and indicate a common ancestor for the MSS. The following six points have been adduced by various previous editors of *The Awntyrs:* [58]

(1) a) The ninth line of stanza 4 (1. 48) is lacking in all four MSS. This is a linking line, important to the structure of the poem, and is the only line missing in all MSS.

      b) *Swyne,* 1. 56, seems to be an interpolation for explicitness by a scribe who did not understand the function of *wilde* as a substantive.

[57] In all of my editorial methods I am indebted to George Kane's discussion of the editorial problems of *Piers Plowman* in the "Introduction" to his recent edition: *Piers Plowman: The A Version,* London, 1960. For an excellent bibliography of textual criticism see pp. 53–54.

[58] The summary here is based on that by Paul Burtness, *A Language Study,* pp. 9–10. The groups of variants throughout the next few sections will be numbered in order to facilitate cross-references from the Critical Notes.

c) *Lost,* l. 462, seems to be a common error since the rhyme requires *lest.*

d) *Layre/leyre,* l. 678, is probably an error for *Ayre* (i.e., Scotland) due to the fact that *l* alliterates in the line.

e) The four MSS may have, as Amours suggests, a common error in l. 145 where *Berell/Berel/ Beryke* is a proper name resulting from the misunderstanding of an original *berel,* the gem. "Most probably the original simply said that she was 'brighter than beryl or than Brangwain, that *bird* so bold.'" (p. 340)

f) "Anacoluthon, l. 134, which Lübke, Amours, and Smith cite to support their postulation of X, is too frequent in Middle English to be conclusively scribal." (Burtness, p. 10)

No single one of these points would be proof of a common ancestor, but taken together they are conclusive. It should become clear later that an hypothesis of copying from a common original is the only adequate explanation for some of the variants in the four MSS.

Before discussing the collation of the MSS, we must consider the possibility that the text has been transmitted orally. First, oral transmission must be distinguished from oral composition (actually recomposition). Oral composition, in the sense in which A. B. Lord uses the term in *The Singer of Tales,* implies that each version of a poem is a distinct "original" created by the singer-poet during his performance, rather than a memorized text. That the MSS of *The Awntyrs* are not the result of this kind of improvisation is obvious from the presence of the common errors outlined above. (Whether the original poem was an oral composition is a different question and is discussed above under "Authorship.") Further, there are no instances among the MSS of the substitution or permutation of themes and motifs which we would expect to result from oral composition.

The question of whether there was oral as well as scribal transmission is more difficult. That there was scribal transmission is shown by the presence of those most venerable of scribal errors, homeoteleuton and homeoarchy.[59] The following lines have been omitted because the scribe was misled by a repeated word or phrase:

(2)   14 L: "Dame Gaynour he ledes" at the end of ll. 13 and 14.

252 T: "Siþene" at the beginning of ll. 252 and 253.

326 L: "þe goste a-wey glides" at the end of ll. 325 and 326.

383–5 L: "His horse" at the beginning of ll. 383 and 386.

495–507 I (stanza XXXIX):   "Gawayne" at the beginning of ll. 495 and 508.

632 T: "The grones" at the beginning of ll. 632 and 633.

There are other variants, however, which might indicate oral transmission. For instance, the occurrence of the same line in two places (ll. 229 and 320) causes T to pick up in the wrong stanza. A more likely indication is the

[59] There is a good description of the way such mechanical errors in transcription come about in Eugène Vinaver, "Principles of Textual Emendation," in *Studies in French Language and Medieval Literature Presented to Professor Mildred K. Pope,* Manchester, 1939, pp. 351–369.

frequent substitution of one formula for another. However, most such variants might also be due to scribes, and the deciding factor in our case is the same as that which George Kane cites for the MSS of *Piers Plowman:*

> None of these manuscripts has the characteristics which, from knowledge of Middle English texts preserved in several versions, one connects with true oral transmission. By such I mean compression at one point and expansion at another, dislocation of matter other than palaeographic, large omissions evidently made for abridgement or from defect of memory, and marked unevenness in the accuracy of reproduction. (p. 144)

Having concluded that the four MSS are different states of one text, descended by a process of copying, we can decide whether it is possible to combine them to produce a text which more nearly represents the original than do the individual MSS. All the variants in our MSS can be divided into those in which we can (with varying degrees of confidence) determine originality and those in which we cannot.[60] It is the existence of the second type of variant which causes many editors to argue against conflation, which is sometimes described as a "patch-job." First, it must be pointed out that we are not referring to conjectural emendation, but to choosing between variants, each of which has *some* MS authority. More importantly,

---

[60] Throughout the discussion of the editorial problems "original" will be used to mean "a reading which derives from the archetype of the four MSS," not the original form of the poem, which is beyond our reach. Also, singular references such as "the scribe" or "T varies here" should always be understood to imply an unknown number of scribes in the process of transmission from the archetype to the MSS.

however, the alternative to conflation in many cases is the
acceptance of a *scribal* "patch-job," the result of chance
and error. We have only what George Kane calls "less
corrupt manuscripts," and, as he says, "to print one of
these without editing it would invest it with quite unmer-
ited authority." [61] The many instances in which we can
determine originality and thus have a basis for emendation will be the subject of the next section. In the remain-
der of this section we discuss those variants which, because we cannot determine the direction of change, define
the kind and degree of difference between a copy-text
edition based on one MS and that based on another.

There are three major types of indeterminate variant.
The most numerous are those involving an article, prep-
osition, conjunction, or other function word not affecting
the sense of the passage. Examples of this type of variant,
which defies analysis, may be readily found in the apparatus. A second type of variant is that which we might
call "formulaic," in which one common formulaic half-
line is substituted for another, again with little or no
change in the basic sense of the passage. The following
examples will indicate their frequency: [62]

(3)   14   Gawayne þe gay   T D
              Gawan the gode   I
        35   ho þe trouthe trowes   D
              quo truly me trowes   I

---

[61] P. 146. For a discussion of just how bad texts may be, with
examples from Old English MSS, see Kenneth Sisam, "The Authority
of Old English Poetical Manuscripts" in his *Studies in the History of
Old English Literature,* Oxford, 1953, pp. 29–44.

[62] We shall be able to resolve some of these variants by other
means. In all instances where a variant occurs in two or more MSS
the quotation is from the first cited, and the others may differ slightly
in spelling or grammatical or dialectal form.

who þat righte trowes   T
ho so righte trowis   L
43 huntynge in hast   D
huntynge with horn(es)   T I L
52 þei durkene and dare   D T
þay droupun and daren   I L
54 for drede of þe dethe   D I L
for þe dowte of þe dede   T
57 in hurstes and huwes   D
in holttis and hillys   T
108 on hide ne on huwe   D I
on hede ne one hare   T
of hide ne of here   L
122 braides oute þe bronde   D I
brawndeche owte his brande   T
137 of figure and face   D
of fegure and of flesche   T L
a figure of flesche   I
146 Of al gamene or gle   D
Of any gamnes or gudis   T
Of alle the gomun and the grythe   I
Of game or gle   L
226 Mary . . . miȝeti   D T
Mary . . . modur   I L
315 walke one my wey   D I L
wende one my waye   T
341 Withe al worshippe and wele   D
With alle the wirchipe to welde   T
With all welthis to wille   I
347 wlonkest in wede   D I
worthiest in wede   L
465 Here my hond I you hiȝte   D
Here my trouthe I ȝow plyghte   T I L

The third type of indeterminate variant is that in which there is a substantive change in the sense of a passage but no basis on which to choose between the variants. Fortunately these are not numerous. All such variants will be mentioned in the notes, and the following will indicate their type:

(4) 407 And whi þou sturne one þi stede stondes so stille. D

And whi þou stonyes on thi stede and stondes so stille. T

Whi þou stedis in þat stid and stondes so stille. I

And whi þou studiest in þis stede and stondes stille. L

529 The bronde was blody þat burneshed was briȝte. D

He bare thruȝe his brenys þat burneyst were bryȝte. I

Þurghe þe blasyng basnet of þat hende wighte. L

607 Grisly one gronde he groned one grene. D

Gallerone fulle greuousely granes on þe grene. I

All grouelonges in grounde gronet on grene. I

To þe ground was cast þat doghty be dene. L

When confronted with variants like these, where originality cannot be determined, the editor must accept the reading of his base MS. Thus a copy-text edition of one MS will differ from that of another in each of these cases. (They will, of course, agree when the original reading is certain.) However, the number of significant variants of this type is very small when compared to the many cases where we have a firm basis for choice. Furthermore, if we choose as our base MS the one which most often preserves the original reading in clear cases, we have a valid basis for accepting its readings when we are in doubt.

2. COMPARISON OF VARIANTS

The fact that we can determine that one variant is more probably original than another is the basis for any attempt to conflate different states of a text. The traditional way of determining originality is the method of recension, by which a stemma of the MSS is constructed and only those readings are accepted which derive from the archetype, as shown by their occurrence in a majority of genetic groups. For reasons which will be discussed in the next section, recension is not possible for the MSS of *The Awntyrs*. Besides, the construction of genetic groups depends on the process of finding "common errors," which necessitates the use of a method to determine originality in individual cases which *precedes* the knowledge of MS relations.[63]

There are two basic assumptions, not always made explicit, on which an editor relies to determine originality. The first is that the archetype of the extant MSS was constructed according to some principles of form and content which allow us to judge readings as to degree of "correctness." [64] This first principle is necessary, but not sufficient,

---

[63] As Archibald A. Hill points out, the failure to acknowledge the circularity of the procedure is one of the main faults of the genealogical method. "Some Postulates for the Distributional Study of Texts," *Studies in Bibliography*, III (1950–51), 65–66.

[64] Hill, in the article quoted above, puts forth a strong argument for excluding from textual criticism any use of "literary excellence"

and must be combined with the second assumption, that a scribe exhibits certain tendencies and leaves certain evidence which can be used to infer the direction of change.

The evidence for judging correctness will vary with every text. In the case of *The Awntyrs,* there are certain formal features of alliteration, rhyme, and linking which give strong evidence for originality. Of course the importance of this evidence depends on the degree to which the formal feature is invariant in the poem. Thus the presence of two alliterating syllables in the first half-line and the end-rhyme are better bases for choice between variants than alliteration in the second half-line and the frequently absent feature of linking. Another aspect of this assumption is that the original was correct grammatically, e.g., that *he* for the female ghost in l. 118L and Gawain's reference to himself as *he* in l. 525I are unoriginal variants. We also expect the poem to make elementary sense —that its reference to people and things be accurate. Thus when MSS T and L refer to an eclipse of the moon

---

as a tool for determining readings. However, in his desire to be completely "scientific" he ignores the important distinction between formal features (such as rhyme and meter), grammatical features, and purely stylistic features. It is only the last (in the most general sense) which I include in my use, below, of the term "literary excellence." Further, Hill says that in ignoring literary evidence he is "following the practice of the most important of all general considerations of manuscript study . . . *The Calculus of Variants,* W. W. Greg, Oxford: Clarendon Press, 1927" (p. 66). But Greg makes it clear that he is only *postponing* the application of any methods of determining originality, of which literary judgment is one facet, until an exact method of classifying and comparing variants can be outlined: "This completes the present sketch of the Calculus of Variants. Its scope is admittedly restricted, since, without the notion of originality, which has to be imported from outside, it can lead to no definite results" (Greg, p. 53).

instead of the sun (1. 94), and to knight instead of king
(1. 644), we suspect that they are in common error.[65]
Another aspect of this first assumption is that in *The
Awntyrs* words common to the alliterative tradition such
as *blonke* and *pade* are more likely to be original than the
variants *stede* and *tade,* and that a formulaic expression
such as *sighed full sore* is to be preferred to *weeped full
sore.* Finally, there is the assumption, which has no place
in textual criticism because of its purely subjective basis,
that a certain reading is better solely on the grounds of
"literary excellence."

   The basis for our second assumption, that we can infer
the *direction* of change, is the knowledge we have of
scribal practices gained from an examination of those
cases where the direction of change is obvious. For example, there are at least 20 instances where MS T has
fulle before an adverb which is not present in the other
three texts.[66] This is clear evidence in our case for the
tendency of scribes to make their text more emphatic
which George Kane has illustrated abundantly from the
MSS of *Piers Plowman.* Kane also makes a rough division
of scribal variants into unconscious, semi-conscious and
conscious substitutions. Unconscious substitutions are
errors due to slips of the eye or pen which the scribe
would have corrected had he been aware of them. These
errors, usually called mechanical, include homeoteleuton,

[65] Hill says that the use of such methods would cause one to
emend "stout Cortez" in Keats' sonnet (p. 69). This might be true
for an editor who is using conjectural emendation rather than choosing between variants, and who ignored all manuscript evidence,
neither of which is true in our case.
[66] Ll. 20, 33, 85, 186, 225, 312, 340, 346, 353, 379, 384, 432,
450, 454, 486, 496, 503, 504, 633.

mentioned above, dittography, etc. They are the easiest to detect and interpret since they leave concrete evidence in the text of the *cause* of the error and also usually confuse the sense.[67] Semiconscious errors are those forced on the scribe by his dialect or idiolect, of which he may or may not have been aware. The example given above, L's use of *he* for *she* (1. 118), may be due to a scribe's unfamiliarity with the form *ho*. Another example is that in which not all the rhyme-words in a stanza have been changed from the dialect of the exemplar to that of the scribe (cf. *duellith*, 1. 4L). Conscious substitutions of one reading for another are more difficult to resolve since their cause is not in the MS or the dialect of the scribe. However, they can often be explained as the result of certain definite scribal tendencies of substitution. The substitution of a familiar word for a poetic, unfamiliar, or difficult word is a practice which can be summed up by the classical textual premise that the more difficult reading is to be preferred.[68] Related to this is the tendency (illustrated above by *fulle*) for scribes to make their text more emphatic. Examples of each type of substitution will be given below.

It is obvious that there are instances where our criterion of correctness conflicts with the assumption that the more difficult reading is to be preferred. However, in most cases there will be other factors which enable us to choose between the variants. For example, MS D has *So siked*

[67] For the mechanics of such errors see Vinaver's article quoted above. For examples in Middle English see Kane, pp. 117–124.

[68] See Vinton A. Dearing's restatement of this familiar principle: "The shorter reading, the harder reading, the harsher reading, the rarer form, the reading at first glance apparently wrong, are probably the earlier." *A Manual of Textual Analysis,* Berkeley and Los Angeles, 1959, p. 17.

he sare in l. 559 while MS I has *So wepputte he fulle sare.*
Now *siked* makes a formulaic phrase with *sare* and alliterates in the line and thus would seem to be a better
reading. However, *wepputte* makes a link with l. 560
(where *w* alliterates), and since the last line of a stanza
often does not alliterate, it too could be a correct reading.
The assumption which determines our choice in this case
is that the more difficult reading is more likely to be
original, and that the scribe of D changed *wepputte* to
siked for the alliteration, not realizing that the link was on
wepputte.

Each of the following groups of variants illustrates one
aspect of the editorial problem. Some groups indicate the
cause of error (confusion of letters) or reason for substitution (difficult word), others the basis for choosing
between variants (rhyme, link, etc.). Since various factors are involved in determining originality, any one
variant could be included in more than one group. For
instance, MS L's *claterid* in l. 132 makes less sense than
MS D's *chatered,* and misses the alliteration on *ch.* However, it is included in the group of mechanical errors
since it is due to the confusion between the letters *ch* and
cl (cf. MS D's *clolle* for *cholle,* l. 114). Thus the inclu-
sion of a variant under a particular heading does not
necessarily imply that that is the sole basis for rejecting
the reading.

The following examples of mechanical scribal error
are quite clear and need no special comment.

(5)   a)   Anticipation of copy (including the omission
           of letters):
           sa savmhellus, 24I; kenettis, 44L (from l. 45);
           droupun, 52IL and droupe, 53L (from l. 54);

106I (picks up the corresponding line from the next stanza); cleying, 119D; skeled, 120D; he helpes, 177D; is (for bitis), 211D; tying, 292D; rebe, 394D (for rybe); scas (anticipation of the *s* in cast), 613D; right (for bright), 645L.

b) Repetition of copy (including dittography): the chace, 63L (rechace, l. 62); Thus, 152I (from l. 151); Lolo, 153L; Fro cite, 211I (from l. 210); fontestone one, 225D; ye yete, 323D (for ye ete).

c) Confusion of letters or minims: clene (for bene), 71L; clolle (for cholle), 114D; clatered (for chaterid), 132L; delices (for delites), 213L; cure (for aure), 253D; glisset (for gliffed), 356IL; brake (for blake), 385D; glomed (for glemed or glowed), 393T; polemus (for poleinus?), 396D; feld (for folde), 500TL; greuut (for gremit?), 524I; þare (for ȝare), 567D; ioy (for roy), 627D.

d) Incorrect word division: a nayre and (cf. D ane errant), 349I; An nanlas (for An anlas), 390I; Arther schayer, 491I; þi none, 628I.

e) Incorrect line division: 400–1T (by putting *to see,* from the end of l. 400 at the beginning of l. 401, the scribe was forced to change ll. 401–403 for the rhyme.)

At the other extreme from mechanical errors are conscious scribal alterations. The most common of these is the substitution of an easier or more familiar term for a difficult or poetic word: [69]

(6)   4 dere] kyng L. 18 hawe] TI; herde D; hye L. 72
        vndre] mydday I. 167 Muse] Loke L. 219 vnder]
        midday L. 298 slake] slade L. 299 ferlyes] chaunce
        L. 331 frithe] fuilde I. 383 *and* 386 horse] stede I.
        390 anlas] mayles T. 398 fresone] fair folower L.
        493 galiard] Dame Gaynour I. 528 bronde] swerd
        L. 536 skriles] sorowis L. 577 bronched hym]
        berus to him I. 590 Stones of iral] Stones of grete
        strengthe L. 606 groueling] doun to L. 612 þat
        cruel] þat kene knyghte L. 616 atteled] wend I.
        643 medlert] world L. 671 batailed] moted T.

Between the clear examples of mechanical error and scribal glossing there are many cases in which the cause of substitution is uncertain. In the following examples the substitution may be a conscious gloss or simply a misreading:

(7)   56 þay werray] þayre werre on I; wery were L. 266
        whele] wele L. 275 fey] fery I. 355 tasses] tassellus
        I. 513 deray] delaye T. 535 waynes at] wayvis at
        L. 591 stiþe] stiff L. 629 blede] bidus I. 641 re-
        synge] T; reysone D.

There is also a body of variants of the type George Kane calls "homoeographs," which "preserve something of the shape of the supplanted, original words or phrases, but little or nothing of their meaning or relation to the context" (p. 132). Kane argues that scribes were reluctant to copy faithfully something they did not understand, even to the point of replacing it with something which

[69] Unless otherwise noted, the *lemma* indicates the reading of **D** and of any MS for which no variant is given.

makes no sense in the context. The following may be
examples of this type:

(8)   87 wonges] L; wlonkes I. 121 todes] dedis T. 265
       king] kynd L. 295 Dorset] desesde I. 353 with
       pane] TL; in poon I. 375 ynoghe] TI; I-nore D.
       408 viser] vesage T. 497 by-lyue] wiþ love L. 661
       saȝtlynge] semblynge T. 668 halle] al holy L.

Another group of substitutions in which it is hard to
distinguish between conscious and unconscious motiva-
tion is that in which the substitute reading may have been
taken from or influenced by the same or a similar word
in the immediate context:

(9)   17 rybees] rebans I (occurs in l. 16). 22 serclet]
       I L; set D (occurs in ll. 21 and 23). 40 burnes]
       barons L (cf. baraynes in l. 41). 132 chaftis] T;
       chalus D (cholle earlier in the line). 147 Gretter]
       greyþer L (greythid later in the line in L). 287 en-
       closed] crownyd L (occurs in l. 288). 379 clere]
       clene T (occurs in l. 378). 418 gyllis] TIL; grylles
       D (occurs in l. 422). 463 Kestes] lukes T (occurs
       in l. 462). 486 wisly] worthely L (occurs in l.
       487). 508 gaily graþed] graythely graþed TL.

The most consistent tendency of scribal substitution in
the MSS of *The Awntyrs* is the attempt to make the text
more explicit. The substitution of synonyms for difficult
words, mentioned above, is one example of this tendency,
but it becomes even clearer when we notice the additions
which the scribes make in their texts. The following examples are typical:

(10)   25 One a mule as þe mylke] One a mule whit as
        þe mylke L. 46 fel] fellede downe T. 109 as a

stone] as stylle as a stone I; stil as a stone L. 218
trentales] trentes of masse I. 283 and 296 Gete
þe] Gete þe wele I. 415 lenge] lende T; lende here
L. 469 leue] leue þe L. 541 þe stede hede] Gauan
stede hede I. 574 þat fautes] þat of fighte fawtis
L. 696 he wedded] Sir Gallerone wedded T.

Many of these additions make the line hypermetrical,
and their effect is to destroy some of the poetic compres-
sion and ellipsis in the poem. One type of poetical license
in particular, the substantive use of an adjective, often
causes one of the scribes to expand the text. Hence such
changes as the following:

(11)   46 femayles] female dure I. 66 þe pruddest in
        palle] þe kyng pruddest in pal L. 391 þat stourne
        vppone stede] þat steryne was one stede T. 502
        gentil] gentille mene T. 612 þat cruel] þat kene
        knyghte L. 641 thiese ryalle] T; þis riall route I.
        657 þo sturne] those knyghtes T; þese sturun men
        I.

Having identified the various types of scribal substitutions, we soon find certain characteristic changes in one
MS or another. These usually involve either the avoid-
ance of a word which the scribe found difficult (examples
a–f), or the use of a favorite formula (examples g–j):

(12)   a)   The word *blonke* occurs four times in the
              poem. In l. 29 MS L omits it completely, in
              ll. 499 and 548 it is replaced by *bodyes/
              body* and in l. 563 by *stede*. It is obvious
              that some scribe in the transmission of L
              did not understand this poetic word.

b)   L replaces *wlonkest* by *worthiest* in ll. 9 and
      347, and *wlonkest I wene* by *semely to seene*
      in l. 696. These are the only occurrences of
      the word.

c)   The word *hapel* occurs six times in the poem
      and in each instance it is either omitted or
      replaced by another word in L (ll. 42, 130,
      131, 488, 586, 698).

d)   Of the two instances of the word *renke* in
      the poem MS I omits it in l. 460 and sub-
      stitutes the word *rengthe* in l. 640.

e)   The word for groves or thickets, spelled
      variously *skuwes, skowes, schaghes* in D,
      seems not to have been understood by the
      scribe of MS T. In one occurrence T sub-
      stitutes *schowys,* changing the meaning con-
      siderably (l. 53), and in the other two
      substitutes *cleues/clewes* (ll. 67 and 129).
      This is a good example of a case where T's
      misunderstanding of the word in two in-
      stances (ll. 67 and 129) gives us strong sup-
      port for rejecting what at first might seem a
      plausible reading in l. 53.

f)   L substitutes synonyms for *wy/wee* in ll.
      334, 405, 639 and 692 and omits it com-
      pletely in l. 365.

g)   MS I has a marked preference for the for-
      mulaic phrase *Gawayne* (or *Gaynour*) *the*
      gode:
      14:    Sir Gawayne þe gay.   D T
             Sir Gawayne the gode.   I

27: Al in gleterand golde. D T L
And thus Dame Gaynour þe gode.
I

157: After Gaynour þe gay Sir Gawyne is
gone. D T L
Thenne Syr Gauan the gode to Gaynour is gone. I

508: Gawyne was gaily graþed in grene.
D T L (TL have graythely for
gaily)
Thenne Syr Gauan þe gode was
graþed in grene. I

598: As al mene sene. D
Wiþ her grey eyen. L
For Gawan þe gode. I

633: The grones of Sir Gawayne greuene
me sare. D
The grones of Sir Gauan þe gode hit
greuis me sore. I

h) MS I also uses the phrase *in mydde þe lyste*
twice where it is a unique variant (ll. 489,
566).

i) MS D has apparently substituted *huntynge
in hast* for *huntynge with hornnes* in l. 43
and for *huntyng in holtis* in l. 711.

j) There are four places in the poem (ll. 342,
368, 381, 444) where MS D uses the word
brandene/brandure (which we should probably read *braudene/braudure,* "embroider,
embroidery"), all of which seem suspect,
and only one of which is supported by another MS (l. 444I).

The significance of these examples is that evidence in clear cases of a typical scribal tendency of substitution gives us a good basis for determining originality in unclear cases.

The absence of one of the formal features of rhyme, link or alliteration, as mentioned above, is good reason to question a reading. However, since these features are not invariant and one MS might innovate to provide a better link or fuller alliteration we must have additional reason to decide that a reading is a scribal error. MS I, for example, usually repeats the linking phrase more completely than the other MSS and in some cases has an unoriginal reading which makes a fuller link (in ll. 66, 125, 456, 607 and 651). The following examples of non-alliterating scribal substitutions are typical of the MSS. It will be seen that in many cases the word replaced is a difficult or poetic word:

(13)   82 sneterand] sliteryng L; slete and T (allit. on *sn* group). 112, 113 radde, rad] TIL; drad D. 115 pade] padok IL, tade T. 124 holt(es)] IL; wode D; hillys T. 225 Folowed] Halowyd L. 367 blunket] plonkete T. 417 gile] lye L (also misses rhyme). 424 vnwylles] vnethankes T (alliteration on *w,* also misses rhyme). 449 braide] prayd I. 653 liȝte] righte L. 710 hore] bare T.

Evidence in the link of an unoriginal reading is difficult to assess because the poem is not consistent, but the following cases are clear examples:

(14)   104 bare] sore L. 207, 208 sayne, say] drye, telle T. 286 knyghte] TIL; king D. 299 ferlyes] chaunce L. 377 knight] wighte L. 533 In stiropes

striȝte] Wiþ tho dyntis y-dighte L. 611, 612 kene, kenely] schene, clenly T. 711 holtis] T; haast D.

Since rhyme is the most consistent formal feature of *The Awntyrs,* instances of words which do not rhyme are strong evidence for rejecting a reading, and in many cases (see for example ll. 22T and 57L) they give us support for rejecting the whole line. The following are representative examples:

(15)   32, 34 felle, telle] fellis, tellis L. 33 rides] rydest I. 57 huwes] hillys T; hound L. 65 to sene] to see I. 163 grone] wise L. 202 is] ware I (perhaps influenced by the -are rhyme in the odd lines). 207 trowe] knewe L. 209, 211 sytis, bytes] T; ywis, is D (D also misses the alliteration in both lines). 253 þing] thingus I. 277 deued] dynyd L (probably due to dyntis, the preceding word). 392 strykelyd on stray] L; his pencelle displaied D. 503 shene] shent L. 542 bi þe rode] I; to þe grounde D. 572 fighte] foȝtun I (due to the force of I's dialect). 573 felde] fildus I. 617 slikes] slydys T.

The alliterative poets of the North and the North-West Midlands tended to alliterate on all four stressed syllables and often had five alliterating syllables in the line. In *The Awntyrs* there are many lines with three alliterating syllables in the first half-line. The following examples of words omitted or changed in one MS are evidence of a scribal tendency to reduce these lines to a regular pattern of two alliterations in the first half-line:

(16)   16 riche] *om.* I. 124 hiȝene] are T. 136 þes wayes] *om.* I. 344 of lote] *om.* I. 360 King crowned in

kithe] þenne our comeliche king I; The crownyd
kyng L. 366 and gay] *om*. I. 563 And boldely]
Þen he I. 639 in þis world] ȝette I. 645 þat burly]
forth L.

There are many examples in *The Awntyrs* of the repetition of the same alliterating letter in successive lines. In
at least one instance this feature seems to have been combined with excessive alliteration within the line to produce
a couplet with ggg/gg alliteration in each line. The first
half of ll. 59 and 60 are as follows:

(17)   59:   They gaf to no gamone   D
                Thay gafe no gamene no grythe   T
                Þay geuen no gomen nyf no grythe   I
                They gyue no game grith   L
        60:    Þe grete grendes in þe greues   D
                Grete hundis   T
                Þe grehoundys in þe grene greues   I
                Grete houndis of þe grasse   L

We can see that MS D has omitted one alliterating syllable
in l. 59 and MS T has omitted one in l. 60, and that the
use of the Northern term *grendes* (*greundes*) has caused
further alterations in I and L in l. 60.

In most of the examples discussed so far we have
demonstrated how one of the variants can be judged unoriginal. However, there are also cases in which we must
choose among three readings where none, or at most one
of them can be shown to be scribal. In this case we attempt to show that one of the readings is more probably
original since it is likely to have given rise to the other
two:

(18)   a)   57 The huntes þei halowe] Hying to halowe
                L; Thay hunte and halowes T; þe hunteres

þei halowe I. The less familiar term for hunters has been changed to the more usual form in I, has been omitted completely by L, and has been changed to a verb in T, producing an uncharacteristic lack of parallelism.

b)   82 sneterand (snawe)] snyterand I; slete and T; sliteryng L. D and I have variant spellings of the correct reading. T has mistaken the present participle for a noun + *and,* perhaps indicating an intermediate error *sleterand.* Both T and L miss the alliteration, which is on the consonant group *sn.*

c)   87 wonges ful wete] L; waymynges wete D; vengeance fulle wete T; wlonkes full wete I. The rare word *wonges,* which, however, occurs elsewhere in this formulaic phrase (see *OED* s. v. *Wang,* sb.[1]) has produced nonsense in T and I, and a poor substitute in D.

d)   212 blendis my blode] TL; bledis my ble D; blynde is my ble I. D has changed an unfamiliar word to a more common one, obviously influenced by *blode,* while I has seen it as two words. (This example may indicate a reading *blendis my ble* in a MS from which D and I, but not T and L, are derived.)

e)   289 þat segge schall ensese him] I; A sege shal he seche D; That sege salle be sesede

T; He shal ensege sikirly L. MS T has a variant of the correct *ensese* (take possession, appoint himself) while D's 'a man shall he seek' and L's 'he shall besiege' are obvious attempts to make sense out of something the scribe did not understand.

f)   349 ane errant kniȝte] ane armed knyghte T; a nayre and a knyȝt I; a knyghte L. MS I's *a nayre and* ('an heir and') could only be derived, perhaps by mishearing during dictation, from D, showing that T's *armed* is a gloss for *errant*.

g)   514 Swyre] schuldir T; swithe L. T's *schuldir* is a gloss for the rare form *swyre,* while L's *swithe* is an attempt to retain the alliteration on *sw,* although it does not seem to make any sense.

h)   Two variants which have so far remained unexplained by previous editors are *swaþel* (540D) and *smyther* (544I). They can only be explained by looking at the larger pattern of scribal variants in the poem:
55 (line omitted in D):
By the streams that   *swyftly*   (TL) flow.
                                  squytherly   (I)
540 (line omitted in T):
With a stroke of the sword
     þat swaþel   (D)   strikes him.
     squeturly   (I)
     þe toþer   (L)
544 (line omitted in T):

> He was *hasty and smert* (D)
> *smyther and smerte* (543I)
> *swithely smert* (L)

It is obvious that *swyftly* and *hasty* are glosses for the same word, *toþer* a weak substitution, and *swaþel* and *smyther* meaningless homoeographs for a word which had some of the letters they share. The difficulty of the word may also have caused the omission of the line in D. The only possible source for all the other readings is L's *swithely* (OE *swīþlīce*), which fits all three contexts, is rare in ME and is similar enough in form to be the source of both *swaþel* and *smyther*.

Another situation in which we can determine originality is that in which one reading is the result of a scribe changing a line in order to make better sense because he has not looked at the following line or lines. We can illustrate this tendency first of all by looking at a line in which the direction of change is not clear. In l. 68 MSS D and I read *Al but Sir Gawayne* while T and L have *Nane bot*. Either reading may be correct, though they are contradictory at first glance, depending on how we construe the following line, which begins with the verb *Beleues,* 'remains.' T and L would read 'No one but Gawain remains with Guenevere' while D and I would read 'They assemble (l. 66); everyone except Gawain, who remains with Guenevere.' I think it probable that the reading of D and I was misunderstood and changed, but either direction is possible. Some further examples of this type of variant follow:

(19)   a)   70 vnder a lefe sale] I; þat lady so smalle
            DTL. The reading of I is supported by l. 71,
            which is the same in all MSS (*Of box and of
            berber bigged ful bene*), and which makes
            no sense without the presence in l. 70 of the
            lefe sale which it describes.

       b)   102–104 The sense of this passage in D is "I
            shall learn the ways that may cure the sor-
            rows of that body bare." The other MSS, not
            looking ahead to ll.103–104, have changed
            'wayes' in l. 102. T changes it to 'ways,
            roads,' construing the line with l. 101, while
            I and L change *wayes* to *woe,* making *bales*
            in l. 103 redundant.

       c)   696–697 MS D reads: There he wedded his
            wife wlonkest I wene/Withe giftes and gar-
            sons Sir Galerone þe gay. MS T substitutes
            Sir Gallerone for *he* in l. 696 (making the
            line too long) to make the reference ex-
            plicit, not seeing the name in the next line.
            Then in l. 697 the scribe has to change *Sir
            Galerone* to *of Sir Gawayn* (referring to the
            gifts).

This concludes my presentation of the evidence for accepting or rejecting variant readings. I have not included
the more complicated variants, all of which will be discussed in the notes. My sole purpose has been to show
that "presumption of originality can be established often
enough to justify a process of editing," which, as George
Kane points out, is the postulate on which an editor must
act (p. 146). The use which is made of the evidence in

my edition of *The Awntyrs* is the same as that which Kane
describes so well in his Introduction:

> The examples set out above will have shown my
> use of the various resources for determining origi-
> nality. I have tried to prevent any of them from
> becoming rules, or arranging themselves in a hier-
> archy. Each crux is unique, and often several con-
> siderations must be weighed in its solution. It will
> then be evident that the authority of a text of this
> kind must vary from line to line; the assurance with
> which originality is determinable, and, indeed, has
> been determined by its editor, must depend on the
> arguments available in any given case and his ability
> to perceive them. It has seemed to me right in hon-
> esty to make this clear. If a 'critical' text is one in
> which the editor has compared the variant readings,
> then mine is critical, but it is not critical in any
> Lachmannian sense of being invested with a mys-
> terious authority that sets it beyond question by its
> users. Therefore I have laid my decisions open to
> examination by full presentation of the evidence and
> an exposition of my grounds for determining origi-
> nality. (p. 165)

3. MANUSCRIPT RELATIONS

Once we have determined the original readings from
among the variants in a number of cases, we can approach
the question of the genealogy of the MSS. The purpose of
constructing a genealogy is that we can then use recension, that is the rejection of readings that do not derive
from the archetype of all the MSS, as our method of editing. This method, sometimes called the Lachmannian

method, is best described in a small book by Paul Maas called *Textual Criticism:*

> The business of textual criticism is to produce a text as close as possible to the original (*constitutio textus*). . . . In each individual case the original text either has or has not been transmitted. So our first task is to establish what *must* or *may* be regarded as transmitted—to make the recension (*recensio*).[70]

The basis for constructing a stemma of the MSS by this method is the identification of genealogical groups by the use of "conjunctive error": "It can be proved that two witnesses (B and C) belong together as against a third (A) by showing an error common to B and C of such a nature that it is highly improbable that B and C committed it independently of each other" (p. 43). In recent years the use of recension has fallen into disfavor with many editors, due largely to the criticisms of Joseph Bédier, Dom Henri Quentin and Giorgio Pasquali.[71] Thus Eugène Vinaver can say: "It is no longer possible to classify manuscripts on the basis of 'common errors;' genealogical 'stemmata' have fallen into discredit, and with them has vanished our faith in composite critical texts" (p. 351).

Leaving aside for now the theoretical basis for the method, we can examine the results of its application to the MSS of *The Awntyrs*. Various students of the poem

---

[70] Translated from the German by Barbara Flower, Oxford, 1958, p. 1. The original is "Textkritik," in *Einleitung in die Altertumswissenschaft,* ed. A. Gercke and E. Norden, Berlin, 1927, I, 2, pp. 1–18.

[71] For a short summary of the works of these three scholars see "Critics of the Genealogical Method" in Joseph M. Manly and Edith Rickert, *The Text of the Canterbury Tales,* Vol. II, Chicago, 1940, pp. 12–18.

have constructed a stemma of the MSS with conflicting results.[72] Paul Burtness, whose study is the most complete, and based on all four MSS, says: "I have not succeeded in establishing a genealogy which will account for all the patterns of correspondence in the MSS and do not believe that a definite genealogy is inferable from the available evidence" (p. 9). The problem is that the evidence of conjunctive error leads to results which indicate that conflation, or contamination of the MSS has obscured the lines of descent. And, as Maas indicates, where contamination is present recension is not possible: "If the first of the assumptions made in #6 does not apply, that is if individual scribes have 'contaminated' several examples, the process of *eliminatio* within the area of these 'contaminations' is greatly hindered, if not made impossible." [73] Rather than attempt to give all the evidence for genealogical groupings I shall give one example of "conjunctive error" for each of the groups which emerges from such a study. The following seven groups are mutually contradictory:

> TD: 96 constans, costantyne] IL; costarde, costardyne TD.
>
> TL: 94 sone] DI; mone TL (*sone* alliterates and gives sense).
>
> DL: 271 whele wryghte] TI; wighte DL (they misunderstand the reference to Fortune).
>
> DI: 158 to þat body hase he broghte that birde]

---

[72] Paul Burtness outlines the results of the studies of Lübke, Amours, and Smith (see Bibliography) and concludes: "Accordingly, on the basis of the same evidence, except that Smith had L where the others did not, Lübke, Amours, and Smith reached mutually contradictory genealogies" (p. 8).

[73] P. 7. See also p. 49: "No specific has yet been discovered against contamination."

        TL; to þe body he her brouȝte and (to) þe
        burde DI.
IL: 356 gliffed] TD; glisset IL.
TDI: 80 felle] L; fellis TDI (incorrect rhyme).
DTL: 70 vnder a lefe sale] I; þat lady so smalle DTL.

It should be clear that the degree to which we can demonstrate the direction of error in the above examples varies greatly, and this is one important reason for rejecting the genealogical method. A more important reason, however, is that in order to decide that a particular reading is in error we must be able to explain its cause, and the more obvious the cause of the error, the more likely it is that it could have arisen independently in more than one MS.[74] The variant reading *glisset* in I and L above (l. 356) due to the similarity between *ff* and *ss* is a good illustration of the problem.

In order to avoid the problems involved in isolating "common errors" various scholars have devised methods of constructing a genealogy based on variational groups of MSS without regard to the direction of variation.[75] In

---

[74] This valuable insight is Greg's: "Though the matter lies beyond my present theme I may point out a curious difficulty that arises when we attempt to infer manuscript relation from supposed originality. To show that a reading is original two main lines of argument are available: that the reading itself is satisfactory, and that it explains the origin of the erroneous alternative. But, as a rule, the easier it is to explain how an error arose, the less valid the assumption that it only arose once. Thus the more likely it is that one alternative is correct, the less certain it is that the other points to common derivation." p. 20, fn. 1.

[75] Dom Henri Quentin's method is the earliest and most complicated. It is presented in his *Essais de Critique Textuelle,* Paris, 1926, and described by J. Burke Severs, "Quentin's Theory of Textual Criticism," *English Institute Annual 1941,* New York, 1942, pp. 65–93. W. W. Greg's logical analysis of the methods of comparing and isolating variants in his *Calculus of Variants* is the basis of two more recent attempts to use a scientific approach, Archibald A.

using one of these methods we must restrict ourselves to what Greg calls "significant variants," that is "those variants which give rise to at least two groups of more than one manuscript each" (p. 20). This is because in any group of variants in which there is a reading supported by only one manuscript (A:B, A:BC, A:BCD, etc.) it is always possible that the single reading is unoriginal, in which case we have no evidence for grouping the other MSS. Since there are four MSS of *The Awntyrs,* we have only three possible types of significant variation, and we have sufficient evidence of the occurrence of each type to prove that none of them gives us support for the construction of a genetic group:

DT:IL

52 durkene, darkys] DT; droupun IL.
141 paynes] DT; penaunce IL.
226 miȝeti] DT; modur IL.
296 wele] IL; *om* DT.
431 frely is] DT; is fre IL.
622 mercy] DT; pety IL.

DL:TI

138 knowene] DL; krysommede TI.
163 graceles] DL; grisely TI.
191 tel] DL; talke TI.
269 kniȝte] DL; kynge TI.
309 riche] DL; kyng TI.

Hill's article on the "distributional study of texts" and Vinton Dearing's *Manual of Textual Analysis,* both noted earlier. The basis for all these methods, the use of variational groups without resorting to "common error," is the same, although their methods for constructing a genealogy from the groups vary considerably.

664 quode þe kynge] TI; *om* DL.
675 his] DL; thi TI.

DI:TL

35 trouthe, truly] DI; righte TL.
42–5 The order of these lines is different in TL than in DI.
68 Al but] DI; Nane bot TL.
100 grome, gome] DI; Gaweayne TL.
289 session, cessione] DI; sesone, sesoun, TL.
413 seid, speke . . . vppone] DI; carpede . . . one TL.
433 lede opone lyue] DI; leueande lede TL.

These examples, even more than those of common error, show that the descent of the MSS is mixed, and that the attempt to construct a stemma on which to base an edition would be useless.[76]

There is one further point concerning the relationship of the MSS. Although the evidence is too large to be cited in full, it will be apparent from the apparatus that T and L agree in a variant reading, often one which is probably unoriginal, far more often than any two other MSS. This is evidence, which must be used with caution, for some connection between these two MSS. Further, of the indications in the MSS of points of division in the text, D has a large capital and I the space for one at l. 508, and they are the only MSS to agree in this way. The only use which will be made of these correspondences is that the agreement of T and L, and, less importantly, of I and D,

---

[76] The distributional method is no more able to deal with contamination than the Lachmannian. See for example postulates VIII and IX in Hill's article, pp. 69–71.

will have less weight in choosing between variants than an agreement which crosses this division.

4. EDITORIAL METHODS

Since recension is not possible for the MSS of *The Awntyrs,* the choices left to the editor are either to reproduce one or more of the texts as faithfully as possible, or to choose one MS as a base and amend it with readings from the other three. Abundant evidence has been given above that the original reading can be determined in a significant number of cases; therefore, the copy-text form has been chosen as the best way of editing the poem. The Douce MS is selected as the base because it is the most complete, and because the number and kind of its errors show it to be less corrupt than the other MSS.

The Lambeth MS is the least satisfactory text of the poem. As mentioned above, the fact that it was copied in a dialect area far removed from the original has caused errors of geographical reference as well as grammatical form. Also, L has conscious substitutions, especially replacement of the alliterative vocabulary, more often than the other MSS, as shown by the groups of examples cited above (see especially No. 6). Frequently these changes have resulted in the loss of a rhyme, link, or alliterating syllable. Some additional examples of the frequency with which the scribe of L has found the text difficult are the following:

> 11 dougheti] dospers. 19 palwerke] perlis. 20 þat þe rayne shedes] þeron þe rayne slidis. 46 ful þike-folde] ful meny-folde. 71 Of box] Wiþ bowis. 319 failene] wantis. 369 fax] forhed. 470 life] self. 471 stond] dele. 615 lymped] happith.

The Ireland MS usually has satisfactory rhymes, links, and alliterations, although the difference in dialect from the original has caused a few changes, e.g., *foʒtun* for *fighte,* an incorrect rhyme in l. 572. In fact the scribe of I was more likely to change the text to produce a "better" reading than the scribes of the other MSS—there are more examples of changes for explicitness, and the links are usually repeated more exactly (often in error). Two further examples of I's willingness to change the text are its frequent addition to the line of "quod he" or an equivalent phrase (though not unusual in ME romances, these phrases are clearly innovations in ll. 137, 209, 222, 265, 313, 365, 410, 414, 417, 434, 515, 525, 551, and 646) and the substitution of a line from another place in the poem to fill an omission in the text or to replace a difficult reading (l. 107a, from 87a; l. 319, from 228; l. 362, from 415; l. 394, from 17; l. 566, from 489).

The Thornton and Douce MSS make far fewer of the more obvious scribal errors than do I and L. T is apparently in the same dialect as the original, but it is not for that reason alone a better text since numerous Midland forms indicate that it derives from a MS copied in another dialect. Because T is the least complete of the MSS, with large omissions caused by damaged or missing leaves, D has been chosen as the base MS.

Since D and T are less corrupt, and may represent different branches of the stemma of the MSS, agreement between them will usually indicate a more original reading. In most other cases, because of the nature of the genealogical evidence outlined above, it is not possible to rely on simple majority agreement among the MSS. Therefore, in the absence of any other indications of originality, the reading of the base MS will be adopted.

This procedure may have resulted in the acceptance of some unoriginal readings, but, since the causes of scribal error are likely to operate identically in more than one MS, we must rely on the MS which we know to be less corrupt. An example of the acceptance of a minority reading is line 210, where T, I, and L agree in having "saints" while D has "sere men." In this case none of the other three texts agrees exactly, and D is best for the meter and alliteration, so we allow it to stand. There are also cases in which the arguments for originality are so numerous and well-balanced that the deciding factor is reliance on our base MS. For an example of a very confusing situation of this kind, see the note to ll. 327–334.

There are a number of passages in the poem in which the order of the lines varies in one or more MS. In these cases the order in D is generally preferable (another indication, along with the fact that it has fewer omissions, that the transmission of D is less corrupt), and in order to collate the text the order of the lines in the other three MSS has been made to agree with that of D. The following listing will indicate where the other MSS differ, and includes six lines which are obvious innovations found in only one of the MSS. The line numbers of D are cited first, followed by the original order of the lines in the other MSS:

42–43:   44–45 in T and L.
44–45:   42–43 in T and L.
205–207:   207, 205, 206 in T, I, and L.
253–255:   252–254 in T; T adds a line after these three lines to make up for the omission of l. 252: "For to come to that blysse that euer more salle laste."

299–303:   299, 302–303, 300–301, 302–303 in T.
            (The scribe started the stanza with the
            third and fourth lines, 302–303, and then
            went back to 300–301, causing the loss of
            ll. 304–305.)

MS L adds a line after l. 333 to make up for the omis-
    sion of l. 326: "Knyghtis *and* squyers on eu*e*rych
    sydis."

MS L adds two lines after l. 346 to make up for the
    omission of ll. 341–342: "þer led hy*m* by þe
    bridal a lady gent *and* small*e*/And to þat renk
    rial he raykid ful right*e*."

362–363:   363–362 in L.

397–398:   398–397 in T (also omits the line corre-
            sponding to 396D).

414–415:   415–414 in T, I, and L.

427–428:   428–427 in I.

465–466:   466–465 in L.

543–545:   544, 545, 543 in I.

588–590:   590, 589, 588 in I.

MS L adds two lines, after ll. 684 and 685, to make
    up for the omission of ll. 680–681: "Vp-on þis
    couen*a*u*n*t if þat þow will*e*/ /In forestis and
    fritthes þat bene so faire."

Also, MS T has written stanzas 18–20 in the order 20,
    18, 19.

The apparatus for the text is intended to be a complete
record of all variants except obvious spelling variations.
The lemma, enclosed by a square bracket, indicates the
reading of the base MS (or the MS from which the line is
taken when D is defective) and of any MS for which a
variant is not recorded, or whose reading has not been

indicated in a larger lemma from that line. When more than one sigil follows a variant, the spelling is that of the first MS cited, and may vary slightly in the others.

The following conventions have been used in the transcription of the text:

a) Unambiguous superscript letters have been lowered without notice: þ^e = þe.

b) Unambiguous suspensions and contractions have been expanded and indicated by underlining: w^t = *with;* þ^u = þou; cōquero² = co*n*quero*ur,* etc. The usual fifteenth-century contractions and suspensions are used, and the MSS are rarely ambiguous. A stroke through the ascender of *h* or *ll* is expanded to *e* when it is clear that it is more than a flourish, although it is often redundant (e.g., *helle, fighte*) and cannot be taken as an indication that the *e* is either etymological or pronounced.

c) Emendation of a MS reading which involves a clear mechanical error of one letter is enclosed in parenthesis and the MS reading is given in the apparatus, e.g., *cleying* = *cley(þ)ing.*

d) All other emendations are enclosed in square brackets, and the MS from which the reading is taken is indicated by having its sigil appear immediately after the lemma in the apparatus.

e) Capitalization and punctuation are added, in part to indicate the interpretation of difficult or ambiguous passages. Word divisions are as in the MSS, except that words separated in the MSS which would not be separated in modern usage are joined with a hyphen (e.g., *with-oute*).

f) Unusual features of MSS other than D, such as deletions, or additions above the line in the original hand, are not noticed unless they bear on the editorial problem.

SELECT BIBLIOGRAPHY

This list includes all works cited, and all relevant material on the poem, but not general references to *The Awntyrs* in literary histories, survey articles, etc.

Ackerman, Robert W. *An Index of the Arthurian Names in Middle English*. Stanford, 1952.

Amours, F. J., ed. *Scottish Alliterative Poems in Riming Stanzas*. STS 27, 38, Edinburgh and London, 1892, 1897.

————, ed. *The Original Chronical of Andrew of Wyntoun*. 6 vols. STS, Edinburgh, 1903–5, 1914.

Andrew, S. O. "Huchoun's Works," *Review of English Studies*, V (1929), 12–21.

Baugh, A. C. "The Middle English Romance: Some Questions of Creation, Presentation, and Preservation," *Speculum*, XLII (1967), 1–31.

Bédier, J(oseph). *La Tradition Manuscrite du Lai de L'Ombre. Reflexions sur L'Art d'Editer les Anciens Textes*. Paris, 1946.

Benson, Larry D. "The Literary Character of Anglo-Saxon Formulaic Poetry," *PMLA*, LXXXI (1966), 334–41.

Bordman, Gerald. *Motif-Index to the English Metrical Romances*. Helsinki (Folklore Fellows Communications No. 190), 1963.

Boswinkel, J. "The Structure of the Aunters of Arthur," *Handelingen van het achtentwitigste Nederlands Filologencongres*. Groningen, 1964, pp. 141–3.

Brock, Edmund, ed. *Morte Arthure*. EETS 8, London, 1871.

Brown, Arthur C. L. "On the Origin of Stanza-Linking in English Alliterative Verse," *Romanic Review,* VII (1916), 271–283.

Brown, Carleton, and Rossell Hope Robbins. *The Index of Middle English Verse.* New York, 1943.

Bülbring, K. "Über die Hs. Nr. 491 der Lambeth Bibliothek," *Herrig's Archiv,* LXXXVI (1891), 383–387.

Burtness, Paul Sidney. *A Language Study of "The Awntyrs off Arthure at the Terne Wathelyn."* Unpublished doctoral thesis, University of Chicago, 1953.

Casson, L. F., ed. *The Romance of Sir Degrevant.* EETS 221, London, 1949.

Catalogue of the Printed Books and Manuscripts bequethed by Francis Douce, Esq. to the Bodleian Library. Oxford, 1840.

Christianson, Clayton P. *"The Awntyrs of Arthure"*: *An Edition.* Unpublished doctoral thesis, Washington University, 1964.

Curschmann, Michael. "Oral Poetry in Mediæval English, French, and German Literature: Some Notes on Recent Research," *Speculum,* XLII (1967), 36–52.

Dearing, Vinton A. *A Manual of Textual Analysis.* Berkeley and Los Angeles, 1959.

Dickens, Bruce. "The Date of the Ireland Manuscript," *Leeds Studies in English and Kindred Languages,* II (1933), 62–66.

Doyle, A. I. "Note 105. Date of a MS in Bibliotheca Bodmeriana," *The Book Collector,* VIII (1959), 69.

French, Walter H., and Charles B. Hale, eds. *Middle English Metrical Romances.* New York, 1930.

Fry, Donald. "Old English Formulas and Systems," *English Studies,* XLVII.3 (June, 1967), 1–12.

Furnivall, Frederick J., ed. *Political, Religious, and Love Poems.* EETS 15, London, 1866.

Greg, W. W. *The Calculus of Variants.* Oxford, 1927.

Halliwell, James Orchard, ed. *The Thornton Romances.* Camden Society 30, London, 1844.

Hanna III, Ralph. *"The Awntyrs off Arthure at the Terne Wathelyne": An Edition Based on Bodleian Library MS. Douce 324.* Unpublished doctoral thesis, Yale University, New Haven, 1967.

Herrtage, Sidney J. H., ed. *The Early English Versions of the Gesta Romanorum.* EETSES 33, London, 1879.

Hibbard, Laura A. *Mediæval Romance in England.* New York, 1924.

Hill, Archibald A. "Some Postulates for the Distributional Study of Texts," *Studies in Bibliography,* III (1950–51), 63–95.

Holthausen, F. (Textual Notes), *Beiblatt zur Anglia,* XXXVI (1925), 187–188.

Hooper, A. G. "The Lambeth Palace MS of 'The Awntyrs off Arthure,'" *Leeds Studies in English and Kindred Languages,* III (1934), 37–43.

————. " 'The Awntyrs off Arthure': Dialect and Authorship," *Leeds Studies in English and Kindred Languages,* IV (1935), 62–74.

Hulbert, James R. "The Sources of *St. Erkenwald* and *The Trental of Gregory,*" *Modern Philology,* XVI (1919), 485–93.

James, Montague Rhodes, and Claude Jenkins. *A Descriptive Catalogue of the Manuscripts in the Library of Lambeth Palace.* London, 1930.

Kane, George, ed. *Piers Plowman: The A Version.* London, 1960.

Kaufmann, Albert, ed. *Trentalle Sancti Gregorii.* (*Erlanger Beiträge zur Englische Philologie,* Vol. III) Erlangen and Leipzig, 1889.

Kurath, Hans, Sherman F. Kuhn *et al.,* eds. *Middle English Dictionary,* Ann Arbor, 1952–.

Kurvinen, Auvo, ed. *Sir Gawain and the Carl of Carlisle in Two Versions.* Helsinki, 1951.

Laing, David, ed. *Select Remains of the Ancient Popular Poetry of Scotland.* London, 1822. Revised J. Small, 1885, W. C. Hazlitt, 1895.

Loomis, Roger Sherman, ed. *Arthurian Literature in the Middle Ages: A Collaborative History.* Oxford, 1959.

Lord, Albert B. *The Singer of Tales.* Cambridge, Mass., 1960. Reprinted as an Atheneum paperback, New York, 1965.

Lübke, H. *Awntyrs of Arthure.* Berlin (dissertation), 1883.

Maas, Paul. *Textual Criticism.* Translated by Barbara Flower. Oxford, 1958. The original is "Textkritik," in *Einleitung in die Altertumswissenschaft,* ed. A. Gercke and E. Norden, Berlin, 1927.

MacCracken, Henry N. "Concerning Huchown," *PMLA,* XXV (1910), 507–34.

Madan, Falconer. *A Summary Catalogue of Western Manuscripts in the Bodleian Library at Oxford,* Vol. IV. Oxford, 1897.

Madden, Sir Frederic, ed. *Syr Gawayne.* London, 1839.

Magoun, Francis P., Jr. "The Oral-Formulaic Character of Anglo-Saxon Poetry," *Speculum,* XXVIII (1953), 446–467. Reprinted in Lewis E. Nicholson, ed., *An Anthology of Beowulf Criticism,* Notre Dame, Indiana, 1963, pp. 189–221.

Manly, John M. and Edith Rickert. *The Text of The Canterbury Tales: II, Classification of the Manuscripts.* Chicago, 1940.

Matthews, William. *The Tragedy of Arthur.* Berkeley and Los Angeles, 1960.

Medary, Margaret P. "Stanza-Linking in Middle English Verse," *Romanic Review,* VII (1916), 243–270.

Menner, R. J. " 'Sir Gawain and the Green Knight' and the West Midland," *PMLA,* XXXVII (1922), 503–26.

Moore, Samuel, Sanford B. Meech, and Harold Whitehall. *Middle English Dialect Characteristics and Dialect Boundaries.* Ann Arbor, 1935.

Murray, James, ed. *The Romance and Prophecies of Thomas of Erceldoune.* EETS 61, London, 1875.

——— et al., eds. *A New English Dictionary on Historical Principals,* 12 vols. and Supplement. Oxford, 1933.

Neilson, George. *Huchown of the Awle Ryale.* Glasgow, 1902.

———. "Crosslinks between *The Pearl* and *The Awntyrs of Arthur,*" *The Scottish Antiquary, or Northern Notes and Queries,* XVI (1902), 67–78.

Oakden, J. P. *Alliterative Poetry in Middle English: I. The Dialectal and Metrical Survey.* Manchester, 1930.

———. Assisted by Elizabeth R. Innes. *Alliterative Poetry in Middle English: II. A Survey of the Traditions.* Manchester, 1935.

Oesterley, Hermann, ed. *Gesta Romanorum.* Berlin, 1872.

Ogden, M. S. *The 'Liber de Diversis Medicinis.'* EETS 207, London, 1938.

Ogle, M. B. "The Orchard Scene in *Tydorel* and *Sir Gowther,*" *Romanic Review,* XIII (1922), 37–43.

Pasquali, Giorgio. *Storia della Tradizione e Critica del Testo.* Florence, 1952.

Paton, Florence Ann. *A Critical Edition of the "Aunturs of Arthur."* Unpublished doctoral thesis, University of Colorado, 1963.

Paton, Lucy Allen. *Studies in the Fairy Mythology of Arthurian Romance.* Boston, 1903.

Pinkerton, John, ed. *Scotish Poems.* London, 1792.

Quentin, Dom Henri. *Essais de Critique Textuelle.* Paris, 1926.

Robson, John, ed. *Three Early English Metrical Romances.* For the Camden Society, London, 1842.

Rumble, Thomas C., ed. *The Breton Lays in Middle English.* Detroit, 1965.

Serjeantson, Mary. "The Dialects of the West Midlands in Middle English," *Review of English Studies,* III (1927), 54–67; 186–203; 319–331.

Severs, J. B. "Quentin's Theory of Textual Criticism," *English Institute Annual 1941,* New York, 1942, pp. 65–93.

———, ed. *A Manual of the Writings in Middle English, 1050–1500.* New Haven, 1967.

Sisam, Kenneth. *Studies in the History of Old English Literature*. London, 1953.

Small, John, ed. *The Poems of William Dunbar*. STS 2 and 4, Edinburgh, 1883–5.

Smith, Pearl. *Classification of Manuscripts of the Middle English Poem "Awnturs of Arthure."* Unpublished M.A. thesis, University of Chicago, 1921.

Smithers, G. V. "Story-Patterns in Some Breton Lays," *Medium Ævum*, XXII (1953), 61–92.

Tatlock, J. S. P. "Dante's Terza Rima," *PMLA*, LI (1936), 895–903.

Trautmann, Moritz. "Der Dichter Huchown und Seine Werke," *Anglia*, I (1878), 109–149.

Vinaver, Eugène. "Principles of Textual Emendation," *Studies in French Language and Medieval Literature Presented to Mildred K. Pope,* Manchester, 1939, pp. 351–369.

Waldron, Ronald A. "Oral-Formulaic Technique and Middle English Alliterative Poetry," *Speculum,* XXXII (1957), 792–804.

Webster, K. G. T. "Galloway and the Romances," *MLN,* LV (1940), 363–366.

Wells, J. E. *A Manual of the Writings in Middle English 1050–1400*. New Haven, Conn., 1916 (with nine supplements to 1945).

Weston, Jessie L. *Romance, Vision and Satire*. Boston, 1912.

THE AWNTYRS OFF ARTHURE
AT THE TERNE WATHELYNE

1 In . . . Arthur] In King Arthure tym*e* T. ane] thys I.

2 By] Be syde I. Turnewathelane] Ternewahethelyn*e*
T; Tarnewathelan I. By . . . telles] In talkyng of his
turmentis þe tale of hy*m* tellis L.

3 Whane] Als TL; þ*at* I. that] TI; and D; *om* L.

4 Withe] *om* L. and] and w*ith* TI. with þe] w*ith* þat T.
dere dwelles] kyng duellith L.

5 To] For to TI. herdes] herd I. had] hase TI. bene]
be L.

6 One] And one T; Tyl on I. to] into I.

7 To falle of þe] Fellun to tho I. falle] felle TL. in] in
þe T; þ*at* in þe L. were] L; and D; wele T; was I.
frydde] frythede T.

8 Faire . . . tyme] T; Fayre by þe firmyschamis D;
Fayre by fermesones I; So faire in felawship L.
fermysone] MS fernysone. in] by TIL.

9 Thus] *om* I. to wode] to þe wode TI; wyde L. arne
þei went] þay weyndun I. þe wlonkest] these wlonkes
I; þe worthiest L.

11 al þe] oþ*er* I. dougheti] dospers L.

12 gayest] graythist I; gaynest L. Sir] *om* L.

I

In the tyme of Arthur ane aunter by-tydde
By þe Turnewathelane—as þe boke telles—
Whane he to Carlele was comen, [that] conquerour
     kydde,
Withe dukes and dussiperes þat with þe dere dwelles,
To hunte at þe herdes þat longe had bene hydde.   5
One a day þei hem dighte to þe depe delles,
To falle of þe femailes in forest [were] frydde,
[Faire in the fer(m)ysone tyme], in frithes and
     felles.
Thus to wode arne þei went, þe wlonkest in wedes,
Bothe þe kyng and þe quene   10
And al þe dougheti by-dene;
Sir Gawayne, gayest one grene,
Dame Gaynour he ledes.

14   *line om* L. Thus] And thus T; Thenne I. þe gay] the
      gode I. Dame] TI; *om* D.

15   glemed] glemith L. fulle] so IL.

16   Withe] That was *with* I. riche] *om* I. ribaynes] rubyes
      L. so] þat T.

17   Rayled . . . rybees] Arayit aur*e with* rebans I;
      Rayed with rybans L. of rialle aray] rycheste of ray
      I. of] one T.

18   of a] was of T. hawe] TI; herde D; hye L. here] þe
      L. hedes] hydys TIL.

19   Of] Wroghte *with* T; Wiþ L. pillour] purpure I; per-
      rey L. of palwerke] and palle T; and palle werke I;
      and perlis L. of perre] and perrye TI; was pelurid L.

20   Schurde] Schruedede TL; Wos schrod I. þat] þeron
      L. shedes] schrydes T; shredes I; slidis L.

21   soþely to] full*e* sothely to T; quo sothely will I.

22   Withe . . . sides] And thus wondirfully was all*e* þe
      wyghtis wedys T. Withe] *om* I. saffres and seladynes]
      selcouþe stonys L. serclet on] IL; set by D. þe] *om*
      I.

23   sette] semyde T. of] *with* I.

24   Saude . . . of] Semlely sewede *with* T; W*ith* ryche
      sa savmhellus of I; With riche seyntis of L.

25   One] Opun I. as] whit as L. þe] *om* L.

26   Gaili] Thus gayli I; Ful gayly L.

II

Thus Sir Gawayne þe gay [Dame] Gaynour he ledes,
In a gleterand gide þat glemed fulle gay,   15
Withe   riche   ribaynes   reuersset—ho-so   righte
  redes—
Rayled withe rybees of rialle aray;
Her hode of a [hawe] huwe, þat here hede hedes,
Of pillour, of palwerke, of perre to pay;
Schurde in a short cloke þat þe rayne shedes,   20
Set ouer withe saffres soþely to say—
Withe saffres *and* seladynes [serclet on] þe sides.
Here sadel sette of þat ilke,
Saude withe sambutes of silke;
One a mule as þe mylke,   25
Gaili she glides.

27 Al . . . golde] And thus Dame Gaynour þe gode I.
    Al] Thus alle TL. in gleterand] gliteryng in L. gayly]
    ful gayly L.

28 gates] gate L. þe(2)] a TI.

29 And þat burne] Nane bot hym selfe T; And a byrne
    I; None but þat berde L. one his blonke] one a
    blonke TI; om L. withe þe quene] that with the
    quene I; by þat birde T; wiþ þe berne L. bides]
    a-bydus I.

30 borne] bore L.

31 He . . . longe] So lung he ledys þat lady I. ladde]
    ledith L. that loghe] I; þe lawe D; þose landeȝ, T;
    þe lawnde L.

32 Vnder] Sythene vndir T; þer at I; þat vndir L.
    lorere] MS lorre; lorere TL; laurialle I. þey] scho
    TIL. a felle] a hille the fellus I; þe fellis L.

33 And] Sir T; om I. withe] and I. ernestly] fulle
    ernestly T. rides] he rydest I.

34 her] om L. þe . . . telle] trewely to telle T; quo truly
    wille telle I; so righte he hem tellis L.

35 tauȝte] told L. ho þe trouthe] who þat righte T;
    quo truly me I; ho so righte L.

37 MS L. D: To ane oke he hem sette.
    T: At his triste was he sett.
    I: Vn-to a tre an (for ar) þay sette.

38 barselette] bracelet L.

39 Vnder] Vndurneth I. þe] þose T.

III

Al in gleterand golde gayly ho glides
Þe gates, with*e* S*ir* Gawayn*e,* bi þe grene welle;
And þat burne on*e* his blonke with*e* þe quene bides,
Þat borne was in Borgoyne—by boke and by belle. 30
He ladde þat lady so longe by [that loghe] sides,
Vnder a lor(e)re þey light*e,* loȝe by a felle.
And Arthur with*e* his erles ernestly rides   f.lb.
To teche hem to her tristres, þe trouthe for to telle—
To here tristres he hem tauȝt*e,* ho þe trouth*e* trowes; 35
Eche lorde with*e*-outen*e* lette
[To a tristre-tre is sette],
With*e* bowe and with*e* barselette,
Vnder þe bowes.

40   Vnder þe] Vndir þose T; Thus vndur I. þei bode þes
burnes] þay byde þan byrnes I; bodyn þe barons L.

41   þes baraynes] þose barrayne T; þe wild bore L. in]
by þe L.

42   haþeles in hiȝ] hirdmene hendely forsothte T; men
hendely L. in] on I.

43   Herken] To herkyn I; Here L. with hornnes] T L; in
hast D; *with* horne I.

44   of here] on kenettis L. in] by þe L.

45   Conforte] Thay recomforthed T; Cumfordun I; To
comfort L. here kenettes] þe knyghtis L. to] and L.

46   fel of þe] fellede downe þe T; felle to þe I; fellid L.
femayles] female dure I. ful þike] feyful thyk I; ful
meny L.

47   Withe . . . felle] W*ith* felle hounndus *and* with
fresche I; Wiþ fele fressh hondis L. felle] MS fele.
þei . . . fare] felonosly þay fare T; þay folo the fare
I; to folow þe fare L.

49   Withe . . . quelles] þay questede and quellys T;
Thay questun þay quellun I. gret] *om* L.

50   Bothe in] By TIL. and] by I.

51   Alle . . . delles] þat þe dere dwellys T. Alle] *om*
IL. dure] MS dur*ere*?

52   þei . . . dare] *And* darkys and darys T. durkene]
droupun IL. dare] daren I.

IV

Vnder þe bowes þei bode, þes burnes so bolde,   40
To byker at þes baraynes in bonkes so bare.
There mighte haþeles in hiȝ herdes be-holde,
Herken huntynge [with hornnes] in holtes so hare;
Þei kest of here couples in cliffes so colde,
Conforte here kenettes to kele hem of care.   45
Þei fel of þe femayles ful þike-folde—
Withe fresshe houndes and fel(l)e þei folowene here
    fare. . . .
Withe gret questes and quelles,
Bothe in frethes and felles,   50
Alle the dure in þe delles
Þei durkene and dare.

53   þen durkene] Alle darkis T; All dyrkyns I; Alle
     droupe L. in . . . skuwes] and to downe schowys T;
     and to þe doun dryvis L.

54   And] TL; þat D; *om* I. drede] þe dowte T. droupes]
     drowpid L. þe (1)] *om* L.

55   *line om* D. And . . . swoghes] T; For þe squyppand
     watur þat squytherly squoes I. stremys] streme L.
     swoghes] sweyvis L. swithely] swyftly TL.

56   þay werray] þayre werre on I; Wery were L. wilde]
     wilde swyne DTIL. and . . . wo] wurchis hom wo
     I; wroght ful of wo L.

57   The . . . huwes] Hying to halowe the hertis with
     hound L. The huntes] Thay hunte T; þe hunteres I.
     þei] and T. hurstes and huwes] holttis and hillys T.
     in, and] by I.

58   And . . . relyes] T; And bluwe rechas ryally þei
     rane D; To þe rest raches þat releues I; Alle þe
     rennyng racchis rayle L. to þe ro] one þaire ray T.
     to] of I.

59   Thay . . . grythe] T; They gaf to no gamone D; þay
     geuen no gomen nyf no grythe I; They gyue no game
     grith L. one] on þe IL. gruwes] *om* L.

60   þe . . . greues] Grete hundis T; þe grehoundys in þe
     grene greues I; Grete houndis of þe grasse L. so]
     fulle T. þei] gane T. greundes] MS grendes.

61   So . . . gone] Thus thies gomes þay ga T; þus
     gladdely þay goe I; They go so gladly L.

V

Þen durkene þe dere in þe dymme skuwes,
[And] for drede of þe dethe droupes þe do;
[And by þe stremys so strange þat swithely swoghes]   55
Þai werray þe wilde and worchene hem wo.
The huntes þei halowe in hurstes and huwes,
[And tille þaire riste raches relyes] to þe ro;
[Thay gafe no gamene, no grythe], þat one grounde
    gruwes;
Þe grete gre(u)ndes in þe greues so gladly þei go—   60
So gladly þei gone in greues so grene.
The king blowe rechas
And folowed fast one þe tras,
Withe many sergeant of mas,
Þat solas to sene.   65

---

62   The . . . blowe] And boldly blawes T. rechas] a
     rechase IL.

63   And] om I. folowed] folowes T. tras] chace L.

64   sergeant] seriandys I. mas] þe mace L.

65   þat] Swylk T. sene] see I.

66   Withe] Thus with TL; þus þat I. þei semble] þay
     semelede TL; to see I. pruddest in palle] kyng
     pruddest in pal L; semelokest of all I.

67   And . . . souerayne] þay soȝt to þayre souerayne I;
     And seke to the game L. within schaghes schene] in
     cleues so clene T; undur þe scha schene I; in shawis
     so shene L.

68   Al but] Nane bot TL. gayest] the gayeste T; graythest I; þe greithest L.

69   Beleues] Was laft I; Levith L. in] in þose T; vndur
     þe I; the L. so] om TI.

70   MS I. By] Vnder DTL. lay] was liȝte D; lighte L.
     vndur a lefe sale] þat lady so smalle DTL (so
     om L).

71   Of . . . of] Wiþ bowis of L. bene] clene L.

72   Fast . . . vndre] Euyn atte þe mydday I. cone falle]
     byfalle L.

73   shal] om TIL.

74   wol] wold I. mele] MS meve; mene T.

75   als] al L.

76   hit were] þe I.

77   þe king was] Sir Gawane was T; Syr Arther wos I;
     was Arthur L.

VI

With*e* solas þei semble, þe pruddest in palle,
And suwen*e* to þe sou*e*rayne *with*in schaghes schene—
Al but S*ir* Gawayn*e*, gayest of all*e*,   f.2a.
Beleues with*e* Dame Gayno*ur* in greues so grene.
[By a lauryel ho lay, vnd*ur* a lefe sale],   70
Of box and of berber bigged ful bene.
Fast byfore vndre þis ferly con*e* fall*e*,
And þis mekel mervaile þat I shal of mene;
Now wol I of þis mervaile mele if I mote:
The day wex als dirke   75
As hit were mydniȝt*e* myrke,
There-of þe king was irke
And liȝt*e* on*e* his fote.

79   to] one TIL. ar] con I. farene] lyghte TL; founde I.
     þes] þose T; þe L.

80   fleene fro] fled to IL; fledde faste to T. forest]
     feritthes L. to þe fawe felle] to þe fewe felles D; and
     to þe fawe fellis T; fro þe fau fellus I; for þe flawis
     þat felle L.

81   MS T. *line om* D. Thay . . . roches] And to re-
     settyng þei ronne L. faste] *om* I. reddour] redeles I.
     þe] *om* IL.

82   For þe sneterand] For þe slete and þe T; For þe
     sliteryng L. þat . . . snelle] T; snartly hem snelles
     D; þat snaypely hom snellus I; þat snowid hem so
     snelle L.

83   There] So I. a . . . lede] I; a lowe one the loughe in
     lede T; a lede of þe lawe in londe D; a lothly to loke
     on lede L. is] *om* L.

84   MS T. *line om* D. the] *om* IL. in] of L. helle] hellus I.

85   And glides] Glydand I; Glode L. Sir Gawayne]
     Dame Gaynoure TIL. þe . . . gayne] the gatis fulle
     gayne T; hyre gates were gayne I; gatys vngayne L.

86   and ȝomerand] ȝamyrly T; ful ȝamerly I; ȝernely L.
     a lowd ȝelle] L; loude ȝelles DI; lowde ȝelleT.

87   ȝaules] ȝellede T; ȝaulit I; lollid L. ȝameres]
     ȝamede T; ȝamurt I; ȝanyd L. wonges ful] L; way-
     mynges D; vengeance fulle T; wlonkes full I. hit
     (2)] and L.

88   withe] ofte T; *om* L. sare] fulle sare T.

VII

Thus to fote ar þei farene, þes frekes vnfayne,
And fleene fro þe forest to þe [fawe felle];   80
[Thay rane faste to the roches for reddoure of þe rayne],
For þe sneterand snawe [þat snayppede þame so snelle].
There come [a lau oute of a loghe—in lede] is not to
    layne—
[In the lyknes of Lucyfere, layetheste in helle]—
And glides to Sir Gawayne, þe gates to gayne,   85
ȝauland and ȝomerand with many [a lowd ȝelle].
Hit ȝaules, hit ȝameres, with [wonges ful] wete,
And seid withe siking sare:
"I bane þe body me bare;
Alas! now kindeles my care,   90
I gloppen and I gretc!"

---

89   bane] ame T. body] byrde I. me] þat þe T; þat
     me IL.

90   Alas] For I. kindeles] comyn is I. care] om L (torn).

91   gloppen] gloupe L. I grete] om L (leaf torn).

92 Then . . . grete] Alle gloppuns and gretys I. Dame] TI; *om* D. gloppenet . . . gay] *om* L (*torn*).

93 *om* L (*torn leaf*). seid to] askede T. is þi good] is þi best I; was his beste T.

94 is] L; es T; ar D; is but I. sone] mone TL.

95 And] *om* L. confortes] comforthede T; comfort L. for] w*ith* T; throgh*e* I; of L.

96 Sir] Ho sayd Syr I. Clegis] Caduke T; Gawayn L. Constantyne] Costantyne I; Costardyne D; Costarde T; Constans L.

97 þes knyȝtes] Thir knyghtis T; They L.

98 þat . . . day] þat levith me þus in desert to do me dye þus þis day L. oonly . . . laft] haue laft me allone I; me hase lefte in this erthe T. one] at TI.

99 With] W*ith* on IL. grisselist] grymlokkest I. grede] grete T (*first written* grede) I.

100 Of þe] At this T; That L. þe grome] S*ir* Gaweayne T; þe gome I; Gawayn L. greue] shal greve L. you] þe IL.

101 For] *om* TL. shal] will*e* IL. þe] ȝone T; þat L.

102 And . . . wete] In ȝone wayes so wete T. þe wayes] hit woe I; his wo L. I shalle] will*e* I I; shal y L.

103 T: If I maye the bales bete.
    I: Gif þat I may hit bales bete.
    L: If y the balis may bete.

104 Of] And I. þe] ȝone T; þat L. bare] sore L.

VIII

Then gloppenet and grete [Dame] Gaynour þe gay,
And seid to Sir Gawene, "what is þi good rede?"
"Hit [is] þe clippes of þe sone, I herd a clerk say,"
And þus he confortes þe quene for his kniȝthede.   95
"Sir Cadour, Sir Clegis, Sir [Constantyne], Sir Cay,
Þes knyȝtes arne vncurtays—by crosse and by crede—
Þat þus oonly haue me laft one my deþe day
With þe grisselist goost þat euer herd I grede."
"Of þe goost," quod þe grome, "greue you no mare,   100
For I shal speke withe þe sprete,
And of þe wayes I shalle wete,   f.2b.
What may þe bales bete
Of þe bodi bare."

105   Bare] Alle bare I. þe] hir T. and] *om* L. to] by IL.

106   I = l. 119.

107   Hit . . . wayment] H*it* ȝaulut hit ȝamurt I (= l. 87a); Hit wonyd and wayvid L. as] lyke TI.

108   But . . . huwe] Þat nowþer one hede ne on hare T; Nauthyr of hyde nyf of heue I; But neiþer of hide ne of here L. on] *om* TL.

109   stemered] stottyde T; stedyt I; starid L. hit ston-ayde] *om* I. hit (2)] and L. hit (3)] *om* L. as] as stylle as I; stil as L. a] *om* L.

110   marred] menet I. hit (2)] *and* L. memered] mo*ur*nede TL; musut I. hit (3)] *om* L. mused] marret I.

111   Agayne þe] Vn to þat T; Vn to þe I; To þat L. Sir] *om* L.

112   He] And I; *om* L. to . . . res] to here rathely L. to it one] T; oute at D; to hit in I. he] TIL; *om* D. radde] ITL; drad D.

113   Rad] IL; Drad D; For rade T. neuer] neuyr ȝette I. ho so] nowe who þat T.

114   On] Opon I. chef] clyft L. þe] her LI. cholle] TIL; clolle D.

115   A pade] A tade T; A padok I; Paddoks L. pikes] pykit TL; prykette I. hir] LT; þe D; a I.

116   Withe] hir TIL. holked] ware holkede TI. ful] *and* I; *om* L.

IX

Bare was þe body and blake to þe bone,   105
Al bi-clagged in clay, vncomly cladde;
Hit waried, hit wayment as a womane,
But on hide ne on huwe no heling hit hadde;
Hit stemered, hit stonayde, hit stode as a stone,
Hit marred, hit memered, hit mused for madde.   110
Agayne þe grisly goost Sir Gawayne is gone;
He rayked [to it one] a res for [he] was neuer [radde]—
[Rad] was he neuer, ho-so righte redes.
On þe chef of þe [cholle]
A pade pikes one [hir] polle,   115
Withe eighen holked ful holle,
That gloed as þe gledes.

---

117   That gloed] Glowand T; And gloet I; They glyme-
      rid L. þe] om TL.

118   a glede] gledis TL; þe gledes I. þere ho] whare scho
      T; qwere hit I; wha*re* he L.

119   Vmbeclipped] Vmbyclede T; Was vmbyclosut I;
      Clothid L. in] TI; hi*m* w*ith* D. in a cloude] *om* L
      (*torn leaf*). of] w*ith* TL; in I. cleþyng] MS cleyng.

120   Serkeled] MS skeled; Cerkelytt T; Was sette aure I.
      Serkeled . . . satt *om* L (*torn leaf*). þat . . . hir]
      T; alle aboute þe D; þ*at* sate to þe I.

121   todes] dɔdis T. one] opon I. my] w*ith* I. fulle] to
      TL. To . . . fulle] *om* L (*torn leaf*).

122   þe] þen þis I. braides] brawndeche T; braydet I.
      þe (2)] his T; a I. *line om* L (*torn leaf*).

123   *line om* L (*torn leaf*). Therefor] For all*e* I. þe] þat
      T; þis I. changed] thoghte it T.

124   hiȝene] hyes IL; are T. þe] *om* T. holtes] I; holt L;
      wode D; hillys T. here] þe L. hedes] TI; hede DL.

125   For . . . bere] þe greundes were all agast of þe
      gryme bere I. þe] þat TL. a] so TL. bere] giere L.

126   The . . . bere] Ful grisly þe goost grynnyd in her
      gere L. The . . . were] þus were þe grehondes I.
      of þe] for þat T.

127   in þe] one the T; on L. bowes] bewes T.

128   T: þat one that gaste gewes.
      I: þat of the gost gous.
      L: That on þe grene growys.

129   I = D. T: Thay clyme in the clewes
      L: Shrikys and showys

X

Al glowed as a glede þe goste þere ho glides,
Vmbeclipped [in] a cloude of cle(þ)yng vnclere,
S(er)keled withe serpentes [þat satt by hir] sides— 120
To telle þe todes þere-one my tonge were fulle tere.
Þe burne braides oute þe bronde and þe body bides;
Therefor þe cheualrous kniȝte changed no chere.
Þe houndes hiȝene to þe [holtes] and here hede(s) hides,
For þe grisly goost made a gryme bere. 125
The grete greundes were agast of þe gryme bere;
Þe birdes in þe bowes,
Þat one þe goost glowes,
Þei skryke in þe skowes,
Þat haþeles may here. 130

---

130 haþeles may] hedows whene þay T; herdus myȝten
hom I; herdis myghte L.

131 Haþelese . . . here] Who þat myghte þat hedows
see T; Alle þe herdus myȝtun here I; Herkenys þat
wil here L. hendeste in haulle] TL; so fer into halle
D; þe hyndest of alle I.

132 chaftis and] T; chalus one D.
    T: How hir cholle chatirede hyr chaftis and hir
      chynne.
    I: Off the schaft and þe shol shaturt to the shin.
    L: Alle her chawlis claterid chille to her chynne.

133 þe] hir þat T. one] and one TI. cone he calle] callus
I.

134 was] were L. crucifiged] claryfiet I. to clanse vs of]
to saue vs fra T; *and* clanser of I.

135 That . . . sothe] Thou spirette saye me the sothe T;
Wys me þou waret wyȝte I; Now wrecche sey me
sothely L. wheþer] whedir þat TL.

136 And whi þou] And whi þat þou T; Querfore that
þou I. walkest] walkes TIL. þes wayes] þis wey L;
om I. þe] thies TIL.

137 I was] Ho sayd ho was I; I was quod she L. of . . .
face] of fegure and of flesche the T; a figure of
flesche I; of figure and flesshe L.

138 krysommede] TI; knowene DL. in] of L.

139 I] And L. haue] hade I. in] of L. knowene for]
knawene kyde fulle T; þat kyd were for I; ful L.

140   T: God hase sent me this grace.
    I: Þus God hase grauntut me grace.
    L: God hath lent me þis grace.

XI

Haþelese miȝt here, [hendeste in haulle],
How chatered þe cholle, þe [chaftis, and] þe chynne.
Þene coniured þe kniȝte, one Crist cone he calle:
"As þou was crucifiged one croys to clanse vs of syne,
That þou sei me þe sothe wheþer þou shalle,   f.3a.
And whi þou walkest þes wayes þe wodes with-in?"   136
"I was of figure and face fairest of alle,
Cristened and [krysommede] with kinges in my kynne—
I haue kinges in my kyne knowene for kene—
God hase me gevene of his grace   140
To dre my paynes in þis place;
I ame comene in þis cace
To speke with your quene.

---

141   paynes] penaunce LI.

142   I . . . cace] And nowe am I commene one a pase
       T. I] And I I.

143   speke] carpe I.

144   Quene] For qwene I; Qwene crownyd L. some
      wile] whilome T; sumtyme L. brighter] wele
      bryghttere T.

145   Berelle] Beryke T. þes] the TI; *om* L.

146   al . . . gle] any gamnes or gudis T; all*e* the gomun
      and the grythe I; game or gle L. one] one the TIL.

147   Gretter] Wele grettere T; Now greyþer L. Dame]
      om TL. of garsone and] of garsomes *and* of T; be
      grete sow*mus* of I; greythid in L.

148   Of . . . plowes] Of paleys prowd of parkis to pay
      L. palaies] pales T; palas I. parkes . . . pondes]
      powndis . . . parkes T. plowes] plewes T.

149   townes . . . toures] toures . . . tounes I. tresour]
      tresoures TI.

150   castelles . . . contreyes] co*n*ntres . . . castell*es*
      TL. of cragges of clowes] countes y ȝow say L.
      cragges] cliffes I. clowes] clewes T.

151   Now] And nowe T; þus I. cauȝte . . . kide] cast
      fro þat tyre L. cauȝte] cachede TI. oute of] fro I.
      to] in T.

152   Into . . . caughte] þus am I cachet to care I. Into]
      In TL. caughte] cachede TL. couched] closyd L.

153   Lo sir] Loo T; Lo þou I; Lo lo L.

154   delfulle] þat T; *om* L.

155   Lete . . . haue] Nowe gyffe me anes T. Lete] To
      lette I.

XII

Quene was I some-wile, brighter of browes
Thene Berelle or Brangwayne, þes burdes so bolde; 145
Of al gamene or gle þat one grounde growes
Gretter þene Dame Gaynour, of garsone and golde,
Of palaies, of parkes, of pondes, of plowes,
Of townes, of toures, of tresour vntolde,
Of castelles, of contreyes, of cragges, of clowes; 150
Now ame I cauȝte oute of kide to cares so colde—
Into care am I caughte and couched in clay.
Lo! sir curtays knyȝte
How delfulle dethe has me diȝte;
Lete me onys haue a sighte   155
Of Gaynour þe gay."

157   After . . . gone] Thenne Syr Gauan the gode to Gayno*ur* is gone I. After] Nowe to T; Aftir Dame L.

158   MS T. so] MS þen*e* so.
> D: And to þe body he her brou3te and to þe burde bright*e*.
> I: Be-fore þe body he hur bro3te and þe byrde bry3te.
> L: And broght*e* to that body the berde so bright*e*.

159   Welcome] Ho sayd welcum I; Welcome art þou L. I-wis] *om* L; scho says T. worthi] þou worthye T; wurlok I; worthily L.

160   Lo] Se L. how] howe þat T. delful] dolfully L. has . . . di3te] þi dame hath*e* y-dight*e* L.

161   I . . . rode] For my rud was raddur I. of] in T; on L. in þe rone] in þe rayne T; of þe ron I; on þe rise L.

162   louched] þ*at* lauchet I; lufely T; lovesom L. so ly3te] I; on*e* hight*e* D; to syghte T; and light*e* L.

163   Now am I] And nowe I am T; Now I am I. a] *om* L. graceles] grisely TI. grone] grymly granes T; grisly in þis wise L.

164   Withe . . . lake] Wiþ Lucifers lymes L. lo3] þus lau I; ful low L.

165   MS T. D: Take truly tent ti3t*e* nowe by me.
> I: þus lau am I ly3te take wittenesse by me.
> L: Thus am y lik Lucifer tend*e* now to me.

166   þi] 3oure TI. foroure] fauoure T.

XIII

After Gaynour þe gay Sir Gawyne is gone,
[And to þat body hase he broghte that birde so bryghte].
"Welcome Waynour, I-wis, worthi in wone,
Lo! how delful dethe has þi dame diȝte!   160
I was radder of rode þene rose in þe rone,
My lere as þe lele louched [so lyȝte],
Now am I a graceles gost and grisly I grone;
Withe Lucyfer in a lake loȝ am I lighte.
[Thus am I lyke to Lucefere, takis witnes by mee]:   165
For al þi fresshe foroure
Muse one my mirrour,   f.3b.
For, king and emperour,
Thus shul ye be.

---

167   T: Nowe moyse one this mirroure.
       I: þat menes of ȝour merur.
       L: Loke on thy mirrour.

168   For] For bothe T; om IL. king] kynge duke I.

169   Thus] Alle thus I; Thus dighte L.

170 þus] And thus T. dethe] ITL; diȝt D. thare . . .
doute] I do ȝo oute of doute IL; takis witnesse by
me T.

171 þere one] And there one T; And therfore I; þerfor
L. take] takis T. while] whils þat TI. art] es T.

172 art] es T. richest araied] richely arrayede T; ray
richest I. in þi] in a T; on L.

173 Haue . . . poer] Hafe þane pete *and* mynd one þe
pore T. whil] LI; *om* D; for T. art of] hase I; art on
L.

174 Burnes and burdes] Quen birdus and birnys I. are
besye] TIL; þat ben*e* D. are] an (*for* ar) I.

175 Whene . . . bamed] Be thy lyf byreft L. Whene]
Quyl I. is] be I. one a] appone T; vn to L.

176 Thane . . . lyghtely] TL; þen*e* lite wyn*e* þe light*e*
D; þay will*e* leue þe ful lyȝteli I.

177 For] And TI; *om* L. þe helpes] MS he helpes;
helpes the TIL. no þing] noght*e* L.

178 þe] For þe I. praier] holy pr*a*yers L. þe] TIL; *om*
D. may . . . pes] chasses the from helle T. þe pes]
þi pece I.

179 þi yete] MS þe þete.
　　T: Of þase þat ȝellis at thi ȝate.
　　I: Those at þou ȝees at thi ȝate.
　　L: On hem þat ȝollyn at thy yate.

180 art set] sittis T.

XIV

Þus [dethe] wil ȝou diȝte, thare you not doute;   170
Þere-one hertly take hede while þou art here,
Whane þou art richest araied *and* ridest in þi route;
Haue pite one þe poer [whil] þou art of powere.
Burnes and burdes [are besye] þe aboute;
Whene þi body is bamed and brouȝte one a bere   175
[Thane wille þay leue the lyghtely] þat now wil þe loute,
For þene (þ)e helpes no þing but holy praiere.
Þe praier of [þe] poer may purchas þe pes:
Of that þou yeues at [þi] (y)ete,
Whan þou art set in þi sete,   180
Withe al merthes at mete,
And dayntes on des.

---

181   merthes] þe myrthes I. mete] thi mete TIL.

182   And . . . des] Some dayntes þou dele T.

183 riche] *om* T; all*e* riche L. on . . . diotes] þat to the
L. are] MS art.

184 And] MS and I (*and so* I); And thus T; Thus L.
danger] dungun I. in dongone] I downe *and* I T; is
done for to I.

185 nedefulle] nedy I. and] TIL; *om* D. one] opon IL.
nighte] heȝte I.

186 þer . . . helle] For in wunny*ng* place is woe for to
duelle (duelle *struck through lightly and* welle
added, lighter ink) I. folo] folowes TL. ferde]
ferdnes L. of helle] full*e* felle T.

187 þei harme] and hewys T; *and* hovis L; þay haue (?
for heaue) I. in] one TIL.

188 in (2)] *om* L.

189 Was . . . wroughte] For I ne wotte I. wroughte]
om L. world] word I. a wofuller] so woful a I.

190 Hit . . . any] I am to tery of L. ful] *om* T. any]
till*e* any T; for a I. turment] tourmenttis TI.

191 Nowe] But now T. wil] wold I. y] some L. turment]
tourm*entes* IL. tel] talke TI. my] these I.

192 hertly one] þou throli opon I.

193 Fonde] Now fande T; And founde I; For L. thi] of
thi TI.

194 Thou] For thou TI.

195 Beware] Be warre now T; To be ware L. be] of I;
wiþ L.

XV

With*e* riche dayntes on des þi diotes are diȝt*e*,
And in danger and doel in dongon*e* I dwelle,
Naxte, and nedefull*e*, [and] naked on*e* night*e;* 185
Þer folo me a ferde of fendes of helle,
Þey hurle me vnhendely, þei harme me in hiȝt*e;*
In bras and in brymston*e* I bren*e* as a belle;
Was neuer wrought*e* in þis world a wofuller wight*e*—
Hit were ful tore any tonge my t*ur*ment to telle— 190
Nowe wil y of my t*ur*ment tel or I go.
Thenk hertly on*e* þis,
Fonde to mende thi mys,
Thou art warned y-wys,
Bewar*e* be my wo!" 195

196   Wo is] Now wo es T; Ways (? *for* wa is) I. þi wo]
þi wirde I; the L. quod] sayd T; coth*e* I.

197   one þing] a worde T. if] and TI.

198   If auþer] Gyff T; Quethir authir I; If eny L. mas]
messes T. miȝte mende] myghte oghte menden*e* T.
þi] þe of I.

199   meble] mobyll*es* T. one] on þe I; of þis L. merthe]
myrthis T.

200   If] Or TIL. of] of these I; or L. bisshopps] bu*n*fetis
L.

201   couentes] couand I. in] in þe I; of L. cloistre] cloy-
st*er*s TL. kele] TIL; kere D.

202   If] For if TI. þou be] þe were I. wonder] m*er*velle
T. is] ware I.

203   al] *om* T; euyr I. burly] baleful (*first* l *at first written* k?) L. is . . . be] es blakenede T; bryȝte is I;
now left is L.

204   I bare] Ho sayd I bare I. hit I layne] to lye T; to
layne IL.

205   a-vowe] adecoue I.

206   And no mane] That none TI; None L. hit but] bot
I *and* TIL.

207   þat] that to T; a IL. þou trowe] þou (MS þ"e) me
troue I; that þow knewe L.

208   T: And þ*er*fore dole I drye.
     I: Quo sotheli will*e* sayne.
     L: The soþe for to sayne.

XVI

"Wo is me for þi wo," quod Waynour, "y-wys,
But one þing wold I wite if þi wil ware:
If auþer matens or mas miȝte mende þi mys,
Or eny meble one molde, my merthe were þe mare:
If bedis of bisshopps miȝte bring þe to blisse,   f.4a.
Or couentes in cloistre miȝte [kele] þe of care.   201
If þou be my moder grete wonder hit is
That al þi burly body is brouȝte to be so bare!"
"I bare þe of my body, what bote is hit I layne?
I brake a solempne a-vowe   205
And no mane wist hit but þowe;
By þat tokene þou trowe
Þat soþely I sayne."

209 Say] Telle T. me now] T; *om* D; me IL. soþely]
q*uod* Gayno*ur* I. may] myȝte I. safe thi sytis] T;
þe sauen*e* y wis D; saue þe from site I; þe mende of
þi sytis L.

210 And] Fro cite I. make . . . singe] garre seke sayntes T; sayntes ger seke sone I; smartly do seke
seyntis L.

211 But] For I. þe] of thase T; þo IL. bites] ITL; is D.

212 Alle . . . es] TL; Al bledis my ble þi bones arn*e*
D; All*e* blynde is my ble þi blode is I.

213 þat is] This es it to T; þese ar I. paramour] *p*ara-
moures TI. listes] and lustis T; þ*at* listus I. delites]
litys T; likes I; delices L.

214 þat] *om* I. has] gerse T; dose I; makiþ L. liȝte and
lenge] now lewd *and* ly L. lenge] T; lynd I; laft D.
loȝ] so lawe T. in] in in I. a] þis T.

215 Al] For alle T. þe] this TIL. thus] TIL; þat D.

216 Withe . . . wormes] This werlde es wandrethe T.
þe wilde] þese wrechut I; þes wykkid L. worche]
wirkis T. wrake] þis wrake IL.

217 Wrake . . . worchene] For wrake it me wirkis now
T; þus to wrake am I wroȝte I; Wrake þei work
me L.

218 thritty] xxx L. trentales] trentes of masse I.

219 vnder] midday L.

XVII

"Say [me now] soþely what may [safe thi sytis],
And I shal make sere mene to singe for þi sake;   210
But þe baleful bestes þat one þi body [bites]
[Alle blendis my blode—thi blee es] so blake!"
"Þat is luf paramour, listes, and delites,
Þat has me liȝte and [lenge] loȝ in a lake;
Al þe welthe of þe world [thus] awey witis   215
Withe þe wilde wormes þat worche me wrake—
Wrake þei me worchene, Waynour I-wys.
Were thritty trentales done
Bytwene vnder and none,
Mi soule [were] socoured [fulle] sone   220
And broughte to þe blys.

---

220 were] TIL; *om* D. socoured] saluede T. fulle] TI;
      withe D; *om* L.

221 to þe] *in* to T; un to IL.

222 To] Ho sayd to I. blisse] þat blys I. þe (2)] that
TIL. boughte] MS broughte. boughte . . . rode]
dere hase the boghte T; boȝt vs with his blode I.

223 þat] As he I; om L. crucifiged] clarifiet I. one] wiþ
L.

224 As þou was] om TIL. candel] candilles T. code]
with code I.

225 Folowed] Halowyd L. in] in a I; in þe L. fonte-
stone] MS fontestone one (? dittography). frely]
fulle frely T.

226 Mary] And Mary I. þe miȝeti] þat es myghty T; his
(our L) modur IL. myldest] and myldeste T; þat
mylde is I.

227 Of . . . barme] That bare þat blysschede T. þe]
þat IL. in . . . borne] was in Bethlem y-born L.

228 Lene] Gyffe T; He gif I; Leve L. þat . . . grete] for
to grete T; to grete I; to L. thy saule] TIL; þe D.
with] with some T; with þe I; wiþ soule do L.

229 And . . . morne] þat may bettir to thi bote on evyn
and a morn L. mynge] mene T; myn I. matens and
masses] messes and matynnes TI.

230 mende vs] mene me T; mede þe L; mynne me I.
myster] menske TL. hit] nowe it T.

231 rest one þe] restith on L.

232 Gyf fast] Gyffe nowe faste T; þou dele fast I; Yeve
part L.

XVIII

"To blisse bring þe þe barne þat boughte þe one rode,
Þat was crucifiged one croys and crowned with þorne;
As þou was cristened and crisomed with candel and code,
Folowed in fontestone frely by-forne;   225
Mary þe miȝeti, myldest of mode,
Of whome þe blisful barme in Bedlem was borne,
Lene me grace þat I may grete [thy saule] with gode
And mynge þe withe matens and masses one morne."
"To mende vs with masses grete myster hit were;   230
For him þat rest one þe rode,
Gyf fast of þi goode   f.4b.
To folke þat failene þe fode,
While þou art here."

---

233   folke] þo I. þe] her L.
234   While] Whylles þat TI.

235   T: Now here hertly one hande I hete the to halde.
      I: Here I hete þe my hond þi hestus to hold.
      L: Here hertly y hote þe wiþ hestis to holde.

236   a . . . masses] messis a mylioun L. masses] masse
      I. thy] TIL; þe D.

237   But . . . worde] T; A D; But on thing I; O word
      L. quod] saide Dame T; om I. wetene I wolde] MS
      I wis yit wetene I wolde; nowe wiete þat I walde
      T; þat I wete wold I; wyten y wolde L.

238   wrathede] wrathes IL; greues T. God] Crist I. at
      þi weting] of any kyns thynge T.

239   Pride] Ho sayd pride I. with þe appurtenaunce]
      with apparementis T; with his purtenans I; in pro-
      cessioun L. as] hase I.

240   Bifore] And enperit to I. peple] om L. appertly]
      TL; apt D; om I.

241   Hit . . . bowes] The (blank space) is fulle T; þese
      ar þe branches full I; þerof þe bowis are L.

242   þat] It T; And L; om I. burnes] mony byrne I. fulle
      boune] I; so bly D; fulle balde T; ful bayne L. his]
      Goddus I.

243   But ho] Who so T; Quo I. þei bene] he es T; is IL.

244   þei be salued] if þay saluen hom I; he sonner salvid
      L. þat] þer I.

245   Er . . . fare] Or the tyme that he come thore L.
      Er] Certis or TI.

XIX

"Here hertly my honde þes hestes to holde—   235
Withe a myllione of masses to make [thy] mynnyng.
[Bot one worde]," quod Waynour, "wetene I wolde:
What wrathede God moste at þi weting?"
"Pride with þe appurtenaunce, as propheteʒ haue tolde
Bifore þe peple [appertly] in here preching;   240
Hit beres bowes bitter—þerof be þou bolde—
Þat makes burnes [fulle boune] to breke his bidding.
But ho his bidding brekes, bare þei bene of blys;
But þei be salued of þat sare,
Er þey heþene fare,   245
They mone wetene of care,
Waynour y-wys."

---

246   They . . . care] He may ban þe body hym bore L.
      mone wetene] knaue I. care] calde care T; mekil
      care I.

247   Waynour] ʒe Waynore I.

248   Wysse] Now wis I; Telle T. quod] sayde T. some
      wey if] a worde if T; gif þat I.

249   bedis] dedis T; bunfaites L. miȝte me best] þat
      myȝte best vs I; may me L. to þe] in to T; to I; vn
      to L.

250   Mekenesse and mercy] Ho sayd mesure and me-
      kenes I. þes arne] scho saide þo are T; þat is I.

251   Haue] TI; And haue L; And siþene haue D. one]
      of IL. þat pleses heuen king] thane plesys þou
      owre kynge T; þat plesus þe kinge I; it is his bid-
      dyng L.

252   Line om T. Siþene . . . chaste] After þis charite is
      chevest and cherisshid moost L. and þene is] to
      þose þat wyn be I.

253   And þene] Sythene after that do T; om I; And
      sethyn L. aure] MS cure; þat is aure I; after L; of
      T. oþer] TI; om DL. þing] thingus I.

254   arne] be L. þe] om L. graceful] gud T; gracius IL.

255   iche sprete] alle sperites T.

256   þis . . . þing] thies sperituale thynges T; this
      spirituallte I; spiritual thingis L. spute þou] spyre
      me T; speke we I; spire þou me L.

257   Whills] TIL; Als D. þi] om L.

258   Hold] Take L. in] in thyne TIL.

259   þou . . . leve] Here shalt þou dwelle L. þou] For
      þou TI. shal] mun I.

260   Heþene] And hethun I; Hennys L.

XX

"Wysse me," quod Waynour, "some wey if þou wost,
What bedis miȝte me best to þe blisse bringe?"
"Mekenesse and mercy, þes arne þe moost,   250
[Haue] pite one þe poer, þat pleses heuen king;
Siþene charite is chef, and þene is chaste,
And þene almesse-dede (a)ure al [oþer] þing;
Þes arne þe graceful giftes of þe holy goste
Þat enspires iche sprete withe-oute speling.   255
Of þis spiritual þing spute þou no mare—
[Whills] þou art quene in þi quert
Hold þes wordes in hert:
Þou shal leve but a stert,
Heþene shal þou fare."   260

261 quod] saide T. þe freke] Gauan I. fondene] fowndis
TIL. to fighte] to þese fiȝtus I.

262 And . . . folke] That ofte foundis the folkes T.
þus] om IL. þe] þese I. one] in TIL.

263 And] That T; om IL. riches . . . reymes] riche
rewmes ouer-rynnes TI; Ridis and rennis in rewmys
L. with . . . eny] agaynes the TI; wiþ e y L. righte]
ryȝtus I.

264 Wynnene] And wynnes TL. in werre] and welthis
T; and wele IL. þorghe] by T; with L. worshippe]
wirchippis T.

265 Your] Scho sayd ȝaure I. king] kynd L. I . . .
kniȝte] and his kene knyȝtus I; knowyn sir knyghte
L. warne] telle T.

266 May . . . strength] þer may no strenȝthe him stir
I. stry] stere TL. withe] of T. while his] whilles þe
T; quen þe I; whil he L. whele] wele L.

267 mageste . . . his] mageste hegheste and maste es
of T. miȝte] myȝtus I.

268 He . . . lowe] Hym shal be tyde a chaunce L. He
shal] Then schall he I. one] appone T; bi I.

269 Thus . . . kynge] TI; And this chiualrous kniȝte
D; þat cheuallerous knyghte L. chef] bycheve L.
a] TIL; þorgh D.

270 False Fortune] TL; Falsely fordone D. False]
Felles I.

271 That . . . wryghte] TI; With a wonderfulle wighte
D; þat wondirful wighte L.

XXI

"How shal we fare," quod þe freke, "þat fondene to fighte
And þus defoulene þe folke one fele kinges londes;
And riches ouer reymes with-outene eny righte— 263
Wynnene worshippe in werre þorghe wightnesse of
    hondes?"
"Your king is to couetous, I warne þe sir kniȝte, f.5a.
May no mane stry him withe strength while his whele
    stondes;
Whane he is in his mageste, moost in his miȝte,
He shal lighte ful lowe one þe se sondes.
[Thus ȝoure cheualrous kynge] chef shalle [a] chaunce;
[False Fortune] in fighte, 270
[That wondirfulle whele wryghte],
Shalle make lordes [lowe] to liȝte—
Take witnesse by Fraunce.

---

272   T: Mase lordis lawe for to lyghte.
      I: þat lau wille lordis gere liȝte.
      L: Makiþ lordis lowe lighte.

273   Take] Takes T. by] at L.

274   Fraunce] For Fraunse I. ȝe . . . your] ferlily wiþ
      L. (hath *struck out after* Fraunce *in MS D*).

275   Frollo] T; Freol D.
      T: The Frollo and þe Farnaghe es frely by leuede.
      I: Frol and his farnet ful fery haue ȝe leuyt.
      L: Folk *and* (*rest of line blank*).

276   MS T. D: Bretayne in Burgoyne al to you bowen*e*.
      I: Bretan and Burgoyn is both*e* in ȝo*ur* bandum.
      L: Britayne and Burgoyne boþ are to yow bowne.

277   And] þ*at* L. with . . . deued] w*ith* þe dyn*e* dreuede
      T; are w*ith* ȝo*ur* dyntis dynyd L.

278   Gyane may] Now may Gian I; Gynys *and* Grece
      may L. þe werre] þ*at* euyr hit I. þe] þ*at* þe T; þ*at*
      L.

279   There . . . londe] Es noghte a lorde in þat lande
      appon*e* lyfe T. There . . . lyue] þ*er* is noȝte lede
      on leue I; They haue no lord L.

280   Romans] ITL; remayns D. ȝow] TIL; one D. with
      ȝow be] be w*ith* ȝou I.

281   with] atte I; alle (*?for* atte) T. þe (2)] þaire T;
      her L. be] schall be I. reued] byrevid L.

282   Then] Amours; MS Thus. ȝour] L; with D.
      T: Thay sall*e* ȝitt be Tybire tymbire ȝow tene.
      I: Hit schall*e* be tynte as I troue and timburt w*ith*
          tene.
      L: þ*er* shal tristily y trowe tymbre ȝour tene.

XXII

Fraunce haf ye frely with your fight wonnene,
[Frollo] and his folke fey ar þey leued;   275
[Bretayne and Burgoyne es bothe to ȝow bowndene],
And al þe Dussiperes of Fraunce with your dyn deued.
Gyane may grete þe werre was bigonene—
There ar no lordes one lyue in þat londe leued;
Yet shal þe riche [Romans] with [ȝow] be aure-
     ronene,   280
And with þe rounde table þe rentes be reued.
[Then] shal a Tyber vntrue tymber [ȝour] tene;
Gete þe, Sir Gawayne,
Turne þe to Tuskayne;
For ye shul lese Bretayne   285
With a [knyghtc] kcne.

---

283   þe] ȝe L; þe wele I.

284   þe] þou T; ȝow L.

285   For . . . lese] For (*blank space*) þou salle T; Or
      lese schalle ȝe I. For] *om* L.

286   With] Thruȝe I. knyghte] TIL; king D.

287   This] A TIL. shal . . . a] sall*e* kenly closen*e* þe
      T; schall*e* kenely croyse þe I; þ*at* is kyndely
      crownyd wiþ L.

288   Carlele] Carelyone T; Carlit I. shal þat comly] *om*
      TI; y say L. be] is L. as] for TI; a L.

289   MS I. D: A sege shal he seche with a cession*e*.
      T: That sege sall*e* be sesede at a sesone.
      L: He shal ensege sikirly þan in þ*at* sesou*n*.

290   þat] *om* I. baret and bale] bale and barete T; baret
      and bro L. to Bretayne] till*e* Ynglande T.

291   Hit] Ther T; ȝe I. in Tuskane be tolde] be told in
      Tuskan I. of þe] of þat TI; for a L.

292   ye shullene turne] torne home T; be turnut I; ye
      shul ride L. fore þe] for that TL; w*ith* that I.
      typing] MS tying.

293   þere] And ther T; þan L.

294   ful rad] full*e* ryghte TL; þe riche I.

295   In] And at T. Dorset] MS Dorset-shire; desesde I.
      doughetest] duȝty I.

296   Gete þe] Gete þe wele I; Gye þe wele L.

297   The] *om* L.

298   In] For in TI. slake] slade L. þou] *om* L.

299   ferlyes] ferly T; chaunce L. shulle] schyn I. falle]
      be falle L.

XXIII

This knight*e* shal be clanly enclosed w*ith* a crowne,
And at Carlele shal þat comly be crowned as king;
[Þat segge schall ensese him atte a session],
Þat myche baret and bale to Bretayn*e* shal bring.   290
Hit shal in Tuskan*e* be tolde of þe treson*e*,
And ye shullen*e* tu*r*ne ayen*e* for*e* þe ty(þ)ing;
Þer*e* shal þe rounde table lese þe renoune,
Beside Ramsey ful rad at a riding.
In Dorset shal dy þe dough*e*test of alle—   295
Gete þe, S*ir* Gawayn*e*,
The boldest of Bretayne;   f.5b.
In a slake þou shal be slayne,
Sich*e* ferlyes shull*e* falle.

300   Suche] But a L. ferlies] ferly TL. fal] *om* I.

301   a knighte] knyȝtus fulle IL.

302   Sir] þer I; *om* T. þe] *om* I. auenaunt honest] LI;
      honest auenant D; auenante þat honeste es T.

303   Shal] MS He shal. I-wys] forsoþe L. woþely] fulle
      wathely T; wrothely L.

304   *line om* T. And] *om* I.

305   *line om* T. þei] *om* L. one a] þat I. þe] þo I. doughe-
      ty] doghtyng L.

306   Suppriset . . . suget] A sheld wiþ a sege L. suget]
      MS surget; sugette T; subiecte I. þat beris of] T;
      he beris hit in D; he berith it of L; þat bere schalle
      of I.

307   A] T; With a DI; Wiþ in a L. engreled of] englorid
      wiþ L. fulle] so I.

308   He . . . sable] Of seluir he it berith L. hit] *om* T.
      soþely to] quo sotheli wille I; the sothe for to L.

309   riche] kyng TI.

310   barne] childe TIL. playes] playes hym T.

311   outray shalle] salle owttraye T; bytray shal L.

312   Fulle derfely] TL; Derfely I; Delfully D. þat] a T.

XXIV

Suche ferlies shulle fal, with-oute eny fable,   300
Vppone Cornewayle coost withe a knighte kene;
Sir Arthur þe [auenaunt, honest] and able,
Shal be wounded, I-wys, woþely I wene;
And al þe rial rowte of þe rounde table,
Þei shullene dye one a day, þe doughety by-dene,   305
Suppriset with a suget, [þat beris of] sable
[A] sauter engreled of siluer fulle shene—
He beris hit of sable, soþely to say;
In riche Arthures halle
The barne playes at þe balle,   310
Þat outray shalle you alle
[Fulle derfely] þat day.

313   Haue] Ho sayd haue I. Gaynour] Dame Gaynour
      TL. Gaynour and Gawayne] Syr Gauan *and*
      Gaynour I. and] *om* L.

314   tome] tyme TIL. tidinges] ʒo tithing*es* I; mo tales
      T. to] TIL; *om* D.

315   I mot walke] For me buse wende T. I mot] For I
      mu*n* I; I must L. þorgh þis wilde] thorowte this T;
      throʒe oute ʒond*ur* I; thurgh þis L.

316   Vn to] TL; In D; For in I. stid] wane T; place I.
      in] is I. for] þ*er* L. welle] TI; dwelle DL.

317   rightwisly] rewfully T; ryʒtewis I. rose] rest I. and
      rest] *and* rente was T; and rose I; *and* raght*e* hym
      L. þe] *om* TL.

318   one þe] quat I. and the dole] TL; and dele I; *om*
      D. yne] on L.

319   Fede . . . fode] Funde to grete my saule w*ith* su*m*
      of þi gode I. Fede] And fede T. failene þe] fawtes
      the T; wantis her L.

320   menge] mene TL; myn I. matens and masses]
      messes and matyns TI. masses] MS masse. in melle]
      I-mele I; y-melle L.

321   *line om* T. Masses] For massus I. arne medecynes]
      be medicine L. to vs] for us I; to hem L. þat bale]
      in bales I.

322   þenke] thing I. þenke a masse] þinkith massis L.

323   eny . . . euer] eu*ere* spicis that L. ye ete] MS ye
      yete; þou ete TIL.

XXV

Haue gode day Gaynour and Gawayne þe gode,
I haue no lenger tome tidinges [to] telle;
I mot walke one my wey þorgh þis wilde wode,   315
[Vn-to] my wonying stid, in wo for to [welle].
Fore him þat rightwisly rose *and* rest one þe rode,
Þenke one þe danger [and the dole] þat I yne dwelle;
Fede folk fore my sake þat failene þe fode,
And menge me with matens *and* masse(s) in melle.   320
Masses arne medecynes to vs þat bale bides;
Vs þenke a masse as swete
As eny spice þat euer ye ete."
With a grisly grete
Þe goste a-wey glides.   325

---

324   With] And thus w*ith* T; þus w*ith* I; And þan wiþ
      L. grisly] gryliche I.

326 *line om* TL. Withe] Noue w*ith* I.

327 *line om* T. And . . . grene] And a sore gronyng
w*ith* a grym bere I. gronyng . . . greues] a gretyng in grevis so L.

328 wyndes] wynde and TI. weders . . . vnhides]
welkyn þe wethur *in* þat tide I. þe (3)] þan*e* T.
vnhides] in hydis T; þ*at* wid is L.

329 þene . . . shene] þe cloude vnclosut þe sune wex
clere I. þene] *om* L. con shene] gan shyne L;
schane schene T.

330 king] knyght*e* L. has blowene] con blau I. and
one] opon I.

331 faire] MS fare. in þe frithe] in firthes T; on þe fuilde
I. þei flokkene] flokkes TL. by-dene] in fere TIL.

332 And al þe] All þat T.

333 T: And melis to her mildely one þaire manere.
  I: Meles to hur mildely opon þayre manere.
  L: And melyd to her mekely on her manere.

334 The] þo I. wise] wightis L. on swilke wondirs] T;
of þe weder D; of the wedering*es* I; of þes wedris
L. for-] a- TL.

335 Prince] The prynces T; Princys I; The prins L.

336 Dame] Gay IL.

337 Went] þay wente I; Rode L. Rondoles] Randolfe
sett T; Rondall*e*sete IL.

338 þaire] TIL; þe D.

XXVI

Withe a grisly grete þe goost a-wey glides,
And goes with gronyng sore þorgh þe greues grene;
Þe wyndes, þe weders, þe welkene vnhides,
Þene vnclosed þe cloudes, þe sone con shene.
The king his bugle has blowene *and* one þe bent
  bides,   f.6a.
His fa(i)re folke in þe frithe þei flokkene by-dene;   331
And al þe rialle route to þe quene rides,
She sayes hem þe selcouþes þat þei hadde þer seene—
The wise [on swilke wondirs] for-wondred þey were.
Prince proudest in palle,   335
Dame Gaynour and alle,
Went to Rondoles halle
To [þaire] supperc.

339   The king] Quen he I. to . . . set] was sett to þe
      supere T. is] was I. and] TIL; *om* D. sale] TL; his
      sale I; halle D.

340   dayntly di3te] swetely of sight*e* L. dayntly] full*e*
      daynetyuousely T; w*ith* dayntethis I.

341   *line om* L. MS T.
      D: With*e* al worshipp*e* and wele me*n*ewith þe
      walle.
       I: W*ith* all welthis to wille *and* wynus to wale.

342   *line om* L. MS I. bacun] *om* T. on] of T.
      D: Briddes branden*e* (? *for* braudene) and brad
      i*n* bankers bright*e*.

343   þere . . . symballe] Right*e* yn so come syphoners
      and symbale L. þere] so I. in a setoler] two setolers
      in T. setoler] MS soteler.

344   A . . . lote] A lufsum lady (he lates *crossed out*
      after lufsum, lady *written above*) I. lote] leyr L.

345   Scho . . . desse] T; Ho raykes vp in a res D; Ridus
      to þe he dese I; He ridith vp to þe deys L.

346   halsed] askede T; askis L. Sir] king IL. hendly]
      full*e* hendely T.

347   Ho] *om* I. þe] þat TL. wlonkest] worthiest L. wede]
      wedis T.

348   Mone] þ*o*u mon I. makeles] moste T.

349   T: Here es comyn*e* ane armed knyghte.
       I: þis is a nayre and a kny3t.
       L: Here comith a knyght*e*.

350   Do] Now do T; þou do I.

XXVII

The king to souper is set, [and] serued in [sale],
Vnder a siller of silke dayntly diȝte,   340
[With alle the wirchipe to welde and wyne for to wale],
[Briddes bacun in bred on brent gold bryȝte].
Þere come in a [setoler] with a symballe,
A lady, lufsom of lote, ledand a kniȝte;
[Scho rydes vp to þe heghe desse] bifor þe rialle,   345
And halsed Sir Arthur hendly one hiȝte.
Ho said to þe souerayne, wlonkest in wede:
"Mone makeles of mighte,
Here commes ane errant kniȝte,
Do him resone and riȝte,   350
For þi manhede."

352   MS T. The . . . his] Mon*e* in þy D; Monli in his
      IL. syttis] þat sittes D; he sate I; he sittis L. his
      (2)] þi D.

353   In] W*ith* I. with pane] TL; in poon I; to pay D.
      prodly] was prudlich*e* I; full*e* p*re*cyousely T. pight]
      dyghte T.

354   *line om* D. MS T.
      I: Trowlt w*ith* trulufes *and* tranest be-tuene.
      L: Tracyd and travercid with*e* trewlovis.

355   tasses were] tasee was T; tassellus were I; lace was
      L. topas] grene silk L. were þere-to] was þ*er* to I;
      þer to was TL. tiȝte] dight*e* L.

356   gliffed] glysset IL. vp] *om* L.

357   beueren] burely T; brode L. on þat burde] opon þe
      birne I.

358   soueraynest . . . in] semelist soueran on sittand *in*
      his I. of al] sir T; for soþe L.

359   segge . . . eȝe] any segge saughe or sene was w*ith*
      T; segge hade soȝte or seen him I; ey saw or sene
      was wiþ L.

360   King . . . kithe] Þenne oure comelich*e* king I; The
      crownyd kyng L. King] Thus the kyng T. carpis
      . . . tille] to her talkyd on hight*e* L. carpis] TI;
      talk*es* D.

361   T = D. I: And sayd þou wurlych wiȝt.
      L: Welcome comely knyght*e*.

362   He . . . righte] Liȝte and leng all*e* nyȝt I (= l.
      415). He] Thou TL.

XXVIII

[The mane in his mantylle syttis at his mete],
In pal pured [with pane], prodly pight,
[Trofelyte and trauerste wythe trewloues in trete];
Þe tasses were of topas þat were þere-to tiȝte.   355
He gliffed vp with his eighen, þat grey were *and* grete,
With his beueren berde, on þat burde bright—
He was þe soueraynest of al, sitting in sete,
Þat euer segge had sene with his eȝe-sighte—
King, crowned in kithe, [carpis] hir tille: 360
"Welcome, worþely wight,
He shal haue resone and righte;
Whe(þ)ene is þe comli kniȝte,   f.6b.
If hit be þi wille?"

---

363 Wheþene] MS Whelene; Wher L. þe . . . kniȝte]
     þat ayre *and* þat knyȝt I; þat worthy wighte L. þe]
     this T.

364 If . . . wille] Atte thi wille righte L. If . . . be]
     And . . . were I.

365 worþiest] wurliche I. wy welde wolde] wede wolde
D; wy myghte welde T; wee wold I; weld wolde L.

366 was . . . gay] þat was glorius I. of a] alle of T; was
of a I; as L.

367 of blunket] of plonkete T; blounkyd L.

368 Botonede . . . besantes] T; Branded (? *for*
brauded) *with* brende golde D. Botonede] Beten
IL. bokeled ful bene] botenyd ful shene L.

369 fax] forhed L. fyne] *om* L. was fretted] frette was
T. in (2)] *and* I.

370 Contrefelet . . . kelle] The conterfelette in a kelle
T; Hir countur felit and hur kelle were I; Contre-
filettid *and* kellyd L.

371 craftly] of crystalle TL; cumly I. al . . . golde]
was clure to be hold I. al] and TL. clere] TL;
clene D.

372 curiouse] glorious L. many] mony a IL. prene] MS
pene; pyne T.

373 *line om* T. perre] enparel I; fairhede L. praysed]
a-praysut I. prise . . . mighte] princes of myȝte I;
prest *and* wiþ knyghte L.

374 Bright] The bryghte T. birdes] barnis L.

375 ynoghe] note ynoghe T; I-nore D; I-nuȝhe I; blisse
her L.

376 Of . . . folde] They waytid manyfolde L. Of] One
T.

XXIX

Ho was þe worþiest wight*e* þ*at* eny [wy welde]
    wolde: 365
Here gide was glorious and gay, of a gresse grene;
Here belle was of blunket with birdes ful bolde,
[Botonede *with* besantes] *and* bokeled ful bene;
Here fax in fyne perre was fretted in folde,
Contrefelet and kelle, coloured full*e* clene;   370
With a crowne craftly, al of [clere] golde;
Here kercheues were curiouse, with many proude
    p(r)ene;
Her*e* per*re* was pr*a*ysed w*ith* prise men*e* of might*e*.
Bright birdes and bolde
Had [ynoghe] to be-holde   375
Of þat frely to folde,
And þe hende knight.

---

377   And] *om* L. þe] MS one þe; one þat TL. hende]
    kene I. knight] wight*e* L.

378 The] That T; þan þe I.

379 his . . . crest] a crest comely I. clere] full*e* clene
T; was clure I; clerly L.

380 His . . . his] And his bright*e* L. brene] brenyes T.
burneshed] was busket I. ful bene] by dene L.

381 a] *om* L. bordur] ITL; brandur*e* (*for* braudure?)
D.

382 were] was T. enclawet ful clene] I; many hit seen*e*
D; enclosed so clene T; closid by dene L.

383 *line om* L. horse] stede I. of . . . ilke] with*e* the
same T. of] w*ith* I. true men] it was T.

384 *line om* L. His] The T; W*ith* a I. so] full*e* T.

385 *line om* L. bore] MS bere. blake] MS brake.
browed ful] and brees ful I; burely and T.

386 horse] stede I. in . . . was] with*e* sendale was
teldede and T; w*ith* sandell*e* of trise was I; trappid
trily wer L.

387 And in] And T; Opon I; Ther was in L. cheuerone]
frounte L.

388 Stode as] As it were L.

389 Als] Als so T. a] any T.

390 An anlas] An nanlas I; And mayles T.

XXX

The knighte in his colours was armed ful clene,
Withe his comly crest clere to be-holde;
His brene and his basnet, burneshed ful bene,   380
With a [bordur] aboughte, al of brende golde;
His mayles were mylke-white, [enclawet ful clene];
His horse trapped of that ilke, as true men me tolde;
His shelde one his shulder of siluer so shene,
With b(o)re-hedes of b(l)ake, browed ful bolde.   385
His horse in fyne sandel was trapped to þe hele,
And in his cheuerone biforne
Stode as ane vnicorne,
Als sharp as a þorne,
An anlas of stele.   390

391 he was] was he TIL. þat stourne] þat steryne was T;
     stif L. vppone] on his IL; one T.

392 Al of] With his I. strynkelyd on stray] L; MS
     strykelyd; his pencelle displaied D; þat stekillede
     was one straye T; stanseld on stray I.

393 His gloues] He T; His ienewbris L. gamesons]
     iaumbis L. glowed] glomede T. a] þe I; om TL.
     glede] gledys TI.

394 With . . . gay] A rayet aure with rebans rychist of
     raye I (cf. l. 17). With . . . rybe] With greyvis and
     his cusshewis L. rybe] MS rebe; rubyes T. graiþed]
     MS graied. bene] were T; ful L.

395 And] With I. schynbaudes] MS schynbandes. þat
     . . . shrede] scharpe for to schrede T; þat shapyn
     were to shede L; scharpest in schredus I.

396 line om T. polans] IL; polemus D. with] with his I;
     and his L. pelidoddes] IL; pelicocus D. were
     poudred] þat powdrid wer L.

397 Withe a] þus with a T; þus I. one] appone TIL. þat
     . . . lede] þat lady gune he lede T; þat louely he
     ledus he ledus (dittography) I; lovely in lede L.

398 freke] swayne T; fauyn I; fawnt L. fresone] fair
     folower L. him folowed] folowede hym T.

399 line om T. fresone] faunt L. a-fered] a frayet I. for
     drede] and ferd I; for fray L.

400 For] om TL. seldene wonte] wont not L. to se]
     om T.

XXXI

In stele he was stuffed, þat stourne vppone stede,
Al of sternes of golde [stry(n)kelyd on stray];
His gloues, his gamesons glowed as a glede,
With graynes of rybe þat grai(þ)ed bene gay;
And his schene schynbaudes, þat sharp were to
    shrede,   395
His [polans] withe [pelidoddes] were poudred to
    pay.   f.7a.
Withe a launce one loft þat louely cone lede;
A freke one a fresone him folowed in fay.
The fresone was a-fered for drede of þat fare,
For he was seldene wonte to se   400
The tablet flure;
Siche gamen ne gle
Saȝ he neuer are.

---

401   T: To see the tabille at his frounte.
      I: A tablet flourre.
      L: Neuere in þe round table.

402   Siche . . . gle] Swilke gammenes was he wonte T.
      gamen ne] game and siche I; game nor L.

403   Saȝ . . . are] Fulle seldome to see T.

404   Arthur . . . hiȝte] þen thenne þe king carput him
        tille I. one (1)] in TL. one (2)] TI; *om* DL.

405   What . . . if] Qwethun art þou wurlich*e* we *and* I.
        wee] wight*e* L. be] were TI.

406   what þou seches] quethun þou come I. seches]
        says L. wheþer] whedir þat T.

407   And] *om* I. sturne . . . stede] stonyes on thi stede
        and T; stedis in þat stid and I; studiest in þis stede
        and L. so] *om* L.

408   He] þen he I. wayued] MS wayned; auaylet I;
        lyfte TL. viser] vesage T. his (2)] þe T.

409   With] And w*ith* TL. he carpes] carpid L.

410   Wheþer þou be] Sayd quethir þou be I; Be þou TL;
        Wheþer þou D. cayser] cayself*e* I.

411   Fore to] To TL. with] one TIL.

412   Fighting] For fyghtynge TIL. to . . . I] þus am I
        fraest *and* I. I fonded] y am fondyn L.

413   Then . . . king] The kynge carpede T; The kyng
        carpis L. seid] speke I. vppone] one TL.

414   If þou be] As þou art I. be] be a L.

415   Lyghte and] TL; Sayd liȝte and I; Late D. lenge]
        lende T; lende here L.

416   And] þou I; *om* L.

XXXII

Arthur asked one hiȝte, [one] herand hem alle,
"What woldes þou, wee, if hit be thi wille?   405
Tel me what þou seches and wheþer þou shalle,
And whi þou, sturne one þi stede, stondes so stille."
He wayued vp his viser fro his ventalle;
With a knightly contenaunce he carpes him tille:
"Wheþer þou [be] cayser or king, here I þe be-calle,   410
Fore to finde me a freke to fight with my fille;
Fighting to fraist I fonded fro home."
Then seid þc king vppone hight,
"If þou be curteys kniȝte,
[Lyghte, *and*] lenge al nyȝte,   415
And tel me þi nome."

417 Mi] He sayd my I. Sir] *om* L. gile] lye L.

418 grettest] grattus I. and] *and* of TI. gyllis] TIL;
     grylles D.

419– MS I.
420 D: Of Connok of Conyngham and also Kyle
        Of Lomond of Losex of Loyan*e* hilles.
     T: Of Konynge of Carryke of Conyngame of Kylle
        Of Lomonde of Lenay of Lowthyane hillis.
     L: Of Connok of Careyk of Coynham of Kylle
        Of Lomound of Leynaux of Lewans hillis.

421 wile] MS wille.
     T: Thou has wonnen thaym one werre with owt-
        trageouse wille.
      I: þat þou hase wonun on werre with þi wrang
        wiles.
     L: And þow wan hem with werre *and* with wrang
        wille.

422 And] *om* I. geuen] ʒaf L. to] *om* TL. þat] and þat
     T. þat my hert] myn hert þerof L.

423 *line om* T. But . . . his] ʒette schall*e* þou wring þi
     I. hondes] MS honde. wyle] q*u*iles I. But] *om* L.

424 he . . . y-wys] he welden*e* my landes T; any we
     schild hom weld I. at] TIL; agayn*e* D. vnwylles]
     MS vmwylles; vnethankes T. (*word crossed out*
     ?wis *before* wys *in D*).

425 Bi . . . worlde] Atte my unnewilles I wis I. welthe]
     wilis L. þe (2)] this TL.

XXXIII

"Mi name is *Sir* Galaron*e*, with*e*-outen*e* eny gile,
Þe grettest of Galwey, of greues and [gyllis],
[Of Carrake, of Cummake, of Conyngame, of Kile,
Of Lonwik, of Lannax, of Laudoune hillus].   420
Þou has wonen*e* hem in werre with a wrange [wile]
And geuen hem to *Sir* Gawayn*e*—þat my hert grylles—
But he shal wring his honde(s) and warry þe wyle
Er he weld hem, y-wys, [at] myn*e* v(n)wylles.
Bi al þe welth*e* of þe worlde, he shal hem neuer
  welde,   425
While I þe hede may bere,
But he wyn*e* hem in were,
With*e* a shelde and a spere,   f.7b.
On a fairc fclde.

_____

426 þe . . . may] may myn hede L. þe] my T.

427 But] MS But if. wyne] may wynne I. in] one TI;
     with L.

428 Withe a] Bothe w*ith* T. a] *om* IL. a(2)] w*ith* TIL.
     spere] scharpe spere I.

429 On] Appone TI.

430   I . . . felde] For in a fyld will I feȝte I. I] In L.
one] yn L. þereto I make] *and þer* to make I my T;
y hote by my L.

431   eny] a L. vppone] one the T; of þis L. frely is
borne] is fre born IL.

432   wold thenke] thynke it full*e* TL.

433   And] *om* L. iche] MS siche. lede . . . lyue] leueande lede TL. wold] wil L.

434   We ar] ȝe we ar I; We be L. in . . . walke] here in
the wode walkande T; in wudlond cothe þe king
and walkes I; in þe wode here walkyng L.

435   To] We TL; For to I. þe] þes L. herdis] TL; herd I;
hertes D. hounde] hundes T.

436   We . . . gamene] Gyf þou be gome gladdest I. in]
one T. we . . . graiþe] we ne hafe no gude graythe
T; now haue we no grayth*e* I; we have here no
graiþ L.

437   But . . . be] ȝet may þou be I.

438   For . . . niȝte] By mydday to morn on shal wiþ the
fight*e* L. For þi] And for thi T. þe] *om* I. þou . . .
the] T; rathe mon þou rest þe I; þenke rest D. al]
alle þe T.

439   Gawayne] Than Gawayne TI. graþest] þe graithest
L; gayeste T.

440   Ledes] Lad IL. oute of] furthe thruȝh*e* I.

441   Into] Vn till*e* TI.

442   Þat . . . was] Was prudlych*e* I; Prowdily L. piȝte]
y-pight*e* LI.

XXXIV

I wol fiȝte one a felde—þereto I make feithe— 430
Withe eny freke vppone folde þat frely is borne.
To lese suche a lordshippe me wold thenke laithe,
And iche lede opone lyue wold laghe me to scorne."
"We ar in þe wode went to walke one oure waithe,
To hunte at þe [herdis] with hounde and with
   horne; 435
We ar in oure gamene, we haue no gome graiþe,
But yet þou shalt be mached be mydday to-morne—
For-þi I rede þe, [þou rathe mane, þou riste the] al
   niȝte."
Gawayne, graþest of alle,
Ledes him oute of the halle, 440
Into a pavilone of palle,
Þat prodly was piȝte.

443 Piȝte . . . prodly] Hit was prudlyche y-piȝte I. it]
TL; *om* D. with] of I.

444 MS T. fulle] *om* L. And (1)] Wiþ L.
D: Birdes braudene aboue in brend golde briȝte.
I: With beddus brauderit o brode and bankers
y-dyȝte.

445 Inwithe] With inne TL; þer inne I. a . . . cham-
bour] a chaumbre chapelle L. a (3)] and ane T;
and IL (a *added above in I*).

446 with] of I. þe] þat T; with a L.

447 His . . . stalle] þay halen vppe his stede had him to
stalle I. was] was sone T. to þe] yn to L.

448 Hay . . . had] And haye hendly heuyde T; Hay
hely þay hade I; Hay hendly þei hevid L. one] vn I.

449 Siþene þei braide vp] Sythene he braydes vp T;
Prayd vp with I. a borde] bordis L. þei] gune T;
couthe I; gan L.

450 Sanapes . . . sighte] With salers and sanapus þay
serue þe knyȝte I. Sanapes and salers] TL; sanape
and saler D. semly] fulle semly T. to] in L.

451 Torches and brochetes] Preketes and broketes T;
With troches and broches I; Torchis and tortys L.
and stondardes] stondyng L.

452 Thus . . . þat] For to serue þe I. Thus] Than TL.

453 his] þe I; þis L. worþely] worthy TL; wurliche I.

XXXV

Piȝte was [it] prodly wiþ purpour and palle,
[And dossours, and qweschyns, and bankowres fulle
   bryghte];
Inwiþe was a chapelle, a chambour, a halle,   445
A chymne wiþ charcole to chaufe þe kniȝte.
His stede was stabled and led to þe stalle,
Hay hertly he had in haches one highte.
Siþene þei braide vp a borde *and* cloþes þei calle,
Sanape(s) and saler(s) semly to sighte,   450
Torches, and brochetes, and stondardes bitwene.
Thus þei serued þat kniȝte,
And his worþely wiȝte,
With riche dayntes diȝte,
In siluer so shene.   455

---

456   In] Thus in I. semely] schene IL. were serued] þay serue þame T; þay serue IL.

457   in . . . and] *and* . . . in I. ful] so LT.

458   And . . . geste] W*ith* lucius drinkes and metis of þe best I. And . . . good] And thus thase gleterande gom*m*es T; And þus þis galyard me*n* L. geste] gestis T.

459   With] *om* I.

460   Whane þe] As tyde as þat I; *And* whan þe L. renke] *om* I. raghte] L; gon*e* DT; rayket I.

461   to . . . kene] callut his councelle þe doȝti be dene I. to] in to T.

462   Loke . . . lordes] Sayse lukes nowe ȝe lordyngs T; And bede vmloke ȝo lording*es* I. lordynges] L; lordes D.

463   with] *om* L. þe] ȝone T; ȝondur I; þis L. kestes you] nowe lukes vs T; cast ȝo I; cast vs L.

464   Sir . . . vs] T; Gawayn*e* þe goode shal hit D. he] hit I. he . . . vs] y wole þe L.

465   Here] þ*er* to I. hond . . . hiȝte] trouthe . . . plyghte TIL. you] þe IL.

466   wolle] sall*e* TL. fight] encountre LI. þe] ȝone T; þat L.

467   In] In þe T.
      I: For to maynteine my ryȝte.
      L: That is hardy and wight*e* (= l. 674).

468   Lorde] My lorde T; ȝe lord I. by] with*e* TIL. your] thi IL.

XXXVI

In siluer so semely were serued of þe best,
With vernage in veres and cuppes ful clene;
And þus Sir Gawayne þe good glades hour geste,
With riche dayntees endored in disshes by-dene.
Whane þe rialle renke was [raghte] to his reste   460
The king to counsaile has called his kniʒtes so
   kene: f.8a.
"Loke nowe, [lordynges], oure lose be not lost,
Ho shal encontre with þe kniʒte kestes you bitwene."
Thene seid [Sir Gawayne, "he salle vs] not greue;
Here my hond I you hiʒte,   465
I wolle fight with þe knighte
In defence of my riʒte,
Lorde, by your leue."

469– *The omissions noted for T in these lines are due to*
483   *a torn leaf in the MS.*

469   leue] leue þe L. þi lates ar] in lystines be L. liȝte]
      om T.

470   *line om* T. nolde] wold notte I. life] self L.

471   quod] coth*e* I. Sir] *om* L. stond with] dele L. stond
      . . . riȝte] *om* T.

472   If he skape] For and he scapette I. hit . . . skorne]
      om T. foule] gret IL.

473   In] And in I. daying] dawnyng L; dawynge T. þe
      (2)] *om* I. day . . . dighte] *om* T. þe (3)] þer I.

474   And] Thaye TL; *om* I. and . . . morne] *om* T. and
      (2)] *om* I. erly] myldelik I. one] by þe L.

475   By þat on] In myd I. on] in L. Plumtone . . .
      piȝte] *om* T. Plumtone land] Plumtun lone I; Plon-
      ton*e* land L. a palais was] a place was L; hor
      paueluns were I.

476   Where] MS were. freke . . . biforne] *om* T. freke
      opone] frekes opon I; freke of þis L.

477   *line om* T. by lyne] on lenthe IL. one þe loȝ] olong
      on þe I; on þat longe L. lande] lawnde I.

478   Thre] Twa TL. soppes de mayne] *om* T. soppes]
      soppus of I; soppys atte L.

479   þei] Was TI. broughte . . . , Gawayne] *om* T.

480   to . . . brayne] *om* T.

481   king . . . commaunde] *om* T. gared] dede L.

XXXVII

"I leue wel," quod þe king, "þi lates ar liȝte,
But I nolde for no lordeshippe se þi life lorne."   470
"Let go," quod Sir Gawayne, "God stond with þe riȝte!
If he skape skaþelese hit were a foule skorne."
In þe daying of þe day þe doughti were dighte,
And herdene matens and masse erly one morne;
By þat on Plumtone land a palais was piȝte   475
W(h)ere neuer freke opone folde had fouȝtene biforne.
Þei settene listes by lyne one þe loȝ lande;
Thre soppes de mayne
Þei broughte to Sir Gawayne,
For to confort his brayne,   480
Þe king gared commaunde.

482 *line om* T. commaunded . . . sone] dede co-
maunde to þe Erl L. kindeli] I; krudely D. erlis
sone] Erle I.

483 *line om* T. Curtaysly . . . þe] For his meculle
curtasy to kepe þe toþer I. kepe to þe] tent to þat L.

484 With . . . dyned] And made him with dayntethis
to dine I. With] *om* L. or] þat T.

485 TL: Withe (*om* L) birdes bakene in brede of (on
L) brynte golde bryghte.
    I: And sythun þis rialle men a-rayut hom
    o-ryȝte.

486 Siþene] And sythene TL; And aftur I. to] vn to T;
om I. Waynour] Dame Waynour T; Quene Waynor
I. wisly] fulle wyesely T; warly I; worthely L. he]
þay I.

487 He] And TIL. laft] beleues I. in . . . warde] withe
hir in warde T. his worthly] þat wurlyche I.

488 After] And thane thies TL; Sethin þe I. hathels] TI;
aither D; boþe men L. in highe] fulle hendely T;
om L. þei] hase T; haue IL.

489 T: At the lycence of the lorde þat lordely gune
lighte.
    I: In mydde þe lyste of þe lawunde þe lordus
    doune liȝte.
    L: And at þe lystis in þe laund lustily þei alighte.

490 All butte] ITL; Bothe D. þes . . . blode] þe stithest
in steroppus þat stode I. þes two] thir T; þe L.

491 þe . . . chaier] King Arther schayer I; The kyng
on highte L. is] was TIL.

XXXVIII

The king commaunded [kindeli] þe erlis sone of Kent,
Curtaysly in þis case take kepe to þe kniȝt.
With riche dayntees or day he dyned in his tente,
After buskes him in a brene þat burneshed was briȝte;
Siþene to Waynour wisly he went,   486
He laft in here warde his worthly wighte.
After [hathels] in highe hour horses þei hent,
And at þe listes one þe lande lordely done liȝte—
[All butte] þes two burnes baldest of blode.   490
Þe kinges chaier is set
[Above] one a chacelet;
Many galiard gret   f.8b.
For Gawayne þe gode.

---

492   Above] LTI; Quene D. one a] in his I; yn a L.
      chacelet] castelet L.

493   T: And many a gaylyarde grett.
      I: And þenne Dame Gaynour grette.
      L: Were meny galyard þat grette.

495–   *Stanza omitted in I.*
507

495   gurdene here] dyghtis thaire T; are dight*e* on L.

496   Al in gleterand] Alle of glet*era*nde T; Alle glyter-
ing in L. gay] full*e* gaye T.

497   T: Twa lordes be lyfe to thaire lystes thaym*e* ledis.
L: To lordis wiþ love he*m* to þe lyst ledis.

498   as] it T. seriant] sergeauntes T.

499   broched] broches TL. þe blonkes] þaire blonkes T;
her bodyes L. þat þe] þ*at* her L; to þaire T. side]
sydes TL.

500   Ayþer . . . spere] Fast þes frekis on this feld
foghetyn yn fere L. folde] felde T. fastned his]
fichede thaire T.

501   in shide] of schene TL. shindre] scheu*e*rede TL. in
shedes] on shredis L.

502   gentil] gentill*e* men*e* T; gentils L. iusted] iustyn L.

503   shindre] sheu*er* T; shyverid L. in] on L. sheldes]
schydes T. so shene] full*e* schene T; þo shent L.

504   And] *om* TL. brighte] full*e* bryghte T.

506   There] Thus TL. encontres] enconterde T.

507   one] on the L.

XXXIX

Gawayne and Galerone gurdene here stedes   495
Al in gleterand golde—gay was here gere;
Þe lordes by-lyue hom to list ledes
With many seriant of mace, as was þe manere.
The burnes broched þe blonkes þat þe side bledis;
Ayþer freke opone folde has fastned his spere;   500
Shaftes in shide wode þei shindre in shedes;
So iolile þes gentil iusted one were.
Shaftes þei shindre in sheldes so shene,
And siþene, withe brondes brighte,
Riche mayles þei riȝte;   505
There encontres þe kniȝte
With Gawyne one grene.

508 Gawyne . . . gaily] Thenne Syr Gauan þe gode was I. gaily] graythely TL. in] one TL.

509 his] *om* TL. engreled] englorid L. fulle] so L.

510 Trifeled . . . tranes] Trayfolede w*ith* trayfoles T; Trowlt w*ith* trulofes I; Tracid *and* travercid L. and] w*ith* L. true-loves] tranest I.

511 on] opon I. a] his L. startand] IT; stargand D; stertelyng L. he] TIL; þat D. one] oute of I.

512– *The omissions noted for T in these lines are due*
520 *to a torn leaf in the MS.*

512 þat oþer in] *om* T. þat oþer] þe tother IL. talkes] takith L. in (2)] with*e* T; tille him in I.

513 Whi . . . þou] *om* T. Whi] And sayd querto I. þou] MS þou þe. on dreghe] so dreȝgh*e* I; on so drighly L. deray] delaye T.

514 He . . . þe] *om* T. him yne at] on L. swyre] schuldir T; swithe L.

515 That . . . to] *om* T. to] eu*er* tille I.

516 The . . . doutwis] *om* T; þe dede of þat doghty *and* his dyntis L.

517 *line om* T. Fifte] Syxti I.

518 *line om* T. swapt] squappes I.

519 *line om* T. The] His IL.

520 And . . . his] *om* T. And . . . shene] Wiþ þat swerde kene L. clef] cleuet I.

XL

Gawyne was gaily graþed in grene,
Withe his griffons of golde engreled fulle gay,
Trifeled withe tranes and true-loves bitwene.   510
On a [startand] stede [he] strikes one stray,
Þat oþer in his turnaying he talkes in tene:
"Whi drawes þou on dreghe *and* makes siche deray?"
He swapped him yne at þe swyre with a swerde kene,
That greued Sir Gawayne to his deþ day;   515
The dyntes of þat doughety were doutwis bydene—
Fifte mayles and mo
The swerde swapt in two,
The canel bone also,
And clef his shelde shene.   520

521– *These lines are missing in T, apparently because a*
604 *leaf was lost in the MS.*

521 clef þorghe] keuet (? *for* keruet) of I.

522 shuldre and] L; þe shiand (? *for* shinand) D.
shuldre . . . shelde] his shild and his shildur I.
and mare] he share I.

523 And] *om* I. þene þe] *om* L. loþely lord] lady loude
D; latelest lord I; loþely þat lord L. lowe] he laghte
L.

524 greches þerwith] grynyd gresily L. greches] grechut
I. gremed] greuut I; gronyd L. ful] wund*ur* I.

525 I shal] Sayd he shuld I. þi] þis I; w*ith* a L. if] and
I. cone] may L. righte] o-ryʒte I.

526 folowed in one] folowiþ on L; fou*n*des in to I. þe]
þat L.

527 blasone . . . brene] blasynet (et *above, lighter*)
and breny I; his blasyng basnet L. were] wos IL.

528 bytand] IL; burlich*e* D. bronde] swerd L. thorghe]
euyn throgh*et* I. him he] he him I; hym L.

529 I: He bare thruʒe his brenys þat burneyst were
bryʒte.
L: þurgh*e* þe blasyng basnet of þat hende wight*e*.

530 gloppened þat] Galaron þe L.

531 Hit . . . ferly] Was no wondur L.

532 I: His stedes startun on straye.
L: þogh*e* he were in affray.

533 I: With steroppus fulle stryʒte.
L: Wiþ tho dyntis y-dight*e*.

XLI

He clef þorghe þe cantelle þat couered þe kniȝte,
Thorghe [shuldre and] shelde a shaftmone and mare;
And þene þe [loþely lord] lowe vppone highte,
And Gawayne greches þerwith and gremed ful sare:
"I shal rewarde þe þi route if I cone rede righte."   525
He folowed in one þe freke withe a fresshe fare;   f.9a.
Þorghe blasone and brene þat burneshed were briȝte,
Withe a [bytand] bronde thorghe him he bare—
The bronde was blody þat burneshed was briȝte.
Then gloppened þat gay;   530
Hit was no ferly in fay;
Þe sturne strikes one stray
In stiropes striȝte.

521–   *om* T.
604

534   Streyte . . . steroppes] Thenne w*ith* steroppus fulle
       streȝte I. Streyte] Sternely L. stoutely] stifly IL.

535   And] *om* I. waynes] wayvis L. als] ryȝte as I.

536   lowde] lofte IL. skrilles . . . skrikes] MS skirles
       . . . skirkes; sorowis . . . shrikys L.

537   þat . . . burne] þe balefull birde I. burly] bold L.
       blenket one] so blenkis in L. his] IL; *om* D.

538   Lordes] Oþ*er* lordus I. of þat laike] þayre laykes
       well I; þat the layke L.

539   And] *om* IL. of his grace] IL; fele sithe D.

540   a] his IL. swithely] MS þat swaþel; squeturly I; þe
       toþ*er* at L. swykes] strykes IL.

541   He . . . þe] Smote of Gauan I. He] And L. stede]
       stedis L. streite] in styd I; wiþ strengþe L. þere]
       quere I.

542   The . . . rode] And þan þe fayr stede fowndrid on
       fote L. bi þe rode] I; to þe grounde D.

543   (*lines 543–544 are mixed in I*)
        I: Gauan was smyther and smerte.
        L: Gawayn grynnyd in hert.

544   MS L. D: Of he were hasty and smert.
        I: As he þ*at* was of herte.

545   of] of his IL.

XLII

Streyte in his steroppes, stoutely he strikes,
And waynes at Sir Wawayne als he were wode;   535
Þene his lemmane on lowde sk(ril)les and sk(ri)kes
Whene þat burly burne blenket one [his] blode.
Lordes and ladies of þat laike likes,
And þonked God [of his grace] for Gawayne þe gode.
Withe a swap of a swerde [swithely] him swykes—   540
He stroke of þe stede hede streite þere he stode;
The faire fole fondred and fel [bi þe rode].
Gawayne gloppened in hert;
[He was swithely smert],
Oute of sterops he stert   545
Fro Grisselle þe goode.

521–   *om* T.
604

547   Grisselle . . . wote] Now is gay Griselle gone þat
       was so good L. wote] ote I.

548   burlokest blonke] best body L; burlokke blonke I.
       bote brede] bare knyghte L. þat] þer I.

549   in . . . bote] rufully ros and raght hym on rood
       (= l. 317) L. for] I; euer to bene D.

550   þe] hym L. if] and I. cone . . . rede] may a righte
       L.

551   Go . . . me] Foche þe I; Go fecche forth L. fairest]
       quod þe freke is fayrest I. fote] food L.

552   may] wull IL. me] þe DI; *om* L. in] in a L. in as]
       in toe so I.

553   þe . . . fole] þi fresun I; þe good stede L. for (2)]
       om L.

554   þe] a I.

555   I mourne] No more L. monture] matyttory I;
       monkyre L.

556   Als] And as I.

557   so goode at] gud in iche I.

558   Ner . . . wede] He bythoghte hym of rede L. Ner]
       Neȝtehond Syr I. wold] I; wax D.

559   So] And L. wepputte . . . fulle] I; siked he D;
       sighid L.

XLIII

"Grisselle," quod Gawayne, "gone is, God wote!
He was þe burlokest blonke þat euer bote brede;
By him þat in Bedeleem was borne [for] our bote,
I shalle venge þe to day if I cone right rede.   550
Go fecche me my fresone fairest one fote,
He may stonde [me] in stoure in as mekle stede;
No more for þe faire fole þene for a risshe rote—
But for doel of þe dombe best þat þus shuld be dede—
I mourne for no monture, for I may gete mare."   555
Als he stode by his stede,
Þat was so goode at nede,
Ner Gawayne [wold] wede,   f.9b.
So [wepputte he fulle] sare.

521–   *om* T.
604

560   Thus wepus] Sore wepput I; He sighyd L. Wo-
       wayne] Syr Wauan I.

561   And . . . enemy] L; Bouun to his enmy I; And
       wenys him to quyte D. is] was IL.

562   þat oþer] þe tother IL. droӡ . . . dreӡt] wiþdrow
       hy*m* dernely L.

563   And boldely] þen he I. broched . . . blonk] plis
       his stede L. one] opon I.

564   þou] we I; ӡe L. forthe] *om* L. day to] day q*uod*
       Gauan to I.

565   is] IL; was D. þe merke of] IL; by þat D.

566   Withe-in . . . listes] In myddes þe lyist I. þe lede]
       on þe lawunde IL. lordly done] þis lordes dou*n* I;
       ful lightly he L.

567   Touard] Aagayn I. his] a L. him] ful L. ӡare] MS
       þare.

568   To] þus to IL. þey bowe] þay boune I; be þei
       boun L.

569   Shene sheldes] Riche mayles L. were] þay I.

570   I: Well ryc*he* mayles wexun rede.
        L: Wiþ brigh*te* brondis y-bred.

571   Many] And mony I. were a-dred] hadun drede I;
       dred L.

572   fighte] foӡtun I.

XLIV

Thus wepus for wo Wowayne þe wighte,   560
[And wendiþ to his enemy] þat wonded is sare;
Þat oþer droȝ him on dreȝt for drede of þe kniȝte,
And boldely broched his blonk one þe bent bare.
"Þus may þou dryve forthe þe day to þe derke nighte,
The sone [is] passed [þe merke of] mydday and mare."
Withe-in þe listes þe lede lordly done lighte;   566
Touard þe burne withe his bronde he busked him (ȝ)are;
To bataile þey bowe withe brondes so brighte;
Shene sheldes were shred,
Brighte brenes by-bled;   570
Many douȝti were a-dred,
So fersely þei fighte.

521– *om* T.
604

573   þei . . . fote] on fote con þai feȝte I. fote] her foot
       L. one þat] opon þe I; on her L. felde] fildus I.

574   fresshe] fryke L. a lyone] ij lions I. fautes þe]
       fawtutte þe I; of fight*e* fawtis his L.

575   Wilele . . . mene] Witturly þer weys I. Wilele]
       Wysely L.

576   *line om* D. MS I. him wontut] wantis L.

577   He . . . yne] He berus to him I; He brochid hym
       L. þe] his I. brode] *om* L.

578   of . . . and] he went þat L. and] *om* I.

579   hit] he I. so] *om* L.

580   þat . . . stondis] þat eiþer for þat stroke stode L.

581   Though] If I. he] y L. stonayed] stonit in I. he . . .
       ful] ȝette strykes he I. strikes] strikyd L.

582   He gurdes to] And gert L.

583   pesayne] polayn L.

584   wanted] MS wanted noȝte.
       I: þat him lakket no more to be slayne.
       L: He went litil to have be slayn.

585   I: Butte þe brede of hore.
       L: He mayed hym þe more.

XLV

Þus þei feght one fote one þat faire felde,
As fresshe as a lyone þat fautes þe fille;
Wilele þes wighte mene þaire wepenes þey welde,   575
[Wete ȝe wele, Sir Wauan him wontut no wille];
He bronched hym yne withe his bronde, vnder þe brode
    shelde,
Þorghe þe waast of þe body, *and* wonded him ille—
Þe swerd stent for no stuf, hit was so wel steled.
Þat oþer startis one bak and stondis stone stille;   580
Though he were stonayed þat stonde he strik*es* ful sare;
He gurdes to *Sir* Gawayne
Thorghe ventaile and pesayne;
He wanted to be slayne
Þe brede of ane hare.   585

521– *om* T.
604

586   I: And þus þe hardy on heyte on helmis þai
       heuen.
       L: Hastily on helmys þan þes hardy gan hewe.

587   þei] *om* I. and] in I. so] IL; *om* D.

588   Shildes one] W*ith* schildus on þer I. þat . . .
       shewe] schomely þay shewen I.

589   Fretted . . . in] Frettut w*ith* I; þ*at* frettyd were
       wiþ L. þei . . . in] þ*at* failis in þe I; faylith in
       þ*at* L.

590   Stones . . . strewe] þ*at* w*ith* stones iraille were
       strencult and strauen I. iral] grete strengthe L.

591   Stiþe] stiff L. þey strike] strykyn L. striȝte] MS
       stiȝt*e;* streȝte I; right*e* L.

592   Burnes] þenne byernes I. þe (2)] þ*at* L.

593   The . . . delfully] So dolefully þo dogh*e*ty wiþ
       dyntis L. The dougheti] þ*at* euyr þese duȝti I.

594–   MS L. Lote] MS Lete.
598   D: Thene gretes Gayno*ur* w*ith* bothe her*e* gray
       ene.
                 For þo douȝeti þat fiȝte
                 Were manly mached of might*e*
                 With*e* oute reson*e* or right*e*
                 As al men*e* sene.

XLVI

Hardely þen*e* þes haþelese on*e* helmes þey hewe,
Þei beten*e* downe beriles and bo*ur*dures [so] bright;
Shildes on*e* shildres, þ*at* shene were to shewe,
Fretted were in fyne golde—þei failen*e* in fight*e;*
Stones of iral þey strenkel and strewe,   590
Stiþe stapeles of stele þey strike don*e* st(r)iȝt*e;*
Burnes bannen*e* þe tyme þe bargan*e* was brewe,   f.10a.
The dough*e*ti with*e* dyntes so delfully were dight.
[Þe dyntis of þo doghty were doutous by-dene;
Bothe Sir L(o)te and S*ir* Lake   595
Miche mornyng þei make;
Gaynor gret for her sake
Wiþ her grey eyen].

I: Hit hurte King Arther in herte and mengit his
      mode
   Bothe Sir Lote and Sir Lake
   Mecull*e* menyng con make
   Thenne Dame Gaynor grette for his sake
   For Gawan þe gode.

521– *om* T.
604

599   Thus] þenne I. gretis] grette Dame IL. withe . . .
yene] þat grete grefe was to sene L. bothe] *om* I.

600   grisly . . . wound] grimliche wouundes I; þat was
grisly woundid L. wound] MS wounded.

601   The . . . was] þenne þe knyȝte þat was curtase I.

602   And] *om* I. he . . . stounde] I; þat sturne oft
stonded D; strikyd þat stound L.

603   þe (2)] IL; *om* D. carf] keruys I; cleviþ L. downe]
droune I.

604   þe] *om* L.

605   (T *resumes*) Swylke . . . tene] Suche a stroke he
hym raght yn a tene L. Swylke . . . tyme] T; With
a teneful touche D. at þat tyme] in þat tyde I.

606   He gurdes] He girdede TL; And gurdes me I.
groueling on] euyn grouelonges on I; doun to the L.

607   T: Gallerone fulle greuousely granes on þe grene.
I: All grouelonges in grounde gronet on grene.
L: To þe ground was cast þat doghty be dene.

608   Als wounded] But al doun L. Als] And als T.

609   Sone buredely] Swiftly vpe T; Wundur rudely I;
Wondir rathely L.

610   fast] in faste T. face] IT; tras D.
I: Fast he foundes atte his face.
L: Coverid vp in that cas.

611   a] his L. kene] schene T.

XLVII

Thus gretis Gaynour withe boþe here gray yene,
For gref of Sir Gawayne, grisly was wound;   600
The knighte of corage was cruel and kene,
And withe a stele bronde [he strikes in þat stounde];
Al þe cost of [þe] knyȝt he carf downe clene,
Þorghe þe riche mailes þat ronke were and rounde;
[Swylke a touche at þat tyme] he taȝt him in tene,   605
He gurdes Sir Galerone groueling on gronde—
Grisly one gronde he groned one grene.
Als wounded as he was,
Sone buredely he ras,
And folowed fast one his [face],   610
With a swerde kene.

612 Kenely . . . keuered] þus þat cruelle and kene
     kerues I. Kenely] Clenly T. cruel] kene knyghte L.
     keuered] couerde hym T.

613 And] om I. withe . . . cautil] as a kene kempe
     kyndely L. cast of þe carhonde] I; scas of care D.
     carhonde] care T. cautil] a cantelle I.

614 T: Fulle ȝerne he wayttis Sir Wawayne þe wighte.
     I: ȝorne waitis with woe Sir Wauan þe wiȝte.
     L: And with strokis rewardiþ Gawayn þe wighte.

615 But] Butte ȝette IL. lymped] limpus I; happith L.

616 line om L. atteled] wend I. haf] hade I. in] with
     TI. (word crossed out, ?fighte, before sliȝt in D)

617 line om L. swapped . . . swange] sleppis on slante
     TI. slikes] slydys T.

618 And] And Sir T; Thenne Sir I. clekis] TI; keppes
     D; blekys L. þe (2)] þat L.

619 þene] And þan L. one loft] so lowde T; low L.
     skrilles] skremes T; ho scrilles I; shrillis L. skrikes]
     shrikis L.

620 Ho gretes one] And sayd to I. Ho] And L. gretes]
     grete TL. Gaynour] Dame Gaynour TIL. gronyng]
     gronyng ful L; granes so T; grones full I.

621 Lady] And saide lady T; þou lade I. makeles]
     makelest I.

622 Haf] Hafe now T. mercy] pety IL. one] of I.
     yondre] ȝone T; ȝondur nobulle I; that L.

623 so] om L.

624 If . . . be] And hit were I.

XLVIII

Kenely þat cruel keuered one hiȝte,
And withe a [cast of þe carhonde] in cautil he strikes,
And waynes at Sir Wawyne, þat worþely wighte—
But him lymped þe worse and þat me wel likes.   615
He atteled withe a slenke haf slayne him in sliȝte;
Þe swerd swapped one his swange and one þe mayle
    slikes,
And Gawayne bi þe coler [clekis] þe kniȝte.
Þene his lemmane one loft skrilles and skrikes,
Ho gretes one Gaynour with gronyng grylle: 620
"Lady makeles of mighte,
Haf mercy one yondre kniȝte,
That is so delfulle diȝte,
If hit be thi wille."

625 Than wilfully] T; þenne wilfull*e* I; Wisly D; Tha*n*
wightly L. Dame] *om* I. to] vn to T.

626 Ho] *om* I.

627 As] Sayd as I. roy] MS ioy. roial richest] ryalle
and recheste T; richist and rialle I; ricchest L. of]
in I.

628 wife wedded] wedut wife I. at] eu*e*re at L. þi] myn*e*
T. owne] none I; *om* L.

629 þes] ȝone T; ȝondur I; þo L. þe] ȝone T; *om* IL. so]
þ*at* TIL. blede] bidus I. þe (2)] ȝone T.

630 arne] be L.

631 here . . . are] schildus *and* shildurs schomfully I.
here] *om* TL. shene sheldes] sharp swerdis L.

632 *line om* T. grones] grevis L. dos] hit dose I; do L.

633 grones] grevis L. Gawayne] Gauan þe gode hit I.
sare] full*e* sare T.

634 Woldest] But wold L. þou] ȝe I; yow L. leve] lufly
TIL.

635 Make] Gare T. þes] the T; ȝondur I; tho L.
accorde] at a-cord I.

636 a] *om* T.

637 For] Till*e* T; To L. here] TL; þer*e* DI.

XLIX

[Than wilfully] Dame Waynour to þe king wente,   f.10b.
Ho cauȝte of her coronalle and kneled him tille: 626
"As þou art (r)oy roial, richest of rente,
And I þi wife, wedded at þi owne wille,
Þes burnes in þe bataile so blede on þe bent,
They arne wery I-wis, and wonded fulle ille;   630
Þorghe here shene sheldes here shuldres are shent—
The grones of Sir Gawayne dos my hert grille.
The grones of Sir Gawayne greuene me sare;
Woldest þou, leve lorde,
Make þes knightes accorde,   635
Hit were a grete conforde
For alle þat [here] ware."

638   Thene] Bot þan TI. spak] hy*m* spake T. Sir] *om*
       TL.

639   neuer . . . bene] þ*er* had be none in world L.
       neuer] no T. in . . . world] ȝette I. had bene] were
       T. half] haluendelle TL; *om* I.

640   Here] And sayd here I. releyse] a reles L. renke] in
       my rentis T; rength*e* I.

641   And . . . resynge] T; And by rial reyson*e* relese D.
       And] *om* I. thiese] þis I; ȝon L. ryalle] riall route
       I. þe] y L.

642   make . . . monradene] y mouthe þe as menys L.
       make] I make TI. with a mylde] mildist of I.

643   As] Als to T; As a L. of] in this TL; on this I.
       medlert] world L. makeles] þ*at* most is IL.

644   stalket] I; talkes TD; callid L. king] knyghte TL
       (L *is corrected to* king, *another hand*). in stid] I;
       one hie DTL. þer] quer*e* I.

645   And] He TL. þat] þe I. þat burly] forth L. briȝte]
       right*e* L.

646   Of] And sayd of I. and] of L; and of I.

647   kneled] knelis TI. þe] þat T.

648   carped] carpis thies T; speke these I; seyd L. one]
       opon I.

649   stode vp] stert vp anon L.

650   commaunded] com*m*andis þe T.

L

Thene spak *Sir* Galerone to Gawayne þe good:
"I wende neuer wee in þis world had bene half so wiȝte;
Here I make þe releyse, renke, by þe rode,   640
[And by-fore thiese ryalle resynge] þe my righte;
And siþene make the monradene *with* a mylde mode,
As mane of medlert makeles of mighte."
He [stalket] touard þe king [in stid] þer he stode,
And bede þat burly his bronde þat burneshed was briȝte:
"Of rentes and richesse I make þe releyse."   646
Downe kneled þe kniȝte
And carped wordes one hiȝte;
The king stode vp-righte
And commaunded pes.   650

651 commaunded . . . cried] comandis þe pese and
cryes T. cried . . . hiȝte] stode vp ryȝte I.

652 was . . . laft] godely he sesutt I; ful goodly left L.

653 T: And þane to þe lystis þe lordis leppis fulle
lyghte.
I: And þen þese lordus so lele þai lepe vp liȝte.
L: Four lordis in to þe laund lepyd ful righte.

654– D: Sir Ewayne fiȝ Griane and Arrak fiȝ Lake
655 Sir Drurelat and Moylard þat most were of
miȝte.
T: Sir Owayne fytȝ Vryene and Arrak fulle rathe
Marrake and Menegalle þat maste were of
myghte.
I: Huaya Fusuryayn and Arrake fylake
Sir Meliaduke þe Marrake that mekill wasse of
myȝte.
L: Sir Eweyn Sir Realle Sir Errak Sir Lake
Sir Marcaduk Sir Marrak þat myche were of
myghte.

656 Boþe . . . trauayled] þese ij traueling I. mene]
knyghtes T. þey . . . take] trewly þay taghte T;
truly vppe þay take I; a twyn þei take L.

657 þo sturne] those knyghtes T; þese sturun men I; þei
þat stound L.

658 T: þay were for bett and for blede þaire wedis
wexe blake.
I: So for brissutte and for bled þayre blees were
so blake.
L: What for bete what for bled þe bernys were
blake.

LI

The king commaunded pes and cried one hiʒte,
And Gawayne was goodly and laft for his sake.
Þene lordes to listes þey lopen ful liʒte—
Sir Ewayne [fytʒ-Vryene] and Arrak fiʒ-Lake,
[Marrake and Mene(duke)], þat most were of miʒ-
    te—   655
Boþe þes trauayled mene þey truly vp take;
Vnnethe miʒte þo sturne stonde vp-riʒte;   f.11a.
What for buffetes and blode here blees wex blake—
Here blees were brosed for beting of brondes.
Withe-outene more lettynge   660
Diʒte was here saʒtlynge;
Bifore þe comly kinge
Þei held vp here hondes.

---

659   line om T. Here . . . brosed] Alle blake was þayre
        blees I; The bernes were blody L. for beting of] for
        betun with IL.

660   more] any I. lettynge] hersing I; rehercyng L.

661   Diʒte . . . saʒtlynge] Was dighte there thiere
        semblynge T. Diʒte] þere diʒte I; Made L.

662   Bifore þe] And that L. þe] þat T.

663   þei . . . hondes] Yaf hem her landys L. þei] And
        T.

664	Here] *om* T; Now here I. þe] IL; to the T; *om* D.
Sir . . . golde] quod þe king Gauan þe bold I. Sir]
om L. with gersone] quode þe kynge tresoure T.
and] of L.

665	Al þe] Alle L; *om* TI. Glamergane] Glomorgans L.
londe] londus ITL. so] fulle I; *and* L.

666	þe . . . of] Wiþ . . . in L. at . . . wolde] to welde
and to wolde T; to weld and þou wold I; to have
and to hold L. at] MS al.

667	Withe] *om* I. Criffones castelles] Gryffones castelle
T; Kirfre castell I; cuntres and castels L. curnelled]
w*ith* colurs I. ful] so T.

668	Eke . . . halle] And þe Husters haulle T; Iche
Hulkers home I; Hulster al holy L.

669	Waterforde] Wakfelde T. wallede] TIL; *in* Wales
D.

670	baronrees] baroners I. Bretayne] Burgoyne T. with]
in L. so] fulle I.

671	arne] is I; be L. batailed] moted T. bene] clene L.

672	I shal] Here I I. endowe] T; doue I; diȝte D; dubbe
L. a] als a T; as I; *om* L. and . . . þe] doghty L.
honde] myne hande T; my hondus I; hondis L.

673	Withe þi] þat L. saȝtil] saȝtun I. þe] ȝone gentille
T; ȝondur I; þat L.

674	so] *om* L. wiȝte] so wiȝte I.

675	relese] resingne I. his] thi TI.

676	graunte] yeve L. londe] londus IL.

LII

"Here I gif [þe] Sir Gawayne, with gersone and golde,
Al þe Glamergane londe with greues so grene;   665
Þe worship of Wales, at wil and a(t) wolde,
Withe criffones castelles curnelled ful clene;
Eke Vlstur halle, to hafe and to holde,
Wayford and Waterforde, [wallede] I wene;
Two baronrees in Bretayne, with burghes so bolde,   670
Þat arne batailed abouȝte and bigged ful bene.
I shal [endowe] þe a duke, and dubbe þe with honde,
Withe þi þou saȝtil with þe kniȝte,
Þat is so hardi and wiȝte,
And relese him his riȝte,   675
And graunte him his londe."

677   Here] Now and here T; Nowe here I. gif] gif þe
        IL. Sir Galerone] hy*m* T. Sir] *om* IL. quod Ga-
        wayne] *om* L. gile] grylle L.

678   and . . . lithes] for sothe I. þe (2)] *om* L. Lauer]
        Lowyke TL; Logher I. (*second* þe *in D struck
        through in different ink*)

679   and] *om* I. Carrake . . . Cummake] I; Commoke
        and Carrike TL; Connok*e* and Carlele D. Kile]
        Kylle TL.

680   *line om* L. T: Als cheualrous knyghte hase cha-
        landchede als ayere. I: Sir to þi seluu*n* and sithun
        to þine ayre. (*"Originally in MS. D.* . . . *he haf
        cheualry, and chalange hit for* . . . , *but altered
        by a second hand" Madden*)

681   *line om* IL. T: The Lebynge the Lowpynge þe
        Leveastre Iles (helle Ile *struck out before* Iles).

682   *line om I.* Withe] Bathe T; Wiþ her L. and . . . so]
        frely and T; frely so L.

683   *line om* T. Vnder] W*i*th þi tille I. your] oure IL.
        to . . . while] þou leng in a qwile I; to lende at
        þi will*e* L. (*here a in D first written* þe, *altered,
        says Madden, by a second hand*)

684   *line om* T. to (2)] *om* L. repaire] þi repare IL. (to
        make *in D first written* a, *altered, says Madden,
        by a second hand*)

685   *line om* T. I . . . refeff] Here I feffe I. him] þe
        TL. in felde] felefold L. in . . . so] frely and I.
        (faire *in D first written* fare, *altered, says Madden,
        by a second hand*)

LIII

"Here I gif *Sir* Galeron*e*," q*u*od G*awayne,* "wi*th*-oute*n*
   any gile,
Al þe londes and þe lithes fro Lauer to Layre:
[Carrake], and [Cummake], Conyngha*m,* and Kile.
Yet if he of cheualry chalange ham for air*e*,   680
Þe Loþ*er,* þe Le*m*moke, þe Loynak, þe Lile,
Wit*he* frethis, and forestes, and fosses so faire—
Vnder yo*ur* lordeship to lenge here a while,
And to þe rounde table to make repaire—
I shall refeff him in felde *in* forest*es* so faire."   685
Boþe þe king and þe quene,
And al þe douȝeti by-dene,
Þorgh*e* þe greues so grene,
To Carlele þei cair*e*.

---

686   Boþe] Than T; Thus L.

687   al þe] oþ*er* I; þe L.

688   þorghe] Throȝgh*e*-owte I.

689   caire] kayrit I; faire L.

690   *line om* I.

691   And] To T; Throghe greuis so grene I. held] I;
      halde TL; al D. þe] his T. one] with I.

692   þe wees] Those knyghtes T; Thes doghty L. þe]
      These I. wounded . . . woþely] wothely woundet I.
      so] fulle T. woþely] wroþely L. I wene] als I wene
      T.

693   Surgenes . . . saued] þenne surgens hom sauyt I;
      Soiournis tul þei be salvid L; Surgeones sauede
      thayme T. soþely to] quo sotheli wynne I.

694   Bothe] *om* I. confortes] comforthede T; cumfordun
      I. þe knightes] thaym thane T; hom kindely IL.

695   Thei . . . dubbed] And sithin dubbut hom I.

696   There] And ther T; And þenne I. he] Sir Gallerone
      T. wlonkest] MS slonkest. wlonkest I wene] þat
      semly *and* schene T; semely to sene L.

697   and] and with I. Sir Galerone] of Sir Gawayne T.

698   þus . . . hende] Thus Gauan *and* Galrun gode
      frindes ar thay I. þus] And thus T. þat . . . hiჳ]
      those hathelles T; þe kyng for ioy L.

699   Whane] And whene T. he was] þay were I. saued]
      saued and T; holle and I; safe and L.

700   Þei] The kyng L. Sir Galerone] hyme sworne to
      Sir Gawayne in T; Galrun in I; hym L.

701   A] And sythene a T.

702   To] Vn-tille TI. lyues ende] ending day I.

LIV

The king to Carlele is comene with kniʒtes so
    kene,   f.11b.
And [held] þe rounde table one rial aray.   691
Þe wees þat werene wounded so woþely, I wene,
Surgenes sone saued, soþely to say;
Bothe confortes þe knightes, þe king and þe quene;
Thei were dubbed dukes bothe one a day.   695
There he wedded his wife, (w)lonkest I wene,
Withe giftes and garsons, Sir Galerone þe gay.
Þus þat haþel in hiʒ with-holdes þat hende;
Whane he was saued sonde,
Þei made Sir Galerone þat stonde,   700
A kniʒte of þe table ronde,
To his lyues ende.

703   Waynour . . . wisely] Dame Gaynour garte besyly
       T; þenne gerut Dame Waynour to I; Gaynor gart
       wightly L. to] TIL; *om* D.

704   þe] manere of T.

705–   *These lines are combined in T and the result reads:*
706   Pristes with processyones and messis to make hir
       menynge.

705   with processione] prouincials I. were] were fulle I;
       þei were L.

706   a . . . masses] massis a mylione L. to . . . þe]
       her modur I. þe] *om* L.

707   Boke-lered mene] Dukes erles barouns and T; Boke
       lornut byrnus and I; Boþe lerid men and L. þe]
       of þe TI; right of þe L.

708   bellus] I; besely D.
       T: Thurghe alle Yglande scho garte make men-
            ynge.
        I: Thro oute Bretan so bold þese bellus con ringe.
       L: Thurghe brood Englond belle dede rynge.

709   þis] And thus this T; And þis I. ferely] ferlyes T.
       in] þus fair in L. Ingulwud] I; Englond D; a T; *om*
       L.

710   Vnder] Be side I. a holte] holtus IL. hore] bare T.

711   a] *om* TL. holtis] TL; a holt I; haast D. is] sulde T;
       oghte LI. to] *om* TL.

712   Thus to] Throȝhe þe I; Thurgh a L. forest] þe
       forestes T. þey] as y L.

LV

Waynour gared wisely write in-[to] þe west,
To al þe religious to rede and to singe;
Prestes with processione to pray were prest,   705
With a mylione of masses to make þe mynnynge;
Boke-lered mene, bisshops þe best,
Þorghe al Bretayne [bellus] þe burde gared rynge.
Þis ferely bifelle in [Ingulwud] forest,
Vnder a holte so hore at a huntyng—   710
Suche a huntyng in [holtis] is noȝte to be hide.
Thus to forest þey fore,
Þes sterne knightes [and] store;
In þe tyme of Arthore
This anter be-tide.   715

713   Þes] *om* T; Wiþ L. sterne knightes] knyȝtus stalwurthe I; stif knyghetis L. and] TIL; in D.

714   In] And in T. Arthore] King Arthore I.

After line 715 in T:
This ferly by-felle, fulle sothely to sayne,
In Yggillwode Foreste, at þe Ternwathelayne.
Explicit.

CRITICAL NOTES

✤✤✤✤

CRITICAL NOTES

Most of the following notes deal with textual problems, though a few are explanatory. The notes should be used in conjunction with the Glossary, since the acceptance of some readings is based on the etymological information given there. Many minor variants of T, I, and L are not mentioned, especially when the cause of the error is obvious. Variants which are discussed in the Introduction will be referred to by citing the number of the variant group (Nos. 1–19 pp. 42–66 above).

The following short titles and abbreviations are used for the works cited:

Alexander. The Wars of Alexander. Edited by W. W. Skeat, EETSES 47, London, 1886.

The Avowing of Arthur. The Avowynge of King Arther, Sir Gawan, Sir Kaye and Sir Bawdewyn of Bretan. Edited by John Robson, *Three Early English Metrical Romances,* London, 1842.

Destruction of Troy. The "Gest Hystoriale" of the Destruction of Troy. Edited by G. Panton and D. Donaldson, EETS 39, 56, London, 1869, 1874.

GGK. Sir Gawain and the Green Knight. Edited by Sir I. Gollancz and Mabel Day, EETS 210, London, 1940.

Golagros and Gawane. Edited by F. J. Amours, *Scottish Alliterative Poems,* STS 27, 38, Edinburgh and London, 1897.

Kyng Alisaunder. Edited by G. V. Smithers, EETS, 227 237, London, 1952, 1957.

MA. Morte Arthure. Edited by Edmund Brock, EETS 8, London, 1865.

Parlement. The Parlement of the Thre Ages. Edited by M. Y. Offord, EETS 246, London, 1959.

Pearl. Edited by E. V. Gordon, Oxford, 1953.

The Wedding of Sir Gawain. The Wedding of Sir Gawain and Dame Ragnell, in *Middle English Verse Romances.* Edited by Donald B. Sands, New York, 1966.

NOTES

1. With this line compare a line at the beginning of *The Wedding of Sir Gawain:* "In the time of Arthoure this adventure betid," (l. 4) and a line near the end of *GGK:* "Þus in Arthurus day þis aunter bitidde" (l. 2522).

2. *Turnewathelane:* "This is still the name of a small *tarn* or lake, which covers about an hundred acres of land in the forest of Inglewood [cf. l. 709], near Hesketh in Cumberland" (Madden). This area is also the scene of a hunt by Arthur in *The Wedding of Sir Gawain* and *The Avowing of Arthur.*

3–4. *Conquerour kydde* and *Dukes and dussiperes* are both frequent formulas in *MA*.

7. *Frydde* is a past participle, as shown by the readings of T, I, and L. D has taken it for a variant spelling of the noun *frithe* which appears in the following line. The reading of L is preferable since it is the most likely source of both *wele* (T) and *was* (I, perhaps caused by the singular form *forest*).

8. *Fermysone tyme:* D, I, and L have corruptions of this hunting term, which occurs elsewhere in ME only in *GGK* (l. 1156) and *MA* (l. 179). This was the closed season on male deer, extending from mid-September to early May.

10–11. The same lines occur at ll. 686–687.

14. *Dame:* supported by link and meter; cf. *MA* 233: "Sir Gaywayne the worthye Dame Waynour he ledys."

16–17. L reverses *rubyes* and *rybans* while I repeats *rebans* in l. 17. For the formula "rayled with rubies" see *MA* 3263, *Alexander* 1538 (Ashmole MS.) and *Parlement* 128.

18. *Herde* (D) and *hye* (I) are poor attempts to gloss the rare Northern form *hawe* (see *OED* s.v. *Haw,* a.).

"*Hydys* [T], conceals, is wrong for the rime: it should be *hedes,* as in D. = protects, Mod. E. *heeds*" (Amours). See *MED* s.v. *hēden,* v., 2b.

20. *Shredes/schrydes* (< OE *scrȳdan,* 'wards off') may be the original reading, as Burtness suggests, but *shedes* rhymes and gives sense.

22. *Set* (D): probably an error due to the occurrence of the word in l. 21 or 23.

T misses rhyme and link and makes little sense without a verb.

24. *Sambutes of silke:* cf. *Kyng Alisaunder* 176 (Bodleian MS.): "Wiþ sadel of gold, sambu of sylk."

27–28. Written as three lines in I, broken after *golde* and *gatys.*

29. Note the grouping of MSS, TL:DI; except for I's *a byrne* and L's *berne,* either may be the original reading.

30. "This must refer to the birth-place of Gawayne's steed, since neither himself nor the Queen were born in Burgundy. Perhaps, however, it is a poetical license, for the sake of the alliteration" (Madden).

31–32. Written as three lines in I, broken after *lady* and *lighte.*

31. Here and in l. 83 I have accepted the reading of I (supported by T in l. 83) because of the ghost's statement in l. 164 that she dwells *withe Lucyfer in a lake.* D's *lawe* may be a scribal mistake for *loghe* or a conscious substitution of 'hill.'

34. *To teche hem to her tristes:* 'to direct or appoint them to their hunting-stations.'

37. An original *tristre-tre,* as in L (cf. *The Wedding of Sir Gawain,* 19: "The king was set at his trestille-tre"), best accounts for the other variants: T omits *tre,* I omits *tristre,* and D substitutes the name of a specific tree.

43. D seems to have substituted the formula *huntynge in hast* both here (where T, I, and L agree against it) and in l. 711 (where it misses the link).

44–45. L's anticipation of *kennettis* in l. 44 is redundant and the substitution of *knyghtis* in l. 45 makes little sense.

47. *Felle:* the MS reading *fele* ('many') destroys the parallelism and is probably a mechanical error (but see the reading in L).

49. The omission of l. 48 probably has caused the variation in this line. It may have contained a reference to the hounds (linking with l. 47) and a verb, and its loss has caused T and I to supply a subject for the passage and change the nouns *questes* and *quelles* to verbs.

52–53. The link here is on *durkene* (variants *dyrkyns/ darkys*), as shown by the fact that I has this verb in l. 53 despite *droupun* in l. 52. *Droupun* is probably an anticipation of the word in l. 54.

53. *"And to downe schowys* [T], and shove, throng to the down. It cannot be the right reading as it contradicts what precedes and follows" (Amours). As mentioned in the Introduction (#12 e), T changes *skuwes* three times. The partial agreement in error between T and L is evidence of a genetic relationship, with the reading of L (missing the rhyme) apparently later. With the reading in D compare *MA* 1723: "in ȝone dyme schawes."

55. The agreement between T and L is *not* evidence of a more original reading and the reading of I is equally possible.

Swithely: see #18 h.

56. *þai werray:* I and L are obvious corruptions of this (difficult?) phrase in D.

Wilde swyne: the original reading was almost certainly *wilde* (see #1 b).

57. See #18 a.

58. "It is difficult to decide which of the three texts [i.e., T, D, or I] comes nearest the original. D. is apparently the best for sense and rime, but the first half of the line anticipates l. 62 [the scribe was probably misled by the similarity of *raches* and *rechas*]. I. is unintelligible and so is T. as it stands. The simplest solution of the difficulty is to change *one thaire raye* [T] into *on the raa;* thus the line would mean, 'and the hounds rally on the roe at their hiding-place,' which suits both the rime and the content" (Amours). This double use of the verb *relyes* [OFr. *relier*] with two objects, *riste* and *ro* is not wholly satisfactory, but the only other alternative is the acceptance of a unique run-over line: 'and to the ro they gave no peace. . . .'

59–60. See #17. *Gamene* may refer to the deer, or be a parallel object with *grythe.*

61. " 'Gomes' [T] is nonsense and corrupt (it is the greyhounds that go)" (Amours). This error causes further variation in MS T in ll. 62–63.

66. I attempts a more complete link by changing *þei semble* to *to see,* which, however, is an incorrect rhyme in l. 65.

L's attempt to make the line more explicit by adding *king* indicates that TD's *pruddest* is the original reading.

68. *Al but:* see Introduction, p. 65.

70. See #19a.

74. *Meve* (D) could be derived from *mele* (by a confusion of *l* and *v* which are very similar in the MS hands) more easily than from *mene,* which may be an attempt by T to create a fuller link (as also in ll. 229–230).

77. *Arthur* in I and L makes a vocalic alliteration, which, however, is not necessary in the wheel and may be an innovation.

79. D and I alliterate, T and L link; there is no basis to choose between the readings.

80–86. The even lines in this stanza rhyme on -*elle,* not -*elles,* as shown by lines 84 (*helle*) and 82 (*snelle.* There is no verb *snelles*).

80. *Fewe* (D) may be simply a variant spelling, or 'few,' an error caused by the incorrect plural form *felles.*

82. D and I change the adverb to a verb to rhyme with the incorrect *felles* in l. 80. I's *snaypely* indicates that L's *snowid* is a substitution for an original *snayppede* (T); cf. *GGK* 2003: "þe snawe snitered ful snart þat snayped þe wylde" (for *sneterand* see #18 b).

83. See note to l. 31. D's *lede* is probably due to the occurrence of the form later in the line. The line means 'there came a light (or flame) out of the lake.'

85. T's reading is suspect because of *fulle,* but either I ('her road was straight') or L ('with unpleasant manners or looks') is possible.

87. *Wonges:* see #18 c.

92. *Dame:* see note to line 14.

94. "*Hit ar,* D., shows that the scribe mistook *clippes* for a plural noun" (Amours).

96. "*Sir Constantine* (the other two names are false readings) was the son of Cador of Cornwall, and was appointed by Arthur to succeed in the reign" (Amours).

100. *Grome:* written g°*me,* indicating an omitted *r,* a likely source of *gome* in I.

102–104. See #19 b.

106. I has written the corresponding line from the following stanza.

107. The first half of this line lacks one alliterating syllable, but since I substitutes l. 87a and L (which has *wonyd*) is usually an inferior MS, it is likely that this was true of the archetype.

109. *Stonayde:* a rare intransitive use of this verb, meaning 'was astonished, bewildered.'

110. *For madde:* 'as if insane'; see *Pearl* 359: "marre oþer madde," and note.

112. *Oute at* (D): D has apparently taken the phrase *one/in a res,* 'on/in a rush,' to refer to a geographical feature, 'out at a rise,' or something similar; compare the same phrase in l. 345. See *rasse* in *GGK* 1570 (glossed as 'smooth bank' from OFr. *ras*) and *Purity* 446 (for which *OED* gives "? peak, projection").

112–113. *Radde/Rad:* see #13.

114. *Clolle* (D): scribal confusion of *cl* for *ch* (see #5c) causes D to miss the alliteration.

115. *Þe* (D)/*a* (I): I, and perhaps D, takes *polle,* 'head,' for 'pole.'

116. *Hir* (TIL) may be original, but the desire to be explicit (*Withe eighen* could refer to the toad in D) may have caused a scribe to substitute for *Withe.*

119. D is obviously wrong here in having the ghost enclose Gawain. The 'cloud of dark clothing' is the smoke which surrounds the burning ghost, earlier described as naked. The smoke, serpents, and toads ('too many to count,' l. 121) are part of the ironic contrast between the beautifully clothed and jewelled queen and her unfortunate mother.

The toad is used here (as elsewhere in ME, see *OED* s.v. *Tade*) as a general name for serpent, fiend, etc., thus its pecking.

120. *þat satt by hir:* D misses one alliterating syllable.

123. *Thoghte it* (T): T understands *chere* in the positive sense of 'good or cheerful thing' instead of the neutral 'countenance or mind.' The reading of D is also supported by the alliteration.

124. *Holtes:* see #13.

125–126. These lines offer two good examples of scribes innovating to make a fuller link. In the first half-line I changes 125 to match 126 and L changes 126 to match 125.

128. *Glowes:* to stare, cf. Scot. *to glour.* The reading of T and I is equally good: "*Gewes* and *gous* [see Glossary]

have been explained by previous editors as mistakes of the copyist dropping the *l* of the word. I prefer to look upon them as the better reading, and I have no doubt the original rimes were something like *bowis, gowis, scowis"* (Amours).

130–131. *Herdis/Herkenys* (L): see #12 c.

131. *So fer into halle* (D): a prosaic substitution to amplify the first half-line, which misses one of the alliterations the formula provides.

132. *"Challus,* D., is another form of the preceding *cholle,* and is therefore a mistake, due to carelessness or ignorance, for *chaftes"* (Amours). See #5a.

134–135. "The transition from *thou* applied to Christ to *thou* addressed to the ghost is abrupt and confusing" (Amours). T, I, and L attempt, with poor results, to make the reference in l. 135 more explicit (note that T alliterates on *s* and I and L on *w*).

138. *Knowene* (DL): may be an unconscious anticipation of the word in l. 139 or an attempt to make a fuller link. All four texts have the formula correctly in l. 224.

140. Any MS could be correct. I's *grauntet* has the same consonant group as *grace,* but if this were the original reading there would be no reason for the other scribes to change it.

142. *Pase* (T): the scribe may have started to write *place* (l. 141).

145. *Berelle:* see #1e.

148, 150. *Pay/say* (L): incorrect rhymes.

151. Cf. *MA* 3513: "Nowe am I cachede owtt of kyth, with kare at my herte."

151–152. Notice that the link on *cauȝte* makes use of its antithetical meanings, 'driven out' (151) and 'caught' (152). A similar use is made of *fare* in ll. 260–261. Another sophisticated feature of the linking in the poem is the use of homonyms, e.g., *bare,* adjective and verb, in ll. 203–204.

157. *Syr Gauan the gode* (I): see #12g.

158. D and I have confused the references to Guenevere and the ghost and are bad metrically.

161. *Rone:* T's *rayne* may be due to the Northern *a*-rhymes; L's (unrhyming) gloss *rise,* 'bough,' shows *rone* to be correct. This line is a very familiar formula in ME romance.

162. T and L, as usual, seem to be related, and since *louched/lauchet* is both more difficult and attested by the base MS we will accept it. Since *lyȝte* alliterates and crosses the usual TL:DI MS grouping it is probably the original reading. The line may then be understood to mean 'my countenance, like the lily, laughed so light,' or 'my countenance was like the lily, I laughed so light.'

163. *Grisely* (TI): an anticipation of the word as it occurs later in the line.

Granes (T) and *wise* (L) are incorrect rhymes.

165. D, which misses the link on *Lucyfere* and makes little sense, looks like the second half-line of the original expanded to make a whole line. I links with the end of l. 164 but supports T in the second half of l. 165.

167–168. Cf. *Golagros and Gawane* 1230–31:
      Baith knyght, king and empriour
      And muse in his myrrour.

167. *Muse: loke* (L) is a gloss and *menes* (I) a homoeograph for this word.

My mirrour: her face, as an example to her daughter.

169. *Dighte* (L): it is more likely that L innovates here to provide a more substantial link, than that T, D, and I (which is the least likely genetic grouping) have dropped such an important word. (See note to l. 676.)

170. "The end of this line [in T], a repetition of the last part of l. 165, is evidently a slip of memory [or eye], as shown by the want of rime" (Amours).

176. "I cannot extract any sense out of the first half of

the line in D." (Amours). The scribe probably started to write *lyghtely* too soon. As it stands we may, as Christianson suggests, read *light* as 'relieve, comfort' (see *OED* s.v. *Light*, v.[1] 3), giving 'then little will comfort you those who now bow to you.' However, the forms *lite* and *wyne* (< *wilne* = will not?) are both unusual.

177. *þe,* MS *he: he* is probably a false start for *helpes,* which then caused *þe* (after *helpes*) to be dropped. *Helpes the* (TIL) is slightly better for the meter.

178–182. "T. is corrupt here wherever it differs from D. and I., as can be seen by the want of alliteration in l. 178, the jarring note of l. 179, and the bad rime of l. 182" (Amours).

178. Christianson suggests that the error in T was caused by the scribe starting to write *chasses* after *pore,* having seen it as *pur.* As with most variants the process of change may have involved two or more successive scribal "corrections."

186. *Fulle felle* (T): probably an innovation for the alliteration.

187. Cf. *Destruction of Troy* 6729: "He hurlet forth vnhyndly, harmyt full mony."

189. *Word* (I): the same error occurs in l. 215.

192. I's attempt to alliterate makes the line a little long.

197. *Worde* (T): alliterates, but, since it is not supported by any other MS it may be an innovation (see also *merveille,* l. 202).

201. *Kere* (D): perhaps a contracted form of *keuere,* 'shield, protect' (Madden), but more probably a scribal error for *kele* (due to the influence of *care*?) as in l. 45.

204, 208. *Lye/drye* (T): the use of *lye* for *layne* in l. 204 causes a change in l. 208 for the rhyme, which makes T miss the link between the stanzas.

209. *þe sauene y-wis* (D): misses the rhyme (probably caused by a misunderstanding of *sytis*), and this causes a similar error in l. 211 (*is* for *bitis*).

212. See #18d.

213. *Paramour:* D and L have the original use of the French phrase, T and I the more common use as a noun.

216. *Werld* (T): may be an attempt to link one line too soon.

The variation between *wilde, wrechut,* and *wykkid* is a good example of a case where we must accept the reading of our base MS because we have no basis for determining originality.

218 *Trentales:* "A trental generally meant a service of thirty Masses for the dead, said every day within the month after the funeral, or on set days during a longer interval" (Amours).

220. *Withe* (D): the line may have been *Mi soule socoured were sone,* and a scribe wrote *with* for *were,* probably misreading a suspension for *er(e)* as *þ.*

222. T misses the rhyme; cf. ll. 231 and 317.

224–225. "These two lines must refer to Guenever's mother in spite of the construction: *as þou was,* D., explains the sense, although it makes the verse too long" (Amours).

228. *Leve me grace to þi sowle wiþ soule do goode* (L): instead of writing *grete* after *to,* the scribe skipped ahead to *þi sowle wiþ.* Then, either the same or another scribe added the superfluous *soule do.* This line is a good example of the nonsense which scribes could produce.

229–230. *Mene* (TI): makes a fuller link, but L's *mede* (l. 230) supports an original *mende.* Cf. *Destruction of Troy* 815: "þat mys to amend is maistur ye go."

230. Notice the conflicting groupings: *myster* (DI): *menske* (TL), and *mene me* (TI): *mende vs* (D): *mede þe* (L).

235. This difficult line may have originally had five alliterating words: *hertly* (DTL), *honde* (DIL), *hete/hote* (TIL), *hestes* (DIL) and *holde* (all MSS). However, the poetic ellipsis of D may have been made more explicit by the addition of *I hete þe* in the other MSS.

237. The tag *I-wis* in D is supplied for the meter after the omission of *worde*.

238. T misses the rhyme and changes the alliteration.

239. *Hase* (I): for *as,* may indicate oral transmission or dictation; cf. *a nayre and,* l. 349 I.

Apparamentis (T): 'clothes, ornaments,' clashes with the metaphor of pride as a tree, and may have caused T to omit *bowes* in l. 241.

240. *Apt* (D): the less familiar French word *appertly* is undoubtedly original.

242. *Boune* (I): another difficult (Norse) word, glossed by D. T may have been influenced by *balde* in l. 241.

244–246. L's spelling *sore* in l. 244 causes a change in ll. 245 and 246 for the *o*-rhymes. Cf. *MA* 932: "Salue hyme of sore."

249. *Dedis* (T): a gloss, makes more obvious sense but does not alliterate (cf. l. 200).

251. *Siþene* (D): probably an anticipation of the word in l. 252.

Heuen: this may be an innovation for explicitness by D.

252. *Chaste:* not changed from Northern *a* to *o* with the other rhymes, causes L to innovate for an *o*-rhyme. The rare use of this form as a noun causes I to change to an adjective, and may be responsible for the omission of the line in T.

253. *Aure:* Amours' emendation.

256. *Spute* (D)/*spyre* (TL)/*speke* (I): any reading is possible, although *speke* looks like a gloss and *spyre* may be due to *spiritual*.

261–267. I has incorrect rhymes in all the odd lines, causing some further changes.

262. "*Foundis* [T] is probably a slip for *defoulis,* due to the occurrence of the same verb in the preceding line" (Amours).

263. The reading of D is correct. *Riches* is a rare verb, occurring only in the alliterative poems, meaning 'to address

oneself to a place' or 'to take one's way' (see *OED* s. v. *Rich* v.²); cf. *GGK* 1898: "Renaud com richchande þurʒ a roʒe greue."

264. *And welthis* (T)/*and wele* (IL): one of these readings is probably derived from the other.

With the reading in D cf. *MA* 516: "Bot who may wynne hym of werre by wyghtnesse of handes," and 3342: "For alle thy wirchipe in werre by me has thow wonnene."

266. *Stry:* variant of *stroy* (see *OED*), apathetic form of *destroy;* the alliteration is on *str* in the first half-line.

268. L apparently innovates to provide a link.

269–273. Although either *king* or *knyght* is possible in l. 269, D has missed the whole point of the allusion to Fortune in the passage and the reading of T and I is correct.

272. *Lowe:* the three rhyming lines in the wheel each have three alliterations in this stanza.

274–275. Compare *MA* 3404–3405:

For Froille and for Ferawnt, and for thir ferse knyghttis,

That thowe fremydly in Fraunce has faye be-leuede,

which are probably the source of these lines in *The Awntyrs*. In l. 275, D and I have substituted *folk* and *farnet* for the second name, but since in *MA* the meaning of the name is uncertain and T's corruption of it senseless, we will let the reading of D stand.

Frely (T)/*fery* (I): corruptions of *fey,* as shown by the reading in *MA*.

276. *Bandum* (I): derived from *bowndene* (T); *bothe* (TIL) alliterates. The reading of D would mean 'Bretans in Burgundy [are] all submissive/bowed to you.'

278. *Grece* (L): due to *grete,* cf. *delices* for *delites,* l. 213.

280. *Remayns* (D): variant spelling or an error for *Romans* (*e* and *o* are very similar in the MS) or a variant spelling of 'realms' (cf. *reymes,* l. 263).

281. *With* (D)/*atte* (I)/*alle* (T): the original may have been *with alle*.

281–282. I incorrectly makes the Romans victorious.

282. *Tyber:* probably influenced by the reference to the Romans, though Arthur never reached Rome. Amours suggests that the original reading was *Tambire* as in *MA* 3902 (also called the *Tanbre* by Wace and Layamon), beside which Mordred camps: "I think the Douce text is right, with the exception of *thus* that should be *then* or *yet:* 'Then shall an untrue, treacherous Tiber bring you sorrow,' . . . This small river is now called the Camel. 'It rises about two miles to the north of Camelford, and flows into the sea below Padstow.'—Madden, note to Layamon, vol. iii, p. 408." (Amours).

283. *þe wele* (I): see #10.

286. *King* (D): the scribe misunderstood the causative meaning of *with* and thus omitted the linking word.

287. *Croyse* (I) seems corrupt, *crownyd* (L) is a gloss, perhaps influenced by the same word in l. 288. Either T 'shall forcefully seize the crown' or D 'shall be neatly, fairly encircled, crowned' is possible, although D is more difficult (cf. *Pearl,* l. 2: "To clanly clos in golde so clere").

289. "[T] = That men shall take possession (of the power) at a certain time, T., or at a sitting, I., unless *session* is a mistake for *sesone,* which is probable. D. is meaningless" (Amours). L has apparently combined *segge* and *ensese* in some way, necessitating *sikirly* for meter and alliteration. See #18e.

291–292. T has no subject in these lines (*ʒe* 291 I, *ye* 292 DL).

291–298. See the Introduction, pp. 26*ff.,* for some of the similarities between these lines and *MA.*

296. *Þe wele* (IL): see #9.

298. *Slade* (L): see #6.

299. *Chaunce* (L): misses link and alliteration; see #6 and #14.

306. *He beris hit in* (D)/*he berith it of* (L): the reference, from l. 308, depends on a prior mention of the *sauter* or shield and is out of place here. The fact that D, I, and L

begin l. 307 with *with* (again indicating a dependence of some kind) and that the link skips a line may indicate a mistake in the order of the lines in the archetype.

308. *Seluir* (L): an attempt to link with l. 307.

310. *Barne:* perhaps an innovation for the alliteration.

312. *Delfully* (D): an obvious gloss.

316. *Stid:* T's *wane* is redundant, probably caused by *wonyng;* I's *place* is a gloss showing that *stid* is original.

Welle: alliterates; DL's *dwelle* is probably taken from l. 318. Amours cites examples of the phrase 'in woe to well' from *Cursor Mundi* and the *York Plays.*

317. *Rest* (D)/*rente* (T)/*raghte hym* (L): any one may be original; cf. ll. 222, 231, and 549L.

318. *And the dole:* cf. l. 184 and *MA* 3067: "To dwelle in dawngere and dole the days of hys lyue."

319. I seems to be a partial repetition of l. 228 due to the similarity of the passages.

320. T picks up the last five lines of stanza XVIII (ll. 230–234) because lines 230 and 320 are almost identical, then adds the last four lines of this stanza, thus missing line 231.

326. Notice that the link is a repetition of ll. 324–325.

327–334. The rhymes of the odd-numbered lines in this stanza present a very difficult problem, and involve an important question of meaning in line 333. First of all, in ll. 327, 329, 331, and 333: D rhymes on *-ene;* I rhymes on *-ere;* T omits 327, rhymes on *-ene* in 329 and on *-ere* in 331 and 333; L rhymes on *-ene* in 327 and 329, and on *-ere* in 331 and 333. Thus in l. 327 D and L agree on *-ene* against I, in l. 329 D, L, and T agree on *-ene* against I, in ll. 331 and 333 T, I, and L agree on *-ere* against D. The acceptance of the majority of readings would indicate that the original had a mixed rhyme and that to be consistent I changed to *-ere* in ll. 327 and 329 while D changed to *-ene* in ll. 331 and 333.

Now in ll. 327 and 329 I probably has an inferior reading (see notes on those lines). In l. 331 the difference is only between the tags *in fere* (TIL) and *by-dene* (D). However, in line 333 the whole line is different: D has the queen as subject, 'she tells them the wonders that they [i.e., she and Gawain] had seen,' while T, I, and L have the *rialle route* as subject, '[they] speak to her mildly in their way.' To confuse matters further, in l. 334 (which should link with 333) T has *swilke wondirs* (DIL have variants of 'weather') which seems to refer to the *selcoupes* of l. 333D.

The arguments for accepting the reading of T, I, and L in l. 333 are as follows: The three MSS agree against D; the tag *in fere* in l. 331 alliterates, indicating the *-ere* rhyme is correct; and *wondirs* in l. 334 does not refer to l. 333D but is due to the form *a-wondred* later in the line and would not have been changed to *weder* if it was originally in D. The argument for accepting D is: the tag *in fere* in l. 331 is an innovation for the alliteration, the rhymes in *-ere* are due to this rhyme occurring in ll. 334 and 339, there is no other instance of mixed rhymes in the poem, and without the reference to *wondirs,* l. 334 in T, I, and L does not connect with the lines preceding or following it.

I have decided to accept the reading of D since it is our base MS, and emend l. 334 to conform with l. 333.

327. *And goes:* makes the line a little long metrically and may be an innovation for the alliteration.

Bere (I): misses the alliteration.

328. *Vnhides:* must have been unfamiliar to the scribes. T's *in hydis* shows D to be correct, I misses the rhyme, and L's substitution adds an alliterating syllable.

329. *Schane schene* (T): an innovation for the alliteration, perhaps due to unfamiliarity with the form of 'shine,' which indicates that D's reading is original.

334. *Wyghtis* (L): see #12g.

337. "The place meant is perhaps Randalholme, 'an ancient manor house near the junction of the Ale with the Tyne' " (Amours, quoting from *The History and Antiquities of Cumberland* by Samuel Jefferson, 1840, p. 120).

339. *Halle* (D): an obvious substitution for *sale*.

340. *Vnder a siller of silke:* cf. *MA* 3194a: "Vndyre a sylure of sylke."

341–342. The scribe of D took *wale* to be 'wall' (either a misunderstanding or because of *halle* in l. 339), and this may have suggested the embroidery in l. 342. The other MSS agree in describing the meal instead of the furnishings. The word *menewith* in l. 341 D is not recorded in the *OED,* and Amours rejects Donaldson's 'right against or flush with.'

Brandene (D): see #12j.

344. *Lote:* confirmed by the deleted *he lates* in I.

345. *Scho rydes vp to þe heghe dese* (T): T, I, and L agree; D has apparently substituted the formula *raykes vp in a res* (from l. 112) for a better alliteration.

346. Notice the conflicting groupings: *halsed* DI: *askede/askis* TL, and *Sir* DT: *King* IL.

349. *Ane armed* (T)/*a nayre and* (I): see #18f.

352. "The direct speech with which the Douce text opens the stanza is evidently out of place here, and the scribe, discovering his mistake, stops short, misses a line, and starts afresh like the other MSS" (Amours).

353. *To pay* (D)/*in poon* (I): D substitutes a tag phrase and I has a homoeograph for the unfamiliar phrase *with pane;* cf. *GGK* 154: "With pelure pured apert, þe pane ful clene."

354. The fact that D lacks this line and that I has substituted (the very similar) line 510 may indicate that they descend from a MS in which the line was missing.

356. *Glysset:* see #5c.

358. *Sir* (T)/*forsoþe* (L): independent innovations, probably to improve the alliteration.

360. *Carpis:* the more difficult reading; D probably innovates for the alliteration in the second half-line.

Highte (L): causes the scribe to change l. 364 for the rhyme.

361, 363. L switches *comely knyghte* and *worthy*

wighte in these lines, making poor sense, since the king is talking to the lady, but making ll. 363 and 365 link.

362. With this line in I compare l. 415.

365. *Wy welde wolde:* 'man would wield, rule.' All four MSS have changed the original slightly but give good evidence of this reading: D runs together *we* and *welde* giving nonsense ('that ever a dress would'?); I omits *welde;* L omits *wy* as usual (see #12g); T has the right sense but the change of *welde wold* to *myghte welde* (perhaps through an intermediate *welde myghte*) destroys the rhyme.

367. *Plonkete* (T): see #13.

368. *Branded with brende golde* (D): D seems to have a preference for this formula, cf. ll. 342 and 485. L's *botoned* in the second half of the line confirms the reading of T in the first half. See #12j.

370. *Contrefelet and kelle:* T changes the first of these unfamiliar terms and L changes both of them from nouns to verbs.

371. *Clene* (D): from l. 370.

Craftly: I's *cumly* supports the reading of D as an adverb; T and L seem to be in common error here.

Was clure to be hold (I): see l. 379b.

375. *I-nore* (D): see #8.

377. *Wighte* (L): see #14.

379. *Clene* (T): see #9.

381. *Brandure* (D): see note to l. 368 and #12j.

382. *"Enclawet ful clene,* I., is the preferable reading; *many hit seene,* D., is a desperate fill-gap; and *enclosede,* T. [from which L seems to be derived], whether we explain it by 'closed in,' 'closely fitting,' or by 'protected by an outer garment,' is evidently a substitution for an original word not understood by the scribe" (Amours). As usual an unfamiliar French term (meaning 'riveted') causes difficulty.

383, 386. *Stede* (I): see #6.

385. *"Browed ful bolde,* D., is the best reading, and is corroborated by *brees* = brows in I" (Amours).

390. *"And mayles of stele* [T] is quite out of place here. The scribe, having first gone wrong in l. 387 by omitting *in* or *on,* was at a loss how to finish his stanza" (Amours). The difficulty of the term *anlas* may also be a factor.

391. *þat steryne was* (T): see #11.

392. *His pencelle displaied* (D): misses the rhyme; see #15.

Stekillede (T): apparently a mispelling of *strykelyd* (L).

393. *Ienewbris* (L): I cannot guess at the cause or meaning of this word.

Glomed (T): see #5c.

Gledys (TI): an incorrect rhyme. Both T and I start a new leaf with this line, which may be to blame for the error (but cf. T's *gledes* in l. 118). However, only I continues with the plural rhymes in ll. 395 and 397 and the errors may be independent.

394. I substitutes line 17. For the phrase 'grains of rubies' as a decoration on gloves, cf. *MA* 3462–3463:

His gloues gayliche gilte, and grauene by the hemmys,
With graynes of rubyes fulle gracious to schewe.

395. *Schynbandes* (D): as the *OED* points out (s. v. *Shinbawde,* sb.) the *n* is an error for *u* in this word.

396. *Polemus:* see #5c.

398. Cf. *MA* 1364–1365:

Bot a freke alle in fyne golde, and fretted in salle,
Come forthermaste on a fresone, in flawmande wedes.

400–403. These lines are corrupt in T because the scribe wrote *to see* at the beginning of l. 401 instead of at the end of l. 400 and changed ll. 402 and 403 to rhyme with *wont.*

404. Compare the reading of I with ll. 360 and 409.

407. See #4.

408. *"He lyfte vpe his vesage,* T., is doubly wrong: the verb spoils the alliteration, and *vesage* is a mistake for *viser"* (Amours).

Wayned (D): as the *OED* says (s. v. *Waive,* v.2),

this is probably an error for *wayued* [ON. *veifa*], used in the sense 'opened' with window in *GGK* 1743. The scribe was probably influenced by *wayne,* ll. 535, 614.

418. "*Grylles,* D., a scribal error for *gylles,* probably because of the verb *grylles* four lines down" (Amours). More likely caused by the *gr* of *grettest* and *greues.*

419, 420. "The three texts agree indifferently well in their lists of Sir Galeron's possessions, but the Ireland MS. is certainly the most reliable. The first line, which is repeated in l. 679, where T. = I., contains four Ayrshire names, Carrick, Cunningham, Kyle, the three divisions of the county, and Cumnock, which was a barony in the fourteenth century, and forms now the two parishes of Old and New Cumnock. 'Lonwik' in the next line I take to be a corruption of Lanrik, the old spelling of Lanark, and 'Laudoune hillus' is Loudoun Hill, half-way between Ayr and Lanark, a well-known spot where the Bruce defeated Sir Aymer in 1307. 'Lomond' is strange as the name of a district, and the 'Lothian hills' are too far east to be parts of the lands of the lord of Galloway. 'Lannax' is of course the Lennox in Dumbartonshire." (Amours).

421. *Wile:* necessary for the rhyme; *wiles* (I) may be due to the *s* in the alternate rhymes; *wille* (TDL) may also be influenced by those rhymes, or by *kylle* (TL) in l. 419.

423. *Quiles* (I): an incorrect rhyme following *wiles* in l. 421.

424. "*At myne vn-thankes* [T] is right enough for the sense, but wrong for the rime. *Vmwylles,* D., is a slip for *vnwylles,* and *agayne* = in spite of. The reading of I. is the most satisfactory in this line and also in the next, as it keeps up the iteration" (Amours). However, the link is on *welde* and the agreement of T, D, and L indicates that I has innovated for a fuller link.

435. *Hertes* (D): no male deer are being hunted; see l. 8 and note.

436. "*No gome graiþe,* D., may mean 'no knight ready

to fight' or 'no knight's apparel' " (Amours). The MSS vary greatly in the second half of the line, but I's *gome* in the first half supports D. T's *gude* is probably a homoeograph for *gome*.

438. L innovates to provide a link.

þenke reste (D): 'think to rest'? This reading makes the line too short, and may be derived from *þou rathe mane reste* by an intermediate *þou renke reste*.

441–442. Compare *MA* 2478: "Pyghte pauyllyons of palle, and plattes in seegge."

444. A very difficult line; I accept the reading of TL because it contains the formula *bankowres . . . bryghte,* half of which is confirmed by D and the other half by I. How this mixture came about, or how the line may be related to l. 342 (*bankers brighte* D, *brent gold bryȝte* TI) I do not know. See also #12j.

443–459. "The hospitality given to Galeron in *AA,* ll. 443–459, bears some striking resemblances in a simpler fashion to the hospitality accorded to Gawain in *GGK,* ll. 852–893. Galeron's 'stede was stabled,' the pavilion 'pighte was it prowdely, withe purpure and paulle' and elegantly furnished with cushions, and 'With inne was a chapelle, a chambir and ane haulle,' together with 'A chymneye with charecole, to chawffene þat knyghte.' Similarly, in *GGK,* the horse of Gawain is cared for when stiff men 'stabeled his stede,' l. 823, and his bower has its rich hangings and cushions, its chapel, and a 'chemné, þer charcole brenned,' and at which he 'achaufed hym chefly.' Both chapel and chimney, it may be noticed, have their purpose in *GGK,* although in *AA* they have no significance at all in the story. In both poems, the guest is thereafter feasted, and the descriptions of the feasts share details and have some similar phrasing: in *AA* 'he braydes vp a burde, and clathes gune calle,' and sets the table with 'sanapes and salers' and silver vessels; in *GGK* they 'telded vp a tabil on tresteȝ ful fayre,' and set it 'wyth a clene cloþe' and with 'Sanap and salure and syluerin sponeȝ.' " (Matthews, pp. 208–209. He quotes from the Thornton text.)

456. *Schene* (IL): a fuller link, perhaps a better reading.

457. *Veres:* I takes this to be another kind of wine, like *vernage,* and changes *in* to *and.*

458. Except for the fact that T has an incorrect rhyme, any of these very different readings could be original. Since they do not seem to be derived from each other the archetype may have been corrupt or missing.

Hour: in this line and l. 488 the symbol for *ur* should perhaps be expanded as *r.*

459. Compare *MA* 199: "With darielles endordide, and daynteez ynewe."

462. *Lost:* see #1c.

463. *Lukes* (T): misses the alliteration; see #9.

464. *Gawayne þe goode* (D): D substitutes this formula for the extra alliteration on *g* (where the original had a crossed pattern *sg sg*) and omits the object of the verb *greues,* producing nonsense.

474. *Myldelik* (I): see #13.

475. L's *place* indicates that *palais* (D), 'enclosure' was the original reading, perhaps mistaken for *palace* in I and thus changed to *paueluns.*

478. *De mayne:* as Amours points out, this phrase may have acquired a false etymology and the meaning 'of strength.' See Glossary and *MED,* s.v. *demeine.*

482. *Krudely* (D): the scribe may have taken the original word to be the *name* of the son of the Earl of Kent (*in* and *ru* would be very similar in the MS).

485. D and I agree in having the knight dress, though they vary greatly, while T and L, repeating l. 342, describe the food. There is no basis to choose so I have accepted the reading of D; perhaps the line was missing in the archetype. See note to l. 368.

With the line in D cf. *MA* 2517: "Buskede in brenyes bryghte to be-halde."

486. A good example of the many minor variants which make little or no change in the sense and are irresoluble.

Worthely (L): see #9.

488. *Hathels:* glossed as usual in L (see #12c). D has apparently substituted a word of similar shape.

489. *Lordely:* explains both *lordus* (I) and *lustily* (L). This line occurs again (1. 566), and I has the same substitution (where it makes the sense wrong) while L changes *lordely* to *lightly* (probably influenced by *lighte*).

The reading of T shows that the scribe did not look ahead to the next line before changing the text.

490. *Bothe* (D): the knights do not alight.

492. *Quene* (D): mistakes the *chacelet* for the queen's chair?

493. *Dame Gaynour* (I): see #6.

497. *Wiþ love* (L): probably first changed to *by love* by some scribe.

499. Compare *Golagros and Gawane* 306: "Thai brochit blonkis to thair sidis brist of rede blude."

Bodyes (L): see #12a.

501, 503. The variants in these lines are all possible except L's *shent* in 1. 503, which does not rhyme (notice the agreement of T and L). The link skips a line and there is nothing in the text to indicate that this is not original.

501. *Schene* (TL): a gloss for *shide,* meaning 'cut, broken,' or an attempt to avoid redundancy by substituting the word for 'bright.'

502. Compare *MA* 2088: "Jolyly this gentille forjustede a-nother."

505. *Riȝte:* Amours suggests that the poet has altered ME *ritten,* 'to cut, break' for the rhyme, and cites *MA* 2137–2138:

> With wyghte wapynez of werre, thai wroghtene one helmes,
>
> Rittez with rannke stele fulle ryalle maylez.

Another use of the word in the same poem in a similar context, but with a spelling closer to that in *The Awntyrs,* indicates that both forms may have been possible; cf. *MA* 1474:

He ryfez the rannke stele, he ryghttez theire brenez.

508. *Graythely* (TL): see #9.

509. *Englorid* (L): metathesis and confusion of *e* and *o*.

510. Compare l. 354.

511. *Stargand* (D): see #8.

513. *Delay* (T): see #7.

514. *Schuldir* (T)/*Swithe* (L): see #18g.

520. The reading of L may have been caused by an earlier scribe changing *shene* to *kene* for the alliteration.

521–22. Compare *MA* 4231–4232:

The cantelle of the clere scheld he kerfes in sondrye

In-to the schuldyre of the schalke a schaft monde large.

522. *Shiand* (D): the scribe ran together *schildre* and *and?*

He share (I): alliterates, but the verb is redundant.

523. D incorrectly has the lady laughing.

527. *Blasynet* (I): *blasyn* was originally written, a variant or error for either *blasone* (D) or *blasyng* (L), and then *et* was added by a scribe who apparently took it for *bacynet.*

529. The wide divergence of the three MSS and the fact that D and I repeat the second half of line 527 exactly may indicate something amiss in the archetype.

532. The unusual use of *sturne* as a noun (as in *GGK* 214) causes I to substitute *stedes* (perhaps influenced by the *stiropes* in l. 533), and L to change both ll. 532 and 533, thus missing the link.

535. *Waynes at:* also in l. 614 D where the other three MSS change it; cf. *Destruction of Troy* 7655: "Ector, wrathed at his wordis, waynit at the king."

537. I takes *blenket* to mean 'looked' instead of 'gleamed, shone'; cf. *GGK* 2315: "& quen þe burne seȝ þe blode blenk on þe snawe."

539. *God . . . grace:* a very frequent formula in ME.

540. *Swithely:* see #18h.

541. *Streite* (D)/*in styd* (I)/*wiþ strengþe* (L): any one may be right.

Stede: uninflected genitive.

542. D and L miss the rhyme.

544. *Swithely:* see #18h.

547. *Good* (L): alliterates and makes a fuller link, but does not rhyme, and causes further errors in ll. 549 and 551.

548. *Body* (L): see #12a. L misses the rhyme in this line, causing a further change in l. 550.

549. L substitutes l. 317.

552–555. There is something wrong in these lines in all three texts. As Amours says, we would expect *me* instead of *þe* in l. 552, and there seems to be a verb wanting such as 'I care' or 'I mourn' in line 553 or 554. However, the three MSS agree and neither line is too short. Perhaps in the original ll. 552 and 553 were assigned to Galeron instead of Gawain, the general sense being: 'he [the Frision] will do you no more good in place of the fair foal [Grisselle] than the root of a rush.' As the lines stand, the best we can do is emend *þe* to *me* and take ll. 553 and 554 as anticipating *I mourne* in l. 555.

558. The reading of I, which makes *wede* a verb, is better for the rhyme, since the form of the adjective is always *wode* (Amours).

559. See Introduction, pp. 52–53.

561. *Wendiþ:* I's gloss of this word by *bouun* shows it to be the original reading. D means 'and intends to requite, repay him who is sorely wounded.'

565. *By þat* (D): misses the alliteration.

Is: the line is part of Gawain's rebuke.

566. *Lordly:* I and L also change this word in l. 489.

567. *þare:* see #5c.

568. *Boun* (L): the adverb shows that L derives from a MS (like I) in which the verb had an -*n*(*e*) ending.

569–570. The occurrence of *riche mayles* in 569 L and 570 I is baffling.

572. *Foȝtun* (I): see p. 74.

574. *Of fighte* (L): see #10.

577. *Berus to him* (I): see #6.

583. *Polayn* (L): 'knee-armor' could hardly be right when coupled with the *ventaile* which is on the front of the helmet.

584. *He wanted to be slayne:* that this was the original reading can be inferred from L's errors. Taking *wanted* to mean 'desired' rather than 'lacked' a scribe added *litil* (this is also the source of *noȝte* in D). *Went* in L is simply a further corruption of *want*. MS I removed the ambiguity of the line by glossing *wanted* with *lakket*.

585. L's reading is an attempt to make sense out of a line which became meaningless after l. 584 was changed.

586–592. I has Midland *-en* endings on the verbs which are the rhyme-words in the even-numbered lines. Hooper suggests the emendation of *was brewe* to *þei brewe* in l. 592 "to complete a normal set of Northern rhymes in *-e* which L and D have otherwise preserved" (*"The Awntyrs off Arthure:* Dialect and Authorship," p. 65).

586. *Haþelese:* replaced, as usual, in I and L.

590. *Of grete strengthe* (L): see #6; perhaps suggested by the *str* alliterations in the second half-line.

591. *Stiff* (L): see #7.

Striȝte: the alliteration is on *str* in the second half-line in both ll. 590 and 591.

594–598. In l. 594 D has anticipated the beginning of the next stanza (l. 599). L is preferable since it is the only MS to link in l. 594, and has a better link than I in l. 598. (Notice, however, that it links with the reading of D in l. 599, where L varies in the second half of the line.) I and L agree in ll. 595 and 596, where L also retains the Northern *þei make*. It is hard to imagine where MS I got l. 594, but l. 598, which rhymes with it, is a favorite formula in this MS (see #12g) and involves a misreading of l. 597 which means "Guenevere wept for *their* sake." Finally, since l. 594 in L = l. 516 it is possible that this line was missing in the archetype.

600. *"Wounded* [D], a wrong rime, should have been written *wound,* which is sometimes found as a past participle" (Amours). This mistake causes D to change l. 602 for the rhyme, where I and L agree in the correct reading.

603. *Cleviþ* (L): Christianson suggests that this is a better reading, the alliteration being on the consonant group *cl.* However, the *cl* in *clene* may have caused L to innovate.

605. *Teneful touche* (D): anticipates *tene* from the end of the line.

606. *Doun to* (L): see #6.

607. *Gallerone* (T)/*grouelonges* (I): probably independent efforts to make a fuller link with l. 606.

609. *Rudely* (I)/*rathely* (L): since they alliterate, one of these may be original, but the change to the rare *buredely* in D is unlikely.

610. For the idiom 'follow someone's face' see *MED* s. v. *Face,* sb.[1]

611–612. *Schene/Clenely* (T): misses the link.

612. *Keuered one hiȝte:* 'recovered, got up.' *One hiȝte* is an adverb 'up, upwards' and takes the place of the usual complement of this verb, *up.*

613. *"With a cast of the carhonde,* I., with a left-handed stroke. The corrupt readings of T. and D. show that the phrase was not understood" (Amours).

614. T and I have Gawain as the subject of this line (reading *waynes* as 'waits'), which makes the sense wrong in l. 615.

616. *Wend* (I): see #6.

617. *Slydys* (T): incorrect rhyme.

618. *Clekis:* the errors of D (which substitutes *keppes,* retaining the alliterating sound) and L (mistake of *bl* for *cl*) show this reading to be correct.

625. *Wisly* (D): misses the oblique link on *wille* and *wilfully*.

627. *Roy ryalle:* Amours gives two instances of this formula in *MA,* ll. 411 and 3200.

628. *None* (I): see #5d.

629. *Bidus* (I): see #7.

635. *þere* (D I): an example of a form which, though incorrect, may be an original reading of the archetype.

639. *ʒette* (I): see #16.

640. *Rengthe* (I): see #12d.

641. *Route* (I): see #11.

Reysone (D): an obvious error for *resynge,* caused in part by the substantive use of the adjective *ryalle.*

642. *Y mouthe þe as menys* (L): this is incomprehensible, but may be a corruption of some form of the phrase "mene thee with mouth." (Christianson reads *monthe* for *mouthe.*)

643. *World* (L): see #6.

644. *Stalket:* better for alliteration and sense. The reading of L looks as if it is derived from T or D.

645. *Forth* (L): see #16.

651. *Stode vp-ryʒte* (I): taken from l. 649 in an attempt to make a fuller link.

654–655. "This list of knights has evidently been suggested by the following passages from *Morte Arthure.* Arthur is arranging his men for the final battle:—

Sir Ewayne, and sir Errake, and othire gret lordes,
Demenys the medilwarde menskefully thare-aftyre,
With Merrake and Meneduke, myghtty of strenghes.

ll. 4075–4077.

Later on the king comes across the dead bodies of his knights:—

Bot whene sir Arthure anone sir Ewayne he fyndys,
And Errake the auenaunt, and other grett lordes,

. . . .

Marrake and Meneduke, that myghty were euer.
ll. 4262–4267.

"*Menegalle* is an unknown name, and is evidently a mistake for *Meneduke* of the *Morte Arthure,* as shown by the reading *Meliaduke* in the Ireland text.

"*Sir Drurelat and Moylard,* D., are found nowhere else" (Amours).

654, 656. *Fulle rathe/taghte* (T): T's error in the names in l. 654 causes a further change for the rhyme in l. 656.

657. *Those knyghtes* (T)/*þese sturun men* (I): see #11.

658. The partial agreement of T, I, and L in these lines indicates that the original may have had two past participles, 'for-bruised' and 'for-bled' (see also *for-betun* in 659 IL).

661. *Semblynge* (T): see #8.

664. *Þe:* T, I and L have the king addressing Gawain directly in the entire speech; see *þe* in l. 672.

667–669. "The castle, hall, and towns mentioned in these lines may have been well-known localities to the author of the poem, but the names have undergone so many changes in passing through the different texts that it is impossible to identify them now. All we can surmise is that those possessions of King Arthur which he gifts [*sic*] to Galeron were situated in the north-west of England, between Wales and Carlisle. The Ireland MS., written in Lancashire, may be nearer the original than the others" (Amours).

668. *Al holy* (L): see #8.

669. *Walled:* parallel with *curnelled* (l. 667), and *bigged* (l. 671); the reading of D is unlikely.

671. *Moted* (T): see #6.

672. *Endowe:* the scribes of D and L either were unfamiliar with the word, or thought the alliteration lacking because of the prefix (which is not written in I).

676. *Yeve* (L): links with l. 677, but since the others

agree against this generally inferior MS, and since linking is frequently missing near the end of the poem, we do not adopt the reading. (See note to 1. 169).

677ff. In D and T Gawain is speaking to Arthur (or the court) while in I and L he addresses Galeron.

677. *Grylle* (L): MS L has incorrect rhymes in the odd-numbered lines of this stanza.

678. *Layre:* see #16.

679. See note to 1. 419.

680–684. There is something amiss in these lines. Robson suggests that ll. 678 and 680 have been transposed, but this does not explain the sudden introduction of ll. 683–684 which seem to require some prior reference to Galeron's stay.

681. "One expects here the same names as in 1. 420, the rime-letter [i.e., the alliteration] being the same, though the end-rime is not. As the two texts [D and T] stand, I am afraid nothing can be made out of them. We need scarcely regret the omission of two lines in I., as they would probably have made confusion worse confounded" (Amours).

689. *Kayrit* (I): an incorrect rhyme.

691. I has omitted line 690, and some scribe has affixed the phrase *greuis so grene* to this line to make a link of sorts with 1. 688, thus making the line much too long.

693. Amours read *sanede* = 'healed' in ll. 693 and 699T.

696–697. For the cause of the reading in T see #19c.

696. D has *s* for *w* in *wlonkest,* perhaps an anticipation of *s* later in the word, but it is interesting to note that the variant readings of T and L alliterate on *s*.

698. I misses the link and rhyme, perhaps because of *hapel,* causing a further change for the rhyme in 1. 712.

700–701. "These lines are too long in T. The last two stanzas of the poem show distinct signs of failure of memory in the author [i.e., scribe] of the Thornton text" (Amours).

703. *Besyly* (T): misses the alliteration on *w*. Can the

variant *besely* in D in l. 708 be merely an interesting coincidence?

707. *Boþe lerid* (L): shows the reading of D and I to be original.

708. Amours says "D. alone yields a certain amount of sense . . . 'The queen caused book-learned men and bishops to have power through all Britain,' " reading *rynge* as a variant of 'reign.' However, *besely* does not make much sense in that context and is probably an error for *bellus*. The ringing of the bells, indicating the saying of masses for the soul of Guenevere's mother, is perfectly understandable.

   In the second half of the line T repeats part of l. 706.

709. *Ingulwud:* see note to l. 2, and the epilogue in T.

710. *Bare* (T): see #13.

711. *Haast* (D): misses the link; see note to l. 43.

713. *And:* T, I, and L agree and the reading 'and brave' is more likely to give rise to a misunderstanding of *sture* as battle ('in battle') than vice versa.

GLOSSARY AND INDEX OF
PROPER NAMES

✤ ✤ ✤ ✤

ABBREVIATIONS

AFr.	Anglo-French
Du.	Dutch
G.	German
Gael.	Gaelic
Gmc.	Germanic
Ir.	Irish
L.	Latin
LG.	Low German
LOE.	Late Old English
ME.	Middle English
Med.L.	Medieval Latin
MLG.	Middle Low German
Mod.E.	Modern English
OE.	Old English
OFr.	Old French
ON.	Old Norse
ONFr.	Northern Dialect of Old French
OScot.	Old Scottish
Scot.	Scottish

GLOSSARY

The Glossary includes all words in the text and the variants, with their etymologies, except for words common in ME (including articles, prepositions and personal pronouns) and words which have essentially the same form and meaning in both ME and ModE. Regularly inflected forms of nouns and weak verbs are not usually listed separately, and frequently occurring items are curtailed and marked *etc.*

All forms of a word are placed under the entry for MS D, which will usually be the most common spelling of the word if there are more than one. The head-word for verbs is the infinitive or present tense, unless neither occurs, in which case the form will be specified (*pt.* = preterite, *pr.p.* = present participle, etc.). Line numbers without an identifying letter indicate MS D, and the form may or may not also occur in the other MSS.

In the alphabetical arrangement *th* and *þ, u* and *v, i* and vocalic *y* are not distinguished. *ȝ* follows *g*.

GLOSSARY

a, *interj.* ah!, 237 [Cf. OFr. *a.*]
able, *adj.* able, 302 [OFr. *able.*]
accorde, *v.* be reconciled, agree, 635 [OFr. *acorder.*]
adecoue, ? for A-VOWE, 205I.
a-dred, *pp. adj.* afraid, 571; **drad,** 112D, 113D [OE. *ofdrad,* pp. of *ofdrēdan.*]
a-fered, *pp. adj.* afraid, 399 (I *a-frayet*) [OE. *afēran.*]
affray, *n.* attack, 532L [OFr. *effrei.*]
agast, *adj.* aghast, 125I, 126 [*a-* + OE. *gæstan.*]
aire, *n.* heir, 363I, 680, 682I [OFr. *eir.*]
aither, *pron.* either, each (of two), 488, 580L (*eiþer*); *adj.* 198 (*auther*), 500 [OE. *ǣgþer.*]
alas, *interj.* 90 [OFr. *a las.*]
almesse-dede, *n.* works of charity, 253 [OE. *ælmesdǣd.*]
anlas, *n.* dagger, spike on a horse's head-armor, 390 [OFr. *alenaz,* with metathesis.]
apparementis, *n.pl.* clothes, ornaments, 239T [OFr. *apareillement.*]
appertly, *adv.* clearly, openly, 240T [OFr. *apert.*]
appurtenaunce, *n.pl.* accessories, belongings, 239 (I *purtenans*) [AFr. *apurtenance.*]

a-praysut, *pp.* valued, appraised, 373I [OFr. *apriser, preisier.*]
apt, *adj.* fit, 240 [L. *aptus.*]
aray, *n.* array, attire, 17, 691; **ray(e),** 17I, 394I [OFr. *arei.*]
araied, *pp.* arrayed, attired, 172; **arayit,** 17I, 394I, 485I; **rayed,** 17L [OFr. *areier.*]
are, *adv.* See OR.
a-right, *adv.* straightaway, 550L [OE. *ariht, on riht.*]
atteled, *pt.* tried, intended to, 616 [Cf. ON. *ætla.*]
a-twyn, *adv.* in two, 656L [ON. *a-* + *tvinnr.*]
auaylet (*vppe*), *pt.* raised, opened, 408I [OFr. *avaler.*]
auenant, *adj.* noble, courteous, 302 [OFr. *avenant.*]
aunter, *n.* adventure, 1, **anter,** 716 [OFr. *aventure.*]
aure. See OUER.
a-vowe, *n.* oath, vow, 205 [OFr. *avouer.*]

bacun, *pp.* baked, 342I, 485T [OE. *bacan.*]
bayne, *adj.* willing, 242L [ON. *beinn.*]
one bak, *adv.phr.* aback, away, 580 [OE. *on bæc.*]
bale, *n.* grief, harm, 290, 321; *pl.* 103 [OE. *bealu.*]

baleful, *adj.* harmful, fierce, 203L, 211; wretched, 537I [OE. *bealuful.*]

bamed, *pp.* embalmed, 175 [OFr. (*em*)*baumer.*]

bandum, *n.* power, control, 276I [OFr. *bandon.*]

bane, *v.* curse, 89, 246L; **bannene,** *pr.pl.* 592 [OE. *bannan.*]

bankers, *n.pl.* tapestries, 342, 444T (*bankowres*) [OFr. *bankier.*]

baraynes, *n.pl.* female deer not bearing at the time, 41 (T *barrayne*) [OFr. *barain.*]

baret, *n.* strife, 290 [OFr. *barat.*]

bargane, *n.* contention, fight, 592 [OFr. *bargaine.*]

barne, *n.* child, 222, 227 (*barme*), 310; **barnis,** *n.pl.* men, 374L [OE. *bearn.*]

baronrees, *n.pl.* baronies, 670 (I *buroners*) [OFr. *baronerie.*]

barons, *n.pl.* 40L, 707T [OFr. *baron.*]

barselette, *n.* a hunting dog trained to follow wounded game, 38 [OFr. *berceret.*]

basnet, *n.* light helmet, 380, 527L [OFr. *bacinet.*]

bataile, *n.* battle, 568, 629 [OFr. *bataille.*]

batailed, *pp.adj.* walled, embattlemented, 671 [OFr. *batailler.*]

be-calle, *v.* call upon (to fight), 410 [*be-* + ON. *kalla,* OE. *ceallian.*]

bede, *pt.* said, commanded, 462I; offered, surrendered, 645 (L *bede forth*) [OE. *bēodan, biddan.*]

bedis, *n.pl.* prayers, 200, 249 [OE. *gebed.*]

be-falle, *v.* happen, 299L; *pt.* **byfalle,** 72L, **bifelle,** 709 [OE. *befallan.*]

be-holde, *v.* behold, see, 42, 371I, 375, 379 [OE. *behealdan.*]

beleues, *v.*[1] remains, 69 [OE. *belīfan.*]

beleues, *v.*[2] leaves, 487I; *pp.* **byleuede,** 275T [OE. *belǣfan.*]

be-lyue, *adv.* quickly, eagerly, 497 [OE. **be līfe.*]

belle, *n.* bell, 30; *pl.* **bellus,** 708IL; cloak, tunic, 367; cauldron, 188 [OE. *belle.*]

ful bene, *formulaic phrase,* full well, pleasantly, quickly, etc., 71, 368, 380, 671 [Unknown.]

bent, *n.* open field, 330, 563, 629 [OE. *-beonet.*]

berber, *n.* barberry, 71 (T *barborane*) [OFr. and L. *berberis.*]

bere, *n.*[1] bier, 175 [OE. *bēr.*]

bere, *n.*[2] noise, clamor, 125, 126, 327I [OE. *gebǣru.*]

bere, *v.* carry, possess, bear, 426; *pr.3sg.* **beres, beris,** 241, 306, 308; **berus to him,** presses to him, 577I; *pt.* **bare,** carried, 584L; gave birth to, 89, 204, 227T; thrust, 528, 529L; **borne,** *pp.* 30, 227, 431, 549 [OE. *beran.*]

beriles, *n.pl.* beryls, 587 (see also note to l. 145) [OFr. *beryl.*]

besantes, *n.pl.* gold (Byzantine) coins, ornaments resembling such coins, 368T [OFr. *besan,* L. *byzantius.*]

besye, *adj.* busy, 174T [OE. *bisig.*]

besyly, besely, *adv.* busily, 703T, 708D [From prec.]

best, *n.* animal, beast, 554; **bestes,** *pl.* 211 [OFr. *beste*.]

bete, *v.* relieve, mend, 103 [OE. *bētan*.]

betene, *pr.pl.* beat (down), 587; **beten,** *pp.* worked by hammering, inlaid, 368I [OE. *bēatan*.]

beting, *n.* beating, 659 [From prec.]

bettir, *v.* ? to improve, 229L [? From the adj.]

beueren, *adj.* beaver-colored, 357 [OE. *beofor*.]

bewes. See BOWES.

by þat, *adv. phr.* by that time, 475, 565 [OE. *bī, þæt*.]

by-bled, *pp.adj.* covered with blood, 570 [OE. *blēdan*.]

bycheve, *v.* ? achieve, 269L [*bi-* + ? OFr. *chevir, chever*.]

bi-clagged, *pp.adj.* covered, bedaubed, 106 [Cf. OScot. *claggit*.]

bides, *v.* stands, waits for, 29, 122, 330; suffers, 321; *pr.pl.* **byde,** 40I, **bidus,** 629I; **bode,** *pt. pl.* 40 (L *bodyn*) [OE. *bīdan*.]

by-dene, *adv.* together, completely, immediately, etc., 11, 305, 459, 516, 687 [Unknown.]

byfalle, bifelle. See BE-FALLE.

byfore, *prep.* before, 72, 240, 633; **byforne,** *adv. in rhymes,* 225, 387, 476 [OE. *beforan*.]

bigged, *pp.* built, 71, 671 [ON. *byggja*.]

bigonene, *pp.* begun, 278 [OE. *beginnan*.]

byker, *v.* attack, 41 [Unknown.]

byreft, *pp.* bereft, taken, 176L; **byrevid,** 281L [OE. birēafian.]

bites, *v.* bites, 211I; **bote,** *pt.* 548; **bytand,** *pres.p.* biting, 528I [OE. *bītan*.]

by-tydde, *pp.* happened, 1, 715; **hym shal by-tyde,** shall befall him, 268L [OE. *be-* + *tīdan*.]

blake, *adj.* black, 105, 212 (pale?), 385, 658 [OE. *blāc, blæc*.]

blakenede, *pp.* blackened, 203T [OE. *blāc*.]

blasynet, *n.* 527I (See note).

blasyng, *adj.* burning, shining, 528L, 529L [OE. *blæse*.]

blasone, *n.* shield with a coat of arms, 527 [OFr. *blason*.]

ble, *n.* complexion, color, 212; **blees,** *pl.* 658, 659 [OE. *blēo*.]

blede, *pr.pl.* bleed, 629 (T *bledis*); *pr.sg.* **bledis,** 212 (? for *blendis*), 499 [OE. *blēdan*.]

blekys, *pr.sg.* turns pale, 618L [OE. *blǣcan*.]

blendis, *pr.sg.* is mixed, stirred, 212T [Cf. ON. *blanda*.]

blenket, *pt.* shone (in his blood), 537 (L *blenkis,* pr.) [Unknown.]

bly, *adj.* happy, 242D [Reduced form of OE. *blīþe*.]

blynde, *adj.* dark, dim, 212I [OE. *blind*.]

blisful, *adj.* blessed, sacred, 227 [OE. *bliss* + *-ful*.]

blysschede, *n.* ? blessed or radiant (one), 227T [Cf. OE. *blyscan, geblētsod*.]

blonke, *n.* horse, 29, 548, 563; *pl.* 499 [OE. *blanca*.]

blounkyd, *pp.* ? for **blunket,** 367L (Paton suggests some form of *blenk* or *blanch,* to shine. Etymology obscure).

blowe, *pt.* blew, 62, 58 (*bluwe*); *pr.* blawes, 62T; *pp.* blowene, 330 [OE. *blāwan.*]

blunket, *n.* white or gray woolen cloth, 367 (T plonkete) [Unknown.]

bode. See BIDES.

boke-lered, *adj.* literate, learned, 707 [OE. *bōc* + *lered.*]

bokeled, *pp.adj.* ornamented with buckles, 386 [OFr. *boucle.*]

bonkes, *n.pl.* hills, slopes, 41 [ON. *bakki.*]

borde, *n.* table, board, 449 (L pl.) [OE. *bord.*]

bore, *n.pl.* boar, 41L [OE. *bār.*]

bore-hedes, *n.pl.* boar-heads, 385 [Prec. + OE. *hēafod.*]

bote, *n.* relief, advantage, 204, 229L, 549 [OE. *bōt.*]

bote, *v.* See BYTES.

botonede, *pp.adj.* ornamented with buttons, 368T [OFr. *boton.*]

boughte, *pt.* redeemed, 222; *pp.* 222T [OE. *bycgan, bōhte.*]

boun(e), *adj.* ready, eager, bound, 242IL, 568L [ON. *būinn.*]

bourdoure, *n.* ornamented border, 381T; *pl.* 587 [OFr. *bordure.*]

bowe, *pr.pl.* turn, go, 568 (I *boune*); bouun, 561I; *pp.* bowen, submissive, 276 [OE. *būgan.*]

bowes, *n.pl.* boughs, 39, 40, 71L, 127 (T *bewes*), 241 [OE. *bōg.*]

bownden, *pp.adj.* bound, 276T [OE. *bindan,* pp. *bunden.*]

box, *n.* boxwood, 71 [OE. *box.*]

bracelet, *n.* ? variant of barse-lette, 38L.

brad, *pp.* roasted, 342 [OE. *brǣdan.*]

brak. See BREKE.

braides oute, *v.* draws, 122 (I pt.); braide vp, *pt.* drew up, set up, 449 [OE. *bregdan.*]

brayne, *n.* brain, 480 [OE *brægn.*]

branded, brandene, *pp.* ? or brauded, braudene, 368D, 342D (See note).

brandure, *n.* ? or braudure, 381D (See note).

bras, *n.* brass, 188 [OE. *brǣs.*]

braudene, *pp.* embroidered, 444 (I *brauderit*) [OFr. *brouder.*]

brawndeche, *v.* brandish, 122T [OFr. *bra(u)ndiss.*]

y-bred, *pp.* ? for by-bled, or *pp.* of OE. *bregdan,* draw, 570L.

brede, *n.*¹ bread, pastry, 342T, 485T, 548 [OE *brēad.*]

brede, *n.*² breadth, 585 [OE. *brǣdu.*]

brees. See BROWES.

breke, *v.* break, 242, 243; brake, *pt.* 205 [OE. *brecan.*]

brene, *n.* coat of chain mail, 380, 485, 527, etc. [ON. *brynja.*]

brene, *v.* burn, 188 (T *burne*); brent, brend, brynt, *pp.* burnt, refined, 342T, 368, 381, etc. [OE. *beornan,* ON. *brenna.*]

brewe, *pp.* caused, prepared, 592 [OE. *brēowan.*]

bro, *n.* ? (Paton suggests a substantive formed from OE. *brēowan,* meaning evil or mischief) 290L.

broches, *n.pl.* candlesticks, 451I [OFr. *broche.*]

broches, *v.* spurs, 499T; broched, *pt.* 563; cut, pierced, 499, 557L [From prec.]

GLOSSARY

brochetes, *n.pl.* candlesticks, 451
[OFr. *brochete.*]
brode, *adj.* broad, 357L, 577,
708L; o-brode, *adv.* widely,
444I [OE *brād.*]
bronched, *pt.* bent down,
crouched, 577 [Cf. OFr. *em-
bonchier.*]
bronde, *n.* sword, 122, 504, 645,
etc. [OE. *brand.*]
brosed, *pp.* bruised, 659 [OE.
brȳsan, OFr. *bruser.*]
browed, *pp.* with eyebrows, 385
[From next.]
browes, *n.pl.* eyebrows, 144;
brees, 385I [OE. *brū.*]
buffetes, *n.pl.* blows, 658 [OFr,
buffe.]
bunfetis, *n.pl.* good deeds, 200L;
bunfaites, 249L [OFr. *bien-
fait.*]
burde, *n.* lady, virgin, 158, 357,
708; birde, 158T; byrde, 89I,
158I, 537I; berde, 29L, 158L;
pl. burdes, 145, 174; birdes,
374 [Unknown.]
buredely, *adv.* as it becomes a
knight to do, properly, 609
[OE. *gebyredlīce.*]
burghes, *n.pl.* towns, 670 [OE.
burh.]
burly, *adj.* stately, noble, strong,
203, 357T, 537, 385T; bur-
liche, 528; burlokke, 548I;
superl. burlokest, 548; *as sb.*,
stout knight, 645 [OE. *bor-
līce.*]
burne, *n.* knight, man, warrior,
29, 122, 174, 490, etc. [OE.
beorn.]
burneshed, *pp.adj.* burnished,
380, 485, 527, etc. [OFr. *bur-
nir, burniss-.*]

buse, *v.* contraction of *behoves;*
me buse wend, I must go,
315T [OE. *behōfian.*]
buskes, *v.* dresses, 485; busked,
pp. hurried, 567; busket, *pp.*
prepared, 380I [ON. *būask.*]

cace. See CASE.
cachede. See CAUȝTE.
caire, *v.* go, proceed, 689; kayrit,
pt. 689I [ON. *keyra.*]
cayselle, ? for CAYSER, 410I.
cayser, *n.* emperor, 410 [OE.
cāsere.]
canel-bone, *n.* collar-bone, 519
[OFr. *canel* + OE. *bān.*]
cantelle, *n.* corner (of the
shield), 521, 613I [ONF. *can-
tel.*]
car, *n.* left hand or side, 613T
[Cf. Ir. *cearr,* Scot. *car.*]
carf, *pt.* cut, carved, 603; keruys,
pr.sg. 603I, kerues, 612I;
keuet, *pt.* ? for keruet, 521I
[OE. *ceorfan.*]
carhonde, *n.* left hand, 613I [See
car.]
carpe, *v.* talk, speak, 143I, 409,
648, etc. [ON. *karpa.*]
case, *n.* chance, circumstance,
483, 610L; cace, 142 [OFr.
cas.]
caste, *n.* throw, stroke, 613T
[ON. *kasta.*]
cast. See KEST.
cauȝte, *pt.* cauȝte of, took off,
626; cauȝte oute of, driven out
of, 151; caught into, seized,
taken into, 152 (T *cachede*)
[ONF. *cachier,* with analog-
ical preterite.]
cautil, *n.* craft, deceit, 613 [OFr.
a. L. *cautēla.*]

certis, *adv.* certainly, 245T [OFr. *certes.*]

cessione. See SESSION.

chacelet, *n.* platform or raised seat, 491 [ME. *chaflet* a. OFr. *eschafau(1)t.*]

chaftis, *n.pl.* chaps, underjaws, 132T (I *schaft*) [ON. *kjaptr.*]

chalange, *v.* claim, dispute, 680 [OFr. *chalonger.*]

challus, chawlus. See CHOLLE.

chambour, *n.* private room, 445 [OFr. *chambre.*]

chasses, *v.* drives or keeps away, 178T [OFr. *chacier.*]

chaste, *adj. as n.* chastity, 252; **chast,** *adj.* 252I [OFr. *chaste.*]

chatered, *pt.* chattered, quivered, 132 (I *shaturt*) [Echoic.]

chaufe, *v.* warm, 446 [OFr. *chaufer.*]

chaunce, *n.* adventure, misfortune, 268L, 269, 299L [OFr. *cheance.*]

chef, *n.* top, 144; **chevest,** *adj.* most important, 252L [OFr. *chef.*]

chef, *v.* achieve, 269 [OFr. *achever.*]

chere, *n.* countenance, manner, 123 [OFr. *chere.*]

cheuerone, *n.* the frontlet of a horse's head armor, 387 [OFr. *chanfrein.*]

chille, ? some form of chill from OE. *ciele,* or, as Paton suggests, a variant of throat, OE. *ceole,* 132L.

chymne, *n.* fireplace, 446 [OFr. *cheminee.*]

chynne, *n.* chin, 132 (I *shin*) [OE. *cin.*]

cholle, *n.* jowl, 114T, 132 (I *shol*); *pl.* **chalus,** 132D, **chawlis,** 132L [? OE. *ceafl, ceole.*]

cladde, *pp.* clothed, 106 [OE. *clǣþan, clādde.*]

clanly. See CLENE.

clanse, *v.* cleanse, purify, 134 [OE. *clǣnsian.*]

clanser, *n.* purifier, redeemer, 134I [From prec.]

clarifiet, *pp.* exalted, transfigured, 134I, 223I [OFr. *clarifier.*]

claterid, *pt.* rattled, 132L [OE. *clatrian,* echoic.]

clef. See CLEVITH.

clekis, *v.* grabs, seizes, 618T [OE. **clæc(e)an.*]

clene, *adj.* clean, pure, bright, 67T, 371, 457, etc.; *adv.* neatly, properly, 370, 378, 382, etc.; **clanly,** 287; **clenely,** 612T [OE. *clǣne, clēne, clǣnlic.*]

clerk, *n.* educated person, cleric, 94 [OE. *clerc.*]

cleþyng, n. clothing, 119 [OE. *clǣþan.*]

cleues, clewes. See CLOWES.

clevith, *v.* cuts, hews, 603L; **clef,** *pt.* 520 (I. *cleuet*), 521 [OE. *clēofan.*]

clyft, *n.* cleft, 114L [OE. *geclyft.*]

clyme, *v.* climb, 129T [OE. *climban.*]

clippes, *n.* eclipse, 94 [OFr. *eclipse.*]

closene, *v.* get possession of, 287T; **closyd,** *pp.* enclosed, 152L [OFr. *close,* pp. of *clore.*]

cloþes, *n.pl.* table-cloths, 449 [OE. *clāþ.*]

clowes, *n.pl.* gorges, ravines, 150; **cleues,** 67T; **clewes,** 129T [OE. **clōh.*]

code, *n.* chrism-cloth, 224 [? OE. **cōd.*]

coler, *n.* collar, neck-armor, 618 [OFr. *coler.*]

colours, *n.pl.* colored devices or dress, 378 [OFr. *color.*]

comli, comeliche, cumly, *adj.* fair, noble, 360I, 363, 371I, 662, etc.; *as sb.* **comly,** 288 [OE. *cȳmlīc.*]

con, *pt. aux.* with the force of ModE. *did,* 72, 133, 329, 397, etc.; the form of this function word is usually *gun* in T and *gan* in L [OE. *cunnan, ginnan.*]

conforde, *n.* comfort, 636 [OFr. *confort.*]

confort, *v.* comfort, 480; **confortes,** *pr.sg.* 95, 694; **conforte,** *pt.pl.* 45; **(re)comforthede,** *pt.* 45T, 95T, 694T [OFr. *conforter.*]

coniured, *pt.* conjured, adjured, 133 [OFr. *conjurer.*]

contrefelet, *n.* some kind of ribbon for the head or headdress, 370; T and L make this into a verb, which Madden glosses "interwoven" [OFr. *contre-* + *filet.*]

contreyes, *n.pl.* regions, countries, 150, 667L [OFr. *contree.*]

coost, *n.* coast, 301; **cost,** side, 603 [OFr. *coste.*]

corage, *n.* courage, 601 [OFr. *corage.*]

coronalle, *n.* crown, coronet, 626 [OFr. *coroune.*]

couched, *pp.* lying, 152 [OFr. *coucher.*]

couentis, *n.pl.* bodies of monks, 201 (I *couand*) [AFr. *covent.*]

couerde, coverid. See KEUERED.

countes, *n.pl.* territories ruled by a count, 150L [AFr. *counte.*]

couples, *n.pl.* pairs of dogs, 44 [OFr. *couple.*]

craftly, *adv.* skillfully made, 371 [OE. *cræftlīce.*]

crest, *n.* plume or other ornament on a helmet, 379 [OFr. *creste.*]

crisomed, *pp.* annointed with chrism (in Baptism), 224; **krysommede,** 138T [OE. *crisma.*]

croyse, *v.* ? perhaps cross, to bless with the sign of the cross, 287I.

crosse, *n.* cross, 97; **croys,** 134, 223 [ON. *kross,* OFr. *crois.*]

cruel, *adj.* stern, valiant, 601; *as sb.* 612 [OFr. *cruel.*]

cumly. See COMLI.

curiouse, *adj.* finely wrought, exquisite, 372 [OFr. *curius.*]

curnelled, *pp.* walled, battlemented, 667 [OFr. *creneler.*]

curtays, *adj.* courteous, 153; **curteys,** 414; **curtase,** 601I [OFr. *curteis.*]

curtaysly, *adv.* courteously, 483 [From prec.]

curtasy, *n.* courtesy, 483I [OFr. *curtesie.*]

cusshewis, *n.pl.* armor for the thighs, 394L [OFr. *cuisseaux.*]

daying, *n.* daybreak, dawn, 473 (T *dawynge,* I *dawnyng*) [OE. *dagung,* ON. **dagning.*]

dayntes, daynteths, *n.pl.* dainties, luxuries, 182, 183, 340I, 454, 459, 484 [OFr. *dainte.*]

dayntly, *adv.* neatly, handsomely, 340 (T *daynetyuousely*) [From prec.]

dame, *n.* lady, mistress, 13, 69,

85, etc.; mother, 160 [OFr. *dame.*]

danger, *n.* bondage, peril, 184, 318 [OFr. *danger.*]

dare, *pr.pl.* lurk, tremble, lie hid, 52 [OE. *darian.*]

darkys. See DURKENE.

dede, *n.*[1] deed, act, 121T, 249T, 516L [OE. *dēd.*]

dede, *n.*[2] See DETHE.

defoulene, *pr.pl.* oppress, 262 [Cf. ME. *foulen,* OFr. *defoler.*]

dele, *v.* deal, give out, 182T, 232I, 471L [OE. *dǣlan.*]

delful, *adj.* doleful, sorrowful, 160 [OFr. *doel* + *-ful.*]

delfulle, *adv.* sorrowfully, 154, 623; **delfully,** 312D, 593; **dolfully,** 160L [Prec. + *-ly.*]

delites, *n.pl.* delights, 213 (L *delices,* scribal error) [OFr. *delit.*]

delles, *n.pl.* small deep valleys, 6, 51 [OE. *dell.*]

de mayne. See SOPPES DE MAYNE.

deray, *n.* disorder, 513 [OFr. *desrei.*]

dere, *adv.* dearly, 222T; *adj. as sb.* worthy, noble one, 4 [OE. *dēore.*]

dere, *n.pl.* deer, wild animals, 51T, 53; **dure,** 46I, 51 [OE. *dēor.*]

derfely, *adv.* fiercely, boldly, 312T [OE. *dearflic,* ON. *djarffiga.*]

dernely, *adv.* secretly, 562L [OE. *derne* + *-ly.*]

des, *n.* dias, 182, 183; **desse,** 345T [OFr. *deis.*]

dethe, *n.* death, 54, 154, 160, 170, etc. (the usual form in T is *dede*) [OE. *dēaþ.*]

deþe-day, *n.* death-day, 98, 515 [Prec. + OE. *dæg.*]

deued, *pp.* stunned, confounded, 277 [OE. *ādēafian.*]

diȝte, *v.* make ready, treat, use, 170; **dighte,** *pr.pl.* 6, **dyghtis,** 495T; **diȝte, dight,** pp. 154, 183, 340, etc.; **y-dighte,** 533L [OE. *dihtan.*]

dymme, *adj.* dark, 53 [OE. *dimm.*]

dyn, *n.* noise, din, 277 [OE. *dyne, dynn.*]

dine, *v.* dine, 484I; **dyned,** *pt.* 484 [OFr. *disner.*]

dynyd, *pp.* deafened, overcome with noise, 277I [OE. *dynnan,* ON. *dengja.*]

dyntes, *n.pl.* strokes, 277L, 516, 533L, 593 [OE. *dynt.*]

diotes, *n.pl.* meals, 183 [OFr. *diete.*]

dirke, *adj.* dark, 75; **derk,** 564 [OE. *deorc.*]

displaied, *pp.* unfurled, 392 [OFr. *despleier.*]

do, *n.pl.* doe, female deer, 54 [OE. *dā.*]

doel, *n.* sorrow, grief, fear, 184, 554; **dole,** 208T, 318I [OFr. *doel.*]

dolfully. See DELFULLE.

dombe, *adj.* dumb, 554 [OE. *dumb.*]

dongone, *n.* dungeon, 184 [OFr. *donjon.*]

dossours, *n.pl.* hangings, tapestries, 444T [OFr. *dossier.*]

doue. See ENDOWE.

dougheti, douȝte, *adj. as sb.* brave or strong knights, 11, 305, 461, 473, etc.; **doughetest,**

superl. adj. as sb., 295 [OE. *dohtig.*]

doute, *v.* doubt, fear, 170 [OFr. *douter.*]

dowte, *n.* dread, fear, 54T [OFr. *doute.*]

doutwis, *adj.* terrifying, 516, 594L [OFr. *doutous.*]

downe, *n.* down, hilly ground, 53T (L *doun*) [OE. *dūn.*]

downe, *v.* ? Amours suggests "languish" from OE. *dwīnan*, 184T.

drad. See A-DRED.

drawes, *v.* draw away, 513; **droʒ,** *pt.* 562 (L *wiþdrow*) [OE. *draʒan.*]

dre, *v.* suffer, endure, 141; **drye,** 208T [OE. *drēogan.*]

dred, *pt.* feared, 571L [OE *drēdan.*]

drede, *n.* dread, fear, 54, 399, 562, 571I [From prec.]

dreuede, *pp.* confounded, 277T [OE. *drefan.*]

dreʒghe, *adv.* aside, back, 513I (L *drighly*); **on dreghe,** *adv. phr.* aback, at a distance, 513; **on dreʒt,** 562 [ON. *drjūgr.*]

dryvis, *pr.pl.* drive, run, 53L; **dryve forthe,** spend, go through, 564 [OE. *drīfan.*]

droʒ. See DRAWES.

droupe, *v.* cower, 53L; **droupes,** 54; **droupun,** 52IL; **drowpid,** *pt.* 54L [ON. *drūpa.*]

dure. See DERE.

durkene, *pr.pl.* lie still or hidden, 52, 53 (T *darkys*, I *dyrkyns*) [OE. *deorcan.*]

dussiperes, *n.pl.* nobles, 4; **dospers,** 11L; the twelve peers of France, 277 [OFr. *douze pers.*]

ey, *n.* eye, 359L; **eighen** *pl.* 116, 356; **ene,** 594D; **eyen,** 598L; **yene,** 599 [OE. *ēage.*]

eiþer. See AITHER.

eke, *adv.* also, 668 [OE. *ēac.*]

enclawid, *pp.* fastened with nails, riveted, 382I [OFr. *enclo(u)er.*]

enclosed, *pp.* enclosed, encircled, 287, 382T [OFr. *enclos,* pp.]

encontre, *v.* encounter, fight, 463, 466L (I *countur*), 506 [OFr. *encontrer.*]

endored, *pp.* glazed with the yolks of eggs, 459 [OFr. *endorer.*]

endowe, *v.* give, enrich with, 762T (I *doue*) [en- + OFr. *douer.*]

engreled, *pp.* having an edge or border of tapering points, 307, 509 [OFr. *engresle.*]

enparel, *n.* dress, 373I [OFr. *aparail.*]

enperit, ? "perhaps for *ensperit,* i.e., inspired" (Robson), "? Cf. *apperen,* be evident" (*MED*), 240I.

ensege, *v.* besiege, 289L [OFr. *ensegiere.*]

ensese, *v.* take possession, 289I [OFr. *enseisir.*]

er, *adv.* See OR.

erles, *n.pl.* earls, 33, 707T; **erlis,** *gen.* 482 [OE. *eorl.*]

ete, *pt.* ate, 323 [OE. *etan.*]

evyn, *n.* evening, 229L [OE. *ēfen.*]

face, *n.* face, 137, 610I (T's *faas* in this line may be "foes") [OFr. *face.*]

fay, *n.* truth, 398, 531 [OFr. *fei.*]

failene, *pr.pl.* lack, are in need of, 233, 319; fail, 589 [OFr. *faillir.*]

fair(e), fayre, *adj.* fair, beautiful, 331, 542, etc.; **fairest,** *superl.* 137, 551; *adv.* 8 [OE. *fæger.*]

fairhede, *n.* beauty, 373L [OE. *fæger* + ME. *-hede.*]

fal(le), *v.*[1] kill, slay, 7; **fel,** *pt.* 46 (T *fellede*) [OE. *fællan;* this verb and the next were confused and fell together in the North.]

fal(le), *v.*[2] befall, happen, 72, 299, 300; **fel,** *pt.* fell down; **felle,** 80L; **fellun to,** *pt.pl.* pursued, 7I, **felle to,** 46I [OE. *feallan;* confused with prec.]

fande. See FONDE.

fare, *n.* business, ado, onset, fight, 47, 399, 526 [OE. *fær.*]

fare, *v.* go, proceed, 47T, 245, 260, etc.; do, fare, 261; **fore,** *pt.* 712; **farene,** *pp.* 79 [OE. *faran.*]

farnet, *n.* "? a. ON. *foru-neyte* company of travelers" (*MED*), 275I.

fastned, *pp.* fixed, 500 [OE. *fæstnian.*]

fauoure, *n.* ? face, beauty, 166T [OFr. *favour.*]

fautes, *v.* be wanting, lacking, 574; **fawtes,** 319T; **fawtutte,** *pt.* 574I [OFr. *fauter.*]

fawe, *adj.* variegated, 80T [OE. *fāh, fāg.*]

fauyn, *n.* ? for FAUNT, 398I; "perhaps we should read *fanyn,* i.e., *fanon,* the knight's banner" (Robson).

fawnt, *n.* boy, squire, 398L, 399L [OFr. *(en)faunt.*]

fax, *n.* hair, 369 [OE. *feax.*]

fecche, *v.* fetch, get, 551 (I *foche*) [OE. *feccan, fetian.*]

feffe. See REFEFF.

fey, *adj.* fated to die, 275 [OE. *fāge.*]

feyful, *adv.* Robson suggests "fatal, deadly," 46I [From prec. ?]

feithe, *n.* vow, 430 [OFr. *feit.*]

fele, *adj.* many, 47L 262, 539D; **felefold,** manyfold, 685L [OE. *fela.*]

felle, *adj.* fierce, bold, 47T, 186T [OFr. *fel.*]

felle, *n.* hill, ridge, 8, 32, 50, etc. [ON. *fjall.*]

felonosly, *adv.* cruelly, keenly, 47T [OFr. *felon.*]

female, *adj.* 46I; *as sb.* **femailes, femayles,** female deer, 7, 46 [OFr. *femelle.*]

fendes, *n.pl.* fiends, 186 [OE. *fēond.*]

ferd, *pt.* feared, 399I [OE. *fǣran.*]

ferde, *n.* host, 186 [OE. *ferd.*]

ferdnes, *n.* ? for FERDE, 186L.

in fere, *adv.phr.* in company, together, 331T, 500L [OE. *gefēra.*]

fery, ? for FEY (D), or FRELY (TL), 275I.

ferly, *n.* wonder, marvel, 72, 299, 531, etc. [OE *fǣrlic.*]

ferly, *adv.* wondrously, 274L [OE. *fǣrlīce.*]

fermysone tyme, *n.* the closed season for hunting the hart and the buck, 8T [AFr. *fermeison.*]

fermesones, ? for FERMYSONE TYME, 8I.

fichede, *pp.* fixed, fastened, 500T [OFr. *fich(i)er.*]

figure, *n.* form, figure, 137 [OFr. *figure.*]

fille, *n.* fill, satisfaction, 411 (of fighting), 574 (of food) [OE. *fyllu.*]

fyne, *adj.* fine, neat, beautiful, 369, 386, 589 [OFr. *fin.*]

firmyschamis, ? for FERMYSONE TYME, 8D.

firthes. See FRITHE.

flawis, *n.pl.* flakes, 80L [Unknown.]

fleene, *pr.pl.* run, flee, 80 (T *fledde,* pt.) [OE. *flēon.*]

flokkene, *pr.pl.* flock, assemble, 331 [OE. *flocc.*]

flure. See TABLET FLURE.

foche. See FECCHE.

fold, *pp.* folded, 369I [OE *fealdan.*]

folde, *n.*¹ plait, fold, 369 [From prec.]

folde, *n.*² earth, land, 431, 476, 500 [OE. *folde.*]

folde, *v.* enfold, embrace, 376 [OE. *faldan.*]

fole, *n.* foal, horse, 542, 553 [OE. *fola.*]

folowed, *pp.* baptized. 225 [OE. *fulwian.*]

folower, *n.* attendant, 398L [OE. *folgere.*]

fonde, founde, *v.* try, go, venture, 79I, 193 (T *fande*), 261, 412, 526I, 610I [OE. *fandian, fundian,* separate verbs, become confused in these senses in ME.]

fondred, *pt.* foundered, stumbled, 542 [OFr. *fondrer.*]

fontestone, *n.* baptismal font, 225 [OE. *font + stān.*]

for-bett, *pp.adj.* beaten, 658T; **for-betun,** 569I [*for-* + OE. *bēatan.*]

for-blede, *pp.adj.* "covered with blood" (Madden), "exhausted with bleeding" (Amours), 658T [*for-* + OE. *blēdan.*]

for-brissutte, *pp.adj.* completely bruised, 658I [*for-* + OE. *brȳsan,* OFr. *bruser.*]

fordone, *pp.* undone, 270D [OE. *fordōn.*]

fore. See FARE.

foroure, *n.* fur, furred garments, 166 [OFr. *forreure.*]

for-þi, *adv.* therefore, 438 [OE. *forþȳ.*]

for-wondred, *pp.* astonished, 334 (T *a-wondirde*) [*for-* + OE. *wundrian.*]

fosses, *n.pl.* trenches, moats, 682 [OFr. *fosse.*]

foule, *adj.* foul, offensive, 472 [OE. *ful.*]

founde. See FONDE.

fray, *n.* ? for AFFRAY, fear, 399L [Cf. OFr. *effrei,* OE. *fǣr.*]

fraist, *v.* try, seek, 412 [ON. *freista.*]

freke, *n.* man, person, warrior, 79, 261, 411, etc. [OE. *freca.*]

frely, *adv.* freely, nobly, 225, 274, 275T, 431, 682T; *as sb.* noble lady, 376 [OE. *frēolīce.*]

fresone, *n.* Friesland horse, 398, 399, 551, 553I [OFr. *frisoun.*]

fresshe, *adj.* strong, vigorous, 47, 526, 574; fresh, 166 [OE. *fersc.*]

fretted, *pp.* adorned, trimmed, 369, 589 [OFr. pp. *frete.*]

frydde, *pp.* enclosed, 7 (T *frythede*) [OE. *friþian.*]

fryke, *adj.* bold, hearty, 574L [OFr. *frique.*]

frithe, frethe, *n.* enclosed wood, 8, 50, 331 (T *firthes*), 682, etc. [OE. *fyrhþ.*]

frounte, *n.* front, forehead, 387L, 401T [OFr. *front.*]

gayne, *adj.* quick, 85T; **gaynest,** *superl. as sb.* 12L [ON. *gegn.*]

gayne, *v.* encounter, oppose, 85 [ON. *gegna.*]

galyard, *adj.* brave, valiant, 458L; *as sb.* 493 [OFr. *gaillard.*]

gamesons, *n.pl.* quilted jackets or tunics worn under the armor, 393 [OFr. *gambeson.*]

gamene, gamone, game, *n.* sport, game, 59, 146, 402, etc. [OE. *gamen.*]

gare, ger(e), *v.* cause, make, 210T, 481, 635T, etc. [ON. *gøra.*]

garsone, *n.* treasure, 147; **gersone,** 664; **garsons,** *pl.* 697 [OE. *gersume.*]

gates, *n.pl.* ways, roads, 27, 85 [ON. *gata.*]

gentille, *adj.* courteous, 502T, 673T; *as sb.* 502 [OFr. *gentil.*]

gere, *n.* armor, gear, 496; attire, ? or manner, countenance, 125L (*giere*), 126L [ON. *gervi.*]

gersone. See GARSONE.

gert. See GURDES.

gete, *v.* get, obtain, 555; *imp.* guard (oneself), 283, 296, [ON. *geta,* OE. *gietan.*]

gewes, *v.* stares, gazes, 128T (I *gous*) [Cf. ON. *gā.*]

gide, *n.* gown, dress, 15, 366 [OFr. *guite.*]

gye, *imp.* guard (oneself), 296L [OFr. *guiier.*]

gile, *n.* guile, 417, 677 [OFr. *guile.*]

gyllis, *n.pl.* glens, ravines, 418T [ON. *gil.*]

girdede. See GURDES.

glades, *v.* entertain, make happy, 458 [OE. *gladian.*]

gle, *n.* pleasure, entertainment, 146, 402 [OE. *gleo.*]

glede, *n.* burning coal, ember, 117, 118, 393 [OE. *glēd.*]

glemed, *pt.* gleamed, shone, 15 (L *glemith,* pr.) [OE. *glǣm.*]

gleterand, *pr.p. adj.* glittering, 15, 27 (L *glideryng*), 458T, 496 [Cf. ON. *glitra.*]

glides, *v.* glides, goes, comes, 26, 27, 85, etc.; **glode,** *pt.* 85L; **glydand,** *pr.p.* 85I [OE. *glīdan.*]

gliffed, *pt.* looked, 356 [Unknown.]

glysset, *pt.* ? for GLIFFED, 356IL.

glode. See GLIDES.

glomede, ? for GLOWEDE, or GLEMEDE, 393T.

gloppen, *v.* fear, 91, 92, 530, 543 [ON. *glūpna.*]

gloues, *n.pl.* gloves, 393 [OE. *glōf,* ON. *glōfe.*]

glowed, *pt.* glowed, gleamed, 118, 393; **gloed,** 117; **glowand,** *pr.p.* 117T [OE. *glōwan.*]

glowes, *v.* stares, 128 [From prec.]

gome, *n.* man, knight, 61T, 100I, 436, 458T [OE *guma*.]

goodly, *adj.* noble, handsome, 652; *adv.* 652IL [OE. *gōdlic*.]

goost, goste, *n.* spirit, ghost, 99, 111, 118, etc.; **gaste,** 125T; **holy goste,** 254 [OE. *gāst*.]

gous. See GEWES.

graceful, *adj.* conveying grace, 254 [OFr. *grace*.]

graceless, *adj.* evil, damned, 163 [From prec.]

graynes, *n.pl.* grains, small bits (of gems), 394 [OFr. *grain*.]

graithe, *adv.* ready, equipped, 436; **grathest,** *superl.* best dressed, 439; **graythist,** 12I **graythest,** 68I (L *greithest*) [ON. *greiþr*.]

graiþed, *pp.adj.* dressed, prepared, 394, 508; **greyþer,** "richer" (Paton), 147L [ON. *greiþa*.]

graythely, *adv.* promptly, readily, 508T [ON. *greiþiliga*.]

graunte, *v.* allow, give, 140I, 676 [AFr. *graunter*.]

greches, *v.* becomes angry, 524 [OFr. *gro(u)chier*.]

grede, *v.* cry out, 99 [OE. *grǣdan*.]

gref(e), *n.* grief, 599L, 600; **grevis,** *pl.* 632L, 633L [OFr. *grief*.]

grehondes, grehoundys. See GREUNDES.

greyvis, *n.pl.* greaves, leg armor, 394L [OFr. *greves*.]

gremed, *pt.* became angry, 524 [OE. *gremian*.]

grene, *adj.* green, 28, 61, 69, etc.; *as sb.* **(one) grene,** on the ground, 12, 507, etc. [OE. *grēne*.]

gresse, *adj.* grass-colored, 366 [OE. *græs*, n.]

grete, *v.*[1] cry, weep, 91, 278; **gret(e), grette,** *pt.* 92, 493, 594I, 599I; **gretyng,** *pr.p.* 327L [OE. *grēotan*.]

grete, *v.*[2] salute, welcome, 228, 319I [OE. *grētan*.]

grete, *n.* shout, cry, 324, 326 [OE. *grētan, grēotan*.]

greue, *v.* grieve, annoy, 100, 238T, 464, 514, 524I (perhaps we should read *gremit* for *greuut*), 632L, 633 [OFr. *grever*.]

greues, *n.pl.* groves, 60, 61, 69, etc. [OE. *grǣfa*.]

greundes, *n.pl.* greyhounds, 60 (I *grehoundys*), 125I, 126 (I *grehondes*) [OE. *grighund*.]

grevis. See GREFE.

griffons, *n.pl.* a fabulous animal having the head and wings of an eagle and the body and hind quarters of a lion, 509 [OFr. *grifoun*.]

grylle, *v.* grieve, anger, 632; **grylles,** 422 [OE. *gryllan*.]

grylle, *n.* anger, harshness, 677L [From prec.]

grylle, *adj.* stern, harsh, 620 [From the verb.]

gryme, *adj.* grim, horrible, 125, 126, 327I; **grymlokkest,** *superl.* 99I [OE. *grim*.]

grymly, *adv.* sternly, horribly, 162T, 600I [OE. *grimlic*.]

grynnyd, *pt.* grimaced, gaped, 126L, 524L, 543L [OE. *grennian*.]

grisly, *adj.* horrible, hideous, 111,

125, 324, etc.; **grisselist,** *superl.*
99; *adv.* 163, 600, 607; **gresily,**
524L [OE. *grislic.*]
grythe, *n.* peace, respite, 59T,
146I [OE. *griþ.*]
grome, *n.* man, 100 [Unknown.]
groueling, *adv.* face downward,
606, 607I [ON. *ā grūfu +
-ling.*]
gurdes, *v.* strikes, spurs, 582 (L
gert, pt.), 606 (T *girdede,* pt.);
gurdene, *pr.pl.* dress, prepare,
495 [Unknown.]

ȝamer, *v.* lament, 107I; **ȝomerand,** *pr.p.* 86 [OE. *geōmerian.*]
ȝamyrly, *adv.* lamentably, 86T
[OE. *geōmerlīce.*]
ȝanyd, *pt.* gaped, 87L [OE. *geo-
nian.*]
ȝare, *adv.* quickly, fully, 567
[OE. *gearwe.*]
ȝaule, *v.* yowl, howl, 87, 107I;
ȝollyn, 179L; **ȝauland,** *pr.p.* 86
(T *ȝollande*) [Unknown.]
ȝe, *interj.* yea, yes, 247I, 434I,
468I [OE. *gē(a).*]
ȝerne, *adv.* earnestly, 614T (I
ȝorne) [OE. *georne.*]
ȝernely, *adv.* eagerly, 86L [OE.
geornlīce.]

haches, *n.pl.* racks, cribs, 448
[OE. *hæc.*]
halen, *v.* draw, haul, 447I [OFr.
haler.]
halowe, *pr.pl.* halloo, shout, 57
[OFr. *hal(l)oer.*]
halsed, *pt.* beseeched, invoked,
346 [OE. *halsian.*]
haluendelle, *adv.* half, 639T [OE.
þe healfan dǣl.]
hande. See HONDE.

hardely, *adv.* boldly, 586 [OFr.
hardi + -ly.]
hardy, *adj.* brave, daring, 467L,
674; *as sb.* 586I [OFr. *hardi.*]
hare, *adj.* hoary, bare, 43; **hore,**
710 [OE. *hār.*]
hast, *n.* haste, 43D; **haast,** 711D
OFr. *haste.*]
hasty, *adj.* quick, 544D [OFr.
hasti.]
hastily, *adv.* quickly, 586L [Prec.
+ -ly.]
haþel, *n.* man, knight, 42, 130,
131, 586, etc. [OE. *hæleþ,
æþele.*]
haue, *v.* ? for HEAVE, 187I.
hawe, *adj.* bluish or gray, 18TI
[OE. *hæwe, hāwi.*]
hede, *n.* care, heed, 171 [From
next.]
hedes, *v.* protects, 18 [OE. *hē-
dan.*]
hedows, *adj. as sb.* hideous or
frightful (person, sight), 130T
131T [OFr. *hidous.*]
hele, *n.* heel, 386 [OE. *hēla.*]
hely, *adv.* ? completely, richly,
448I [OE. *hēah, hēahlīce.*]
heling, *n.* covering, clothing, 108
[OE. *helan,* v.]
helmes, *n.pl.* helmets, 586 [OE.
helm.]
hende, *adj.* courteous, gentle,
377, 529L; **hendest,** *superl.*
131T, *as sb.* 698 [OE. *gehende.*]
hendely, *adv.* courteously, fairly,
well, 42T, 346, 448T, 488T
[From prec.]
hent, *pt.* took, 488 [OE. *hentan.*]
herde, *adj.* ? bright, 18D [OE.
heard.]
here, *v.* hear, 94, 99, 130, etc.;

one **herand**, in the hearing of, 404T [OE. *hēran.*]
herken, *v.* listen, 43; **herkenys**, ?, 131L [OE. *hercnian.*]
hersing. See REHERCYNG.
hert, *n.* heart, 258, 422, 543, 594, 632 [OE. *heorte.*]
hertly, *adv.* heartily, 171, 192, 235, 448 [From prec.]
hertes, *n.pl.* male deer, 57L, 435D [OE. *heorot.*]
hestes, *n.pl.* promises, 235 [OE. *hǣs.*]
hete, *v.* promise, 235T (I *hote*); **hote**, 430L; **hiȝte**, *pt.* 465 [OE. *hātan.*]
heþene, *adv.* hence, 245, 260 (L *hennys*) [ON. *heþan.*]
heuyde, *pp.* raised, lifted, 448 [OE. *hebban.*]
hewe, *v.* hew, cut, 187T, 586 [OE. *hēawan.*]
hide, *n.* skin, hide, 108 [OE. *hȳd.*]
in hydis, ? for UNHIDES, 328T.
hye, *adj.* intense, 18L; **in hiȝ**, *adv. phr.* on high, above, 42, 698 [OE. *hēah.*]
in highe, *adv. phr.* in haste, quickly, 488 [OE. *hīgian.*]
one **hiȝte**, one **highte**, *adv.phr.* above, aloft, 162D, 187T, 346, 404, 648, 651; **in hiȝte**, 187; **vppone hight(e)**, 413, 523; one **hiȝte**, up, upwards, 612 [OE. *hēahþu.*]
hiȝene, *pr.pl.* hasten, rush, 124; **hying**, *pr.p.* 57L [OE. *hīgian.*]
hiȝte. See HETE.
hirdmene, *n.pl.* attendants, retainers, 42T [Cf. OE. *hīredman, heord.*]
hode, *n.* hood, 18 [OE. *hōd.*]

holked, *pp.adj.* sunk, put out, 116 [Cf. MLG. *holken.*]
holle, *adj.*[1] hollow, 116 [OE. *holh.*]
holle, *adj.*[2] entire, sound, 699I [OE. *hāl.*]
holt(e), *n.* wood, grove, 43, 57T, 124I, 710, 711T [OE. *holt.*]
honde, *n.* hand, 235, 264, 423, etc.; **one hande**, at (my) word, 235I [OE. *hond.*]
honest, *adj.* honorable, 302 [OFr. *honeste.*]
hore. See HARE.
hote. See HETE.
hovis, *v.* ? for HEWES, or HEAVES, 187L; Paton suggests OE. **hofian*, float, soar.
huntes, *n.pl.* hunters, 57 (I *hunteres*) [OE. *hunta.*]
hurle, *v.* throw, drive violently, 187 [Cf. LG. *hurreln.*]
hurstes, *n.pl.* woods, groves, 57 [OE. *hyrst.*]
huwe, *n.* hue, color, 18; complexion, 108D [OE. *hīw.*]
huwes, *n.pl.* steep glens, ravines, 57 [OE. *hōh.*]

iaumbis, *n.* armor for the legs, 393L [OFr. *jambeau.*]
ienewbris, *n.pl.* ? 393L; Paton suggests that this is some form of *vambrace*, which is a covering for the lower arm.
ille, *adv.* badly, 578, 630 [ON. *illr.*]
in-withe, *prep.* within, 445 [OE. *in, wiþ.*]
in melle, **y-melle**, *adv. phr.* amid, among, 320 [ON. *i milli.*]
I-nore, ? for YNOGHE, 375D.
ioy, *n.* joy, 698L [OFr. *joye.*]

iolile, *adv.* heartily, joyfully, 502 [OFr. *joli* + *-ly.*]

iral, *n.* some kind of precious stone, 590 (I *iraille*) [Unknown.]

irke, *adj.* annoyed, 77 [Unknown.]

iusted, *pt.* jousted, fought, 502 [OFr. *juster.*]

I-wys, y-wis, *adv.* indeed, certainly, 194, 217, 247, 424, etc. [OE. *gewis.*]

kele, *v.* cool, relieve, 45, 201T [OE. *cēlan.*]

kelle, *n.* hair net or headdress, 370 [OFr. *cale.*]

kellyd, *pt.* ? for KELLE, *n.* 370L.

kempe, *n.* champion, warrior, 613L [OE. *cempa.*]

kene, *adj.* brave, strong, 139, 286, 301, etc. [OE. *cēne.*]

kenely, *adv.* bravely, 287T, 612 [OE. *cēnlīce.*]

kenettes, *n.pl.* hounds, 44L, 45 [ONFr. *chienet.*]

kepe, *v.* defend, maintain, 483I; **keppes,** *pr.3sg.* stops, seizes, 618D [Late OE. *cēpan.*]

kepe, *n.* care, heed, 483 [From prec.]

kercheues, *n.pl.* kerchiefs, 372 [OFr. *couvrechief.*]

kere, *v.* ? for KELE, 201D.

keruet, keuet. See CARF.

kest, *pt.pl.* threw, set off, 44; **cast,** *pp.* 151L, 607L; **kestes,** *imp.* decide, 463D [ON. *kasta.*]

keuered, *pt.* succeeded in rising, 612; **coverid,** 610L; **couerde hym,** 612T may be covered himself up [OFr. *covrer, recovrer,* OE. *ācofrian.*]

kide, *n.* country, home, 151; **kithe,** 360 [OE. *cȳþþ.*]

kydde, *pp. adj.* known, famous, 3, 139T [OE. *cȳdde.*]

kindeles, *v.* is aroused, 90 [ON. *kynda.*]

kyndely, *adv.* kindly, graciously, 287L, 482I, 613L, 694IL [OE. *gecyndelic.*]

kynne, *n.* kin, family, 138, 139 [OE. *cynn.*]

kithe. See KIDE.

kneled, *pt.* knelt, 626, 647; **knelis,** *pr.3sg.* 627T [OE. *cnēowlian.*]

knowene, *pp.* known, 138D, 139; **knawene,** 265L; *pt.* **knewe,** 207L, **knaue,** 246I [OE. *cnawan.*]

krysommede. See CRISOMED.

krudely, ? for KINDELY, 482D (perhaps both substitutions for a proper name.)

ladde. See LEDE, *v.*

laft. See LEUE, *v.*²

laghe, *v.* laugh, 433; **louched,** *pt.* 162; **lowe,** 523 [OE. *hlæhhan.*]

laike, *n.* fight, contest, 538 [ON. *leikr.*]

layne, *v.* deny, hide, 83, 204 [ON. *leyna.*]

laithe, *adv.* unpleasant, loathesome, 432; **layetheste,** *superl.* 84T; **latelest,** 523I [OE. *lāþ,* ON. *leiþr.*]

late, lates. See LETE, LOTE.

lau, *n.* flame, light, 83I (T *lowe*) [ON. *loge.*]

lau, *adj.* See LOƷE.

lawnde, *n.* field, forest clearing, 31L; **lawunde,** 477I, 489I [OFr. *launde.*]

laurialle, lauryel. See LORERE.

lawe, *n.* hill, slope, 31D, 83D [OE. *hlāw.*]

lede, *n.* man, person, 83, 433, 279I, 566; **in lede,** *adv. phr.* in the land, among the people, 83T, 397L [OE. *lēode.*]

lede, *v.* lead, 13, 14, 397, etc.; *pt.* **ladde,** 31, **lad,** 440I, **led,** 447; **ledand,** *pr.p.* 344 [OE. *lǣdan.*]

lefe-sale, *n.* leafy bower, 70I [OE. *lēaf, sæl.*]

lele, *n.* lily, 162 [OE. *lilie.*]

lele, *adj.* loyal, 653I [OFr. *leel.*]

lemmane, *n.* lady-love, 536, 619 [OE. *lēof, man.*]

lende, *v.* stay, dwell, 414T, 683L; **lynd,** 214I [OE. *lendan.*]

lene, *v.* give, grant, 228; **lent,** pp. 140L [OE. *lēnan.*]

lenge, *v.* dwell, stay, 214T, 362I, 415, 683 [OE. *lengan.*]

lenthe, *n.* length, 477I [OE. *lenþu.*]

lepe, leppis. See LOPEN.

lere, *n.* face, complexion, 162, 344L [OE. *hlēor.*]

lerid, *pp. adj.* learned, 707L [OE. *leornian.*]

lese, *v.* lose, 285, 293, 432; **lost,** *pp.* 462, **lorne,** 470 [OE. *(for) lēosan.*]

lete, *v.* let, allow, 155; **let go,** stop, let go your hold, 471; **late,** ? let yourself, or error for *light and,* 415D [OE. *lǣtan.*]

lette, *n.* delay, hindrance, 36 [OE. *lettan,* v.]

lettynge, *n.* delay, 660 [Prec. + *ing.*]

leue, *n.* permission, 468 [OE. *lēaf.*]

leue, *v.*[1] believe, 275, 469 [OE. *gelēfan.*]

leue, *v.*[2] leave, 69L, 98L, 176T, 228L; **leued,** *pt.* 279; **laft,** 487, 652 (left off, stopped); **laft, left,** *pp.* 69I, 98, 203L, 214, 275I [OE. *lǣfan.*]

leve, *v.* live, 259; **leueande,** *pr.p.* 433T [OE. *lifian.*]

leve, *adj.* dear, 634 [OE. *lēof.*]

lewd, *adj.* evil, 214L [OE. *lǣwede.*]

lycence, *n.* permission, 489T [OFr. *licence.*]

life, *n.* life, 175L 470; **lyues,** *gen.* 702; **on lyue,** *adv. phr.* alive, 279D [OE. *līf.*]

lyfte, *pt.* lifted, 408T [ON. *lyfta.*]

lighte, *v.* alight, descend, fall, 32, 70, 272, etc.; ? relieve, comfort, 176D [OE. *līhtan.*]

lighte, *adj.* light, unconcerned, 162L, 469 [OE. *lēoht.*]

lyȝte, liȝte, *adv.* lightly, 162I, 653; **lite,** ? 176D; **lyghtely,** 176T; **lightly,** 566L [OE. *lēohte, lēohtlīce.*]

likes, *v.* pleases, 615; **likes,** 213I, 538 [OE. *līcian.*]

lyknes, *n.* likeness, 84T [OE. *līcnes.*]

lymes, *n.pl.* limbs, 164L [OE. *lim.*]

lymped, *pt.* befell, 615 [OE. *limpan.*]

lynd. See LENDE.

by lyne, *adv. phr.* with methodical accuracy, 477 [OE. *līne,* OFr. *ligne.*]

lyone, *n.* lion, 574 [OFr. *liun.*]

list, *n.* list, tilting area, 477, 497, 566, etc. [OE. *liste.*]

listes, *n.pl.* lusts, pleasures, 213 (T *lustis*) [OE. *lust.*]

lystines, ? for LYSTES, 469L.

lite, *adv.* ? lightly, or little, 176D

lithes, *n.pl.* people, vassals, 678 [ON. *lỹþr.*]

litil, *adv.* little, 584L; **lite,** ? 176D [OE. *lỹtel.*]

litys, *v.* for DELITES, 213T.

lyues. See LIFE.

lo, *interj.* 153, 160 [OE. *lā.*]

one loft, *adv.phr.* aloft, above, 397, 536I, 619 [OE. *on lofte.*]

loghe, *n.* lake, pond, 31I, 83I [OE. *luh,* cf. Gael. *loch.*]

loȝ, *adj.* low, 477 [ON. *lāgr.*]

loȝ(e), *adv.* low, down, 32, 164, 214; **lowe,** 268, 272 (T *lawe*); **lau,** 165I [From prec.]

lollid, *pt.* ? rocked, drooped, 87L [?Imitative.]

lopen, *pt.* leaped, 653 (L *lepyd;* T *leppis,* I *lepe,* pr.) [ON. *hlaupa,* OE. *hlēapan.*]

lordely, *adv.* nobly, 489, 566 [OE. *hlāfordlic.*]

lordynges, *n.pl.* lords, 462I [OE. *hlāfording.*]

lordshippe, *n.* domain, sovereignty, 432, 470, 683 [OE. *hlāfordscipe.*]

lorer(e), *n.* laurel tree, 32 (I *laurialle*), 70 (I *lauryel*) [OFr. *laurier.*]

lose, *n.* praise, fame, 472 [OFr. *los.*]

lost. See LESE.

lote, *n.* look, manner, 344; **lates,** pl. 469 [ON. *lāt.*]

loþely, *adj.* repulsive, 523L; *as sb.* ? 83L [OE. *lāþlic.*]

louched. See LAGHE.

loude, *adv.* loudly, 619T; **one**

lowde, *adv.phr.* aloud, loudly, 536 [OE. *hlūde.*]

loute, *v.* bend, bow to, 176 [OE. *lūtan.*]

lowe. See LAGHE, LAU, LOȝE.

lucius, *adj.* luscious, delicious, 458I [Unknown.]

luf, *n.* love, 213; **love,** 497L [OE. *lufu.*]

luf, *v.* love, 213T [OE. *lufian.*]

lufly, lufely, *adj.* lovely, 162T, 634T; **louely,** *as sb.* 397 [OE. *luflic.*]

lufsom, *adj.* lovely, 344; **lovesom,** 162L [OE. *lufsum.*]

lustis. See LISTES.

mached, *pp.* matched in combat, 437; equal, 596 [OE. *gemæcca,* n.]

madde, *adj.* insane, demented, 110 [OE. *gemǣdd.*]

mayed, *pt.* dismayed, 585L [ONFr. *amaier.*]

maynteine, *v.* defend, keep, 467I [OFr. *maintenir.*]

makeles, *adj.* matchless, 348, 621, 643 [OE. *gemæcca.*]

manere, *n.* manner, way, 333T, 498; kind, sort, 704T [OFr. *manere.*]

manhede, *n.* manhood, bravery, 351 [OE. *man* + ME. *hede.*]

manyfolde, *adj.* many, various, 376L; **meny folde,** 46L [OE. *manigfeald.*]

mantylle, *n.* mantel, 352 [OE. *mantel.*]

marred, *pt.* was confused, distressed, 110 [OFr. *marrir,* OE. *merran.*]

mas, masse, n. Mass, 198, 229, 321, etc. [OE. *messe.*]

mas, mace, *n.* mace, 64, 498 [OFr. *masse.*]

matens, *n.pl.* matins, morning prayers, 198, 229, 320, 474 [OFr. *matines.*]

matyttory, *n.* ? for MONTURE, 555I.

meble, *n.* movables, goods, 199 (T *mobylles*) [OFr. *moeble.*]

mede, *v.* reward (? for *mende*), 230L [OE. *mēd,* n.]

medecynes, *n.pl.* remedies, 321 [OFr. *medecine.*]

medlert, *n.* world, earth, 643 [OE. *middel* + *eorþ.*]

mekely, *adv.* meekly, 333L [ON. *mjūkr* + *-ly.*]

mekenesse, *n.* meekness, 250 [ON. *mjūkr* + *-ness.*]

mele, *v.* speak, 74, 333T [OE. *mǣlan.*]

melle. See IN MELLE.

memered, *pt.* stammered, muttered, 110 [Echoic.]

mende, *v.* atone for, make reparation for, 193, 198, 209L; free from sin, 230 (perhaps a form of *OED mind, v.*³, remember) [OFr. *amender.*]

mene, *v.* have in mind, remember, 229T, 230T, 320T; mention, express, 73, 74; menes, complains, laments, 167I; menet, *pt.* 110I [OE *mǣnan.*]

menewith, ? up against, 341D.

menge. See MYNGE.

mengit, *pt.* troubled, 594I [OE. *mengan.*]

menyng, *n.* moaning, lamenting, 596I [OE. *mǣnan.*]

menys, ? ; Paton glosses "human being, man" from OE. *mennisc,* 642L.

menske, *n.* honor, 230T [ON. *mennska.*]

merke, *n.* mark, 565I [OE. *mearc.*]

merthe, *n.* mirth, joy, 181, 199 (T *myrthis,* pl.) [OE. *myrgþ.*]

mervaile, *n.* marvel, wonder, 73, 74; mervelle, 202T [OFr. *merveille.*]

messe. See MAS.

mesure, *n.* moderation, 250I [OFr. *mesure.*]

mete, *n.* meal, food, 181, 352, 458I [OE. *mete.*]

in myd, in mydde(s), *prep. phr.* in, amid, 475I, 489I, 566I [OE. *in midd.*]

myn, *v.* commemorate, remember, 229I, 320I; mynne, 230I [ON. *minna.*]

mynd, *v.* remember, 173T [OE. *gemynd.*]

mynge, *v.* remember, commemorate, 229; menge, 320 [OE. *myn(e)gian.*]

mynnyng, *n.* commemoration of a departed soul, 236, 706; menynge, 708T [ON. *minna.*]

myrke, *adj.* dark, 76 [OE. *mirce.*]

mirrour, *n.* mirror, example (figurative), 167 [OFr. *mirour.*]

myrthis. See MERTHE.

mys, *n.* offense, misdeed, 193, 198 [OE. *missan, v.*]

myster, *n.* need, 230 [OFr. *mestier, mester.*]

mobylles. See MEBLE.

mode, *n.* mood, temper, mind, 226, 642, 594I [OE. *mōd.*]

moder, *n.* mother, 202, 226I, 706I [OE. *mōdor.*]

moyse. See MUSE.

on mold, *adv. phr.* on earth, in the world, 199 [OE. *molde.*]

monkyre, *n.* ? for MONTURE, 555L.

monradene, *n.* homage, 642 [OE. *mannrǣden.*]

monture, *n.* mount, 555 [OFr. *monteure.*]

moted, *pp.adj.* moated, 671T [OFr. *mote.*]

mouthe, *v.* ?, 642L; Paton glosses "declare" from OE. *mūþ, n.*

muse, *v.* look, stare, ponder, 110, 167 (T *moyse*) [OFr. *muser.*]

a nayre, for AN AYRE, 349I.

a nanlas, for AN ANLAS, 390I.

naxte, *adj.* nasty, foul, 185 [Cf. Du. *nestig.*]

nede, *n.* need, want, 557 [OE. *nēd.*]

nedefulle, *adj.* in need, 185 (I *nedy*) [Prec. + *-fulle.*]

ner, *adv.* nearly, almost, 558 [ON. *nǣr.*]

nyʒte, *n.* night, 415, 438, 564; one nighte, *adv.phr.* at night, 185 [OE. *niht.*]

none, *n.* noon, 219 [OE. *nōn.*]

note, *n.* business, employment, 375T [OE. *notu.*]

oke, *n.* oak, 37D [OE. *āc.*]

onys, *adv.* once, 155 (T *anes*) [OE. *ān.*]

one bak, one hande, one loft, etc. See BAK, HANDE, LOFT, etc.

oonly, *adj.* alone, lonely, 98 [OE. *ānlic.*]

or, *conj.* before, 191; er, 245, 424; or, *prep.* 484; are, *adv.* previously, 403 [OE. *ǣr*, ON. *ār.*]

ote. See WOTE.

ouer, *adv.* over, around, 21; aure, 17I, 120I [OE. *ofer.*]

ouer-rynnes, *v.* overruns, 263T; aure-ronene, *pp.* 280 [Prec. + OE. *rinnan*, ON. *rinna.*]

outray, *v.* overcome, 311 (T *owttraye*) [AFr. *outreier.*]

owttrageouse, *adj.* excessive, violent, 421T [OFr. *outrageus.*]

pade, *n.* toad or frog, 115 (I *padok*) [OE. *pade*, ON. *padda.*]

pay, *v.* please, satisfy, 19, 148L, 353D, 396 [OFr. *paier.*]

palais, *n.* enclosure, enclosed land, 475; palaies, *pl.* 148 (L *paleys;* TI *pales,* is probably "fences") [OFr. *pal(e)is.*]

palle, *n.* rich cloth, 19T, 66, 335, 441, 443; pal, 353; palwerke, 19 [OE. *pæll, weorc.*]

pane, *n.* fur, 353T [OFr. *pane.*]

paramour, *adv.phr.* by way of sexual love, 213; *n.* lover, 213I (T pl.) [OFr. *par amour.*]

parkes, *n.pl.* enclosed royal lands, 148 [OFr. *parc.*]

pase, *n.* journey or pace, step, 142T [OFr. *pas.*]

pavilone, *n.* pavilion, large tent, 441; paueluns, *pl.* 475I [OFr. *pavillon.*]

peliddoddes, *n.pl.* peridots, a name of the chrysolite, 396I; pelicocus, 396D [OFr. *peritot.*]

pelurid, *pp.* furred, 19L [OFr. *pelure.*]

pencelle, *n.* pennon, streamer, 392D [OFr. *penoncel.*]

perre, *n.* jewelry, 19, 369, 373 [OFr. *perrie.*]

254

GLOSSARY

pes, *n.* peace, 178, 650, 651 [OFr. *pais.*]

pesane, *n.* gorget of mail, 583; "so named from Pisa, where the gorgets were probably first fabricated" (Madden).

pight, piȝte, *pp.* set, pitched, adorned, 353, 442, 443, 475 [ON. *pikka,* ME. *picchen.*]

pikes, *v.* stabs, 115 [OE. *picung* < **pician?*]

pillour, *n.* fur, 19 [OFr. *pelure.*]

pyne. See PRENE.

pite, *n.* pity, 173, 251, 622I [OFr. *pite.*]

plis, ? 563L; perhaps a variant form of the verb "ply" from OFr. (*a*)*plier.*

plyghte, *v.* pledge, promise, 465T [OE. *plihtan.*]

plonkete. See BLUNKET.

plowes, *n.pl.* a measure of land equal to about fifteen or twenty acres, 148 (T *plewes*) [LOE. *plōh,* ON. *plōgr.*]

polans, *n.pl.* knee-armor, 396I; **polayns,** 583I [OFr. *polain.*]

polemus, ? as Madden suggests, probably a minim-error for *poleinus,* see POLANS, 396D.

polle, *n.* head, 115 [Du. *polle.*]

poon, *n.* ? for PANE, 353I; "like a peacock's tail ? *Paon,* Fr." (Robson).

poudred, *pp.adj.* sprinkled, ornamented, 396 [OFr. *poudrer.*]

prayd, *v.* ? for BRAYD, 449I.

praysed, *pp.* praised, 373 [OFr. *preisier.*]

preketes, *n.pl.* spikes to stick candles on, 451T [Anglo-Latin *prikettus.*]

prene, *n.* pin, 372 (T *pyne*) [OE. *prēon.*]

prest, *adj.* ready, prepared, 705 [OFr. *prest.*]

prest, *n.* priest, 373L; **prestes,** *pl.* 705 [OE. *prēost.*]

prykkette, *pp.adj.* stuck, impaled, 115I [OE. *prician.*]

prise, *adj.* dear, worthy, 373 [OFr. *pris.*]

prodly, *adv.* proudly, 353, 442, 443 [OE. *prūd, prūtlīce.*]

proude, *adj.* proud, rich, 148L, 372; **pruddest, proudest,** *superl.* 66, 335 [OE. *prūt, prūd.*]

pured, *pp.adj.* of fur, trimmed or cut down so as to show one color only, 353 [OFr. *purer.*]

purpour, *n.* purple cloth, 443; **purpure,** 19I [OE. *purpure.*]

quelles, *n.pl.* slayings, slaughters, 49 [From next.]

quellys, *pr.pl.* kill, destroy, 49T (I *quellun*) [OE. *cwellan.*]

quert, *n.* health, well-being, 257 [ON. **kvert.*]

questede, *pr.pl.* hunted, searched, 49T (I *questun*) [OFr. *quester.*]

questes, *n.pl.* searches, pursuits, 49 [OFr. *queste.*]

quethun, qwethun. See WHEþENE.

quyte, *v.* requite, repay, 561 [OFr. *quiter.*]

qweschyns, *n.pl.* cushions, 444T [OFr. *coissin.*]

raches, *n.pl.* hunting dogs which pursue their prey by scent, 58T, 81I [OE. *ræcc,* ON. *rakki.*]

rad, *adv.* quickly, soon, 294 [OE. *hrǣde*.]

rad(de), *adj.* afraid, awed, 112T, 113T [ON. *hrǣddr*.]

radder. See REDE, *adj.*

raght, *pt.* reached, went, 317L, 460L, 549L; reached, gave, 605 [OE. *rǣcan, rǣhte*.]

ray, rayed. See ARAY, ARAIED.

raye, ? for OF RAY, or ROY, 172I.

raye, *n.* "track ?" (Madden), 58T; perhaps an error for *raa*, No. form of roe.

rayke, *v.* go, betake oneself, 112, 345, 460I [ON. *reika*.]

rayled, *pp.adj.* set, adorned, 17 [OFr. *reiller*.]

rane, *pt.pl.* ran, 58D, 81I (L *ronne*); **rennyng,** *pr.p.* *adj.* 58L [OE. *rinnan*, ON. *rinna*.]

ras. See ROSE.

rathe, *adj.* quick, hasty, 438T, 654T [OE. *hraþe*.]

rathely, *adv.* quickly, 112L, 609L [OE. *hraþlīce*.]

rechas, *n.* the call for the hounds to assemble, 58D, 62 [OFr. **rachat*, cf. *rachater*.]

reddoure, *n.* severity, harshness, 81T [ONFr. *reddur*.]

rede, *adj.* red, 570I; **radder,** *comp.* 161 [OE. *rēad*.]

rede, *n.* advice, counsel, 93, 558L [OE. *rǣd*.]

rede, *v.* understand, think, 16, 113, 525, 550; advise, counsel, 438; read, say mass, 704 [OE. *rǣdan, rēdan*.]

redeles, *adj.* without counsel, helpless, 81I [OE. *rǣdlēas*.]

refeff, *v.* re-enfeoff, re-invest, 685 (I *feffe*) [AFr. *refeffer*.]

rehercyng, *n.* recounting, repeti-

tion, 660L (I *hersing*) [OFr. *rehercer*.]

reymes, *n.pl.* realms, 263 (L *rewmes*) [OFr. *reaume*.]

releyse, *n.* release, grant, 640, 646 [OFr. *relais*.]

relese, *v.* release, cede, 641, 675 [OFr. *relesser*.]

relyes, *pr.pl.* assemble, rally, 58T (I *releues*, L *rayle*) [OFr. *relier*.]

remayns, *n.pl.* ? for Romans, or realms, 280D.

rengthe, *n.* ? for RENKE (D), or RENT (T), 604I.

renke, *n.* man, knight, 460, 640 [OE. *rinc*, ON. *rekkr*.]

rennyng. See RANE.

rente, possession, source of income, 281, 627, 640T, 646 [OFr. *rente*.]

rente, *pp.* rent, torn, 317T [OE. *rendan*.]

repaire, *n.* stay, 684 [OFr. *repaire*.]

res, *n.* rush, run, 112, 345 [OE. *rǣs*, ON. *rās*.]

resettyng, *n.* refuge, shelter, 81L [OFr. *recetter*.]

reued, *pp.* taken away, 281 [OE. *rēafian*.]

reuersset, *pt.* faced, trimmed with another material, 16 [OFr. *reverser*.]

rewmes. See REYMES.

rial(le), *adj.* royal, noble, 17, 304, 460, etc.; *as sb.* royal person, 345, 640I, 641T [OFr. *real, roial*.]

ryally, *adv.* royally, 58D [Prec. + *-ly*.]

rybe, *n.* ruby, 394; **rybees,** *pl.* 17; **rubyes,** 16L [OFr. *rubi*.]

riches, *v.* proceed, ride, 263D [OE. *reccan,* ON. *rykkja.*]

riding, *n.* track or lane by or through a wood, 294 [OE. *rīdan* + *-ing.*]

righte, *adv.* justly, properly, 16, 113, 525, etc. [OE. *rihte.*]

rightwisly, *adv.* righteously, 317 [OE. *rihtwīslīce.*]

riȝte, *v.* See note, 1.505.

rynge, *v.* ring, summon to service with a bell, 708 [OE. *hringan.*]

rise, *n.* branch, 161L [OE., ON. *hrīs.*]

ro, *n.* roe, 58 [OE. *rā.*]

roches, *n.pl.* rocks, cliffs, 81T [OFr. *roche.*]

rode, *n.¹* complexion, 161 [OE. *rudu.*]

rode, *n.²* rood, cross, 222, 231, 317, etc. [OE. *rōd.*]

roye, *n.* king, 627 [OFr. *roy.*]

rone, *n.* bush, thicket, 161 [ON. *runnr.*]

ronke, *adj.* strong, heavy, 604 [OE. *ranc.*]

ronne. See RANE.

rose, *pt.* rose, got up, 317, 549L; **ras,** 609 [OE. *rīsan, rās.*]

rote, *n.* root, 553 [ON. *rōt.*]

route, *n.* stroke, blow, 525 [? cf. OE. *hrutan.*]

route, rowte, *n.* company, 172, 304, 332, 641I [OFr. *route.*]

rubyes. See RYBE.

rudely, *adv.* violently, swiftly, 609I [OFr. *rude* + *-ly.*]

sable, *n.* heraldic black, 306, 308 [OFr. *sable.*]

sadel, *n.* saddle, 23 [OE. *sadol.*]

safe. See SAUE.

saffres, *n.pl.* sapphires, 21, 22 [OFr. *safir.*]

saȝtil, *v.* become reconciled, 673 (I *saȝtun*) [Cf. LOE. *sæht,* ON. *sāttr.*]

saȝtlynge, *n.* reconciliation, 661 [From prec.]

sake, *n. in phrase,* for someone's sake, on their behalf, 210, 319, 597I, 652 [ON. *fyrir sakir.*]

sale, *n.* hall, 339T [OE. *sæl.*]

saluen, salued. See SAUE.

salers, *n.pl.* salt-cellars, 450 [OFr. *sal(i)ere.*]

sambutes, *n.pl.* saddle-cloths, 24 [OE. *sambue.*]

sanapes, *n.pl.* over-cloths, 450 [OFr. * *sa(u)ve-nape.*]

sandel, *n.* a rich silk, 386 (T *sendale*) [OFr. *cendal.*]

saude, *pp.* sewed, 24 (T *sewede*) [OE. *seowian.*]

saue, *v.* heal, protect, save, 134T; **safe,** 209T; **saued,** *pt.* 220 (T *salued*), 244 (I *saluen*), 693, 699 [OFr. *sauver, salver.*]

savmhellus, ? for SAMBUTES, 24I.

sauter, *n.* heraldic emblem in the form of a St. Andrew's cross, formed by a bend and a bend sinister crossing each other, 307 [OFr. *saut(e)oir.*]

scapette. See SKAPE.

scas, ? for CAST, 613D.

schaft, schaghes, schane. See CHAFTIS, SKUWES, SHENE.

schene, *adj.* cut, broken, 501T [Cf. OE. *scēnan.*]

schene. See SHENE.

scheuer, *v.* shiver, shatter, 501T, 503T [Gmc. root **skif*-.]

schydes, *n.pl.* split or cut pieces of wood, 503T [OE. *scīd.*]

schynbaudes, *n.pl.* armor for the legs [Unknown.]

schomely, *adv.* shamefully, 588I; schomfully, 631I [OE. *scamu,* ON. *skomm.*]

schowys, *pr.pl.* shove, throng, 53T, 129L [OE. *scūfan.*]

schrydes, *v.* protects, covers, 20T (I *shredes*) [OE. *scrȳdan.*]

schurde, *pp.* clothed, dressed, 20 (T *schruedede,* I *schrod*) [OE. *scrūd, n.*]

scorne, *n.* mockery, insult, 433; skorne, 472 [OFr. *escarn.*]

scrykes, scrilles. See SKRYKES, SKRILLES.

sege, segge, *n.* man, knight, 289, 306L, 359 [OE. *secg.*]

seyntis, *n.pl.* girdles, 24L [OFr. *ceint.*]

seke, *v.* pursue, follow, go, 67L, 210T; seche, look for, 289D, 406; soȝt, *pt.* 67I, 359I [OE. *sēcan.*]

seladynes, *n.pl.* probably celidonies, 22D [OFr. *celidoine.*]

selcouþe, *adj.* strange, marvelous, 22L; *as sb.* wonders, 333 [OE. *seldan* + *cūþ.*]

semble, *v.* assemble, 66 (T *semelede,* pt.) [OFr. *assembler.*]

semblynge, *n.* meeting, 661T [Prec. + *-ing.*]

semly, *adj.* fair, beautiful, 450, 696T; semely, 456; semelist, semelokest, *superl.* 66I, 358I [ON. *sǣmiligr.*]

sendale. See SANDEL.

sere, *adj.* several, separate, 210 [ON. *sēr.*]

sergeant of mace, *n.* an inferior executive officer carrying a mace as a badge of office, 64;

seriant of mace, *pl.* 498 [OFr. *sergent, serjent, mace.*]

serkeled, *pp.adj.* set about in a circular pattern, 120; serclet, 22I [OFr. *cercler.*]

sesede, *pp.* invested with power, 289T [OFr. *seisir.*]

session, *n.* term or session of court, 289I (D *cessione*) [OFr. *session.*]

setoler, *n.* player on the citole, a stringed instrument, 343 (T pl.) [OFr. *citole.*]

sewede. See SAUDE.

shaftes, *n.pl.* shafts, spears, 501, 503 [OE. *sceaft.*]

shaftmone, *n.* half-foot, 522 [OE. *sceaftmund.*]

shapyn, *pp.* shaped, arranged, 395L [OE. *scapen,* pp.]

share, *pt.* sheared, cut, 522I [OE. *sceran.*]

shaturt. See CHATERED.

shedes, *v.* repels, keeps off, 20, 395L [OE. *scēadan.*]

shedes, *n.pl.* splinters, fragments, 501 [OE. *gescēad.*]

shene, schene, *adj.* bright, fair, 67, 307, 395, etc. [OE. *scēne.*]

shene, *v.* shine, 329 (I *shyne*); shinand, *pr.p.* shining, 522; schane, *pt.* 329T [OE. *scīnan.*]

shent, *pp.* injured, destroyed, 631; ? scribal error, 503L [OE. *scendan.*]

shewe, *v.* look at, see, 588 [OE. *scēawian.*]

shiand, ? for SHINAND, 522D.

shide, *adj.* cut, split, 501 [OE. *scīd.*]

shin. See CHYNNE.

shindre, *v.* shiver (apart), 501, 503 [? Echoic.]

shol, showys. See CHOLLE, SCH-
OWYS.

shrede, v. splinter, cut, 569;
shred, pp. 395 [OE. scrēadian.]

shredis, n.pl. shreds, splinters,
501L; schredus, 395I [OE.
*scrēad, scrēade.]

shrikys, shrillis. See SKRYKES,
SKRILLES.

shulder, n. shoulder, 384, 514T,
522I; shildres, shuldres, pl.
588, 631 [OE. sculdor.]

siked, pt. sighed, 559; sighyd,
560L [OE. sīcan.]

siking, n. sighing, 88 (TL pr. p.)
[From prec.]

sikirly, adv. surely, 289L [OE.
sicorlīce.]

siller, n. canopy, 340 [OFr. si-
leure.]

symballe, n. cymbal, 343 [OE.
cymbal.]

syphoners, n.pl. ? symphoners,
343L [Cf. OFr. symphonier.]

sytis, n.pl. sorrows, cares, 200T
(I site, sg.) [ON. sūt.]

sithe, n. dat. pl. times, 539 [OE.
sīþ.]

skape, v. escape, 472 (I scapette,
pt.) [ONFr. escaper.]

skaþelese, adj. unharmed, 472
[ON. skaþi + -less.]

skorne. See SCORNE.

skryke, v. screech, shriek, 129;
skrikes, 536 (L shrikys), 619
(L shrikis) [ON. skrǣkja.]

skrilles, v. screams, shrieks, 536,
619 (L shrillis) [Cf. G. schril-
len.]

skuwes, n.pl. groves, thickets, 53;
schaghes, 67; skowes, 129 [ON.
skogr, OE. scaga.]

slade, n. valley, 298L [OE. slæd.]

slake, n. hollow, gap. 298 [ON.
slakki.]

on slante, adv.phr. aslant, 617T
[OE. on + ON. sletta.]

slenke, n. stroke, blow, 616 [Cf.
ME. sleng, adj., ON. slengja.]

sleppis, v. slips, 617T [Cf. MLG.
slippen.]

slete, n. sleet, 82T [OE. *slēt, cf.
MLG. slote.]

sliȝte, n. cunning, skill, 616 [ON.
slǣgþ.]

slikes, v. slides, glances, 617 [Cf.
MLG. sliken.]

sliteryng, pr.p. adj. ? from OE.
slidrian, slip, slide, or OE.
slīþan, injure, wound, 82L.

smartly, adv. quickly, 210L
[From next + -ly.]

smert, adj. quick, 544 [OE.
smeart.]

smyther, ? for SWITHELY, 544I.

snaypely, adv. sharply, severely,
82I [ON. sneypiliga.]

snayppede, pt. cut, nipped, 82T
[ON. sneypa.]

snartly, adv. sharply, severely, 82
[ON. snart, adj.]

snawe, n. snow, 82 [OE. snāwe.]

snelle, adv. keenly, 82T [OE.
snell, snellīce.]

snelles, v. ? for SNELLE, 82D.

sneterand, adj. falling, 82; see
OED snite, sb.,² a spit or sprin-
kling of rain [Unknown.]

socoured, pp. relieved, 220 [OFr.
socorre.]

soiournis, v. sojourns, stays, 693L
[OFr. sojorner.]

solas, n. comfort, joy, 65, 66
[OFr. solas.]

solempne, adj. solemn, 205 [OFr.
solempne.]

some-wile, *adv.* at one time, formerly, 144 (L *sumtyme*) [OE. *sum + hwīl.*]

sonde, *adj.* sound, healthy, 699 [OE. *gesund.*]

sondes, *n.pl.* sands, 268 [OE. *sand.*]

soppes de mayne, *n.pl.* pieces of bread of fine quality, dipped in water or wine, 478 [OE. *sopp,* OFr. *pain demeine.*]

souerayne, *n.* king, sovereign, 67, 347; **soueran,** 358I; **soueraynest,** *superl.adj.* 358 [OFr. *soverain.*]

sowmus, *n.pl.* sums, amounts, 147I [OFr. *somme.*]

speling, *n.* sparing, 255 [OE. *spelian.*]

spyre, *v.* ask, inquire, 256TL [OE. *spyrian.*]

sprete, *n.* spirit, ghost, 101, 255; **spirette,** 135T [OFr. *esperit(e),* AFr. *spirit.*]

spute, *v.* dispute, discuss, 256 [OFr. *desputer.*]

squappes. See SWAPPED.

squeturly, squytherly, ? for SWITHELY, 55I, 540I.

squyppand, *adj.* sweeping, flowing, 55I [Cf. ON. *svipa.*]

squoes. See SWOGHES.

stalket, *pt.* walked, stalked, 644I [OE. **stealcian.*]

stalwurthe, *adj.* stalwart, 713I [OE. *stælwierþe.*]

stanseld, *pt.* ornamented, with bright colors or pieces of precious metal, 392I [OFr. *estanceler.*]

stapeles, *n.pl.* fastenings, 591 [OE. *stapol.*]

stargand, ? for STARTAND, 511D.

startis, *v.* starts, jumps, 532I, 580; **stert,** *pt.* 545; **startand,** *pr.p.adj.* 511I (L *stertelyng*) [OE. *styrtan, *steortian.*]

stede, *n.* stead, service, use, 552 [OE. *stede.*]

stedyt, *pt.* stayed, stopped, 109I (perhaps an error for *stottyde,* T) [OE. *stede,* n., cf. ON. *steþja.*]

stekillede, ? for STRENKILLEDE, 392T; perhaps a variant of *OED* steek, v.², fix, fasten.

steled, *pp.* overlayed, pointed, or edged with steel, 579; **stelun,** *pp.adj.* 602I [OE. *stȳle,* n.]

stemered, *pt.* staggered, stumbled, 109 [OE. *stamerian.*]

stent, *pt.* stopped, 579 [OE. *styntan.*]

stere, *v.* move, displace, 266T (I *stir*) [OE. *styrian.*]

sternes, *n.pl.* stars, 392 [ON. *stjarna.*]

stert, *n.* moment, 259 [OE. *styrtan, *steortian,* v.]

stid, *n.* place, 316, 407I, 541I, 644I [OE. *stede.*]

stif(f), *adj.* strong, stout, 391L, 591L, 713L [OE. *stīf.*]

stifly, *adv.* strongly, violently, 534I [Prec. + *-ly.*]

stir. See STERE.

stiropes, sterop(pe)s, *n.pl.* stirrups, 490I, 533, 534, 545 [OE. *stigrāp.*]

stiþe, *adj.* strong, 591; **stithest,** *superl.* 490I [OE. *stīþ.*]

stondardes, *n.pl.* tall candlesticks, 451 [OFr. *estandard.*]

stonde, *n.* time, occasion, 581, 700; **stound(e),** 602I, 657L [OE. *stund.*]

stonyes, v. is astounded, 407T; stonayde, stonded, pt. 109, 602; stonayed, pp. 581 [Cf. OFr. estoner.]

store, adj. brave, stout, 713 [ON. stŏrr, OE. stŏr.]

stottyde, pt. stopped, faltered, 109T [Cf. OFr. estoutoier, estoteier.]

stound(e). See STONDE.

stoure, n. fight, battle, 552 [AFr. estur.]

stoutely, adv. bravely, strongly, 534 [OFr. estout.]

on stray, adv.phr. astray, about, 392T, 511, 532 [OFr. estraie.]

strange, adj. strong, 55T [OE. strang.]

strenkel, v. scatter, 590; strencult, strynkelyd, pp. adj. 590I, 392L [Obscure.]

strewe, v. scatter, 590; strauen, pp. 590I [OE. strewian.]

stry, v. destroy, 266 [Aphetic from OFr. destruire.]

striȝte, adv. straight, directly, immediately, 533, 591; streyte, 534, 541 [OE. streccan.]

studiest, pr.2sg. stare, muse, 407L [OFr. estudier.]

stuf, n. material, 579 [OFr. estoffe.]

stuffed, pp. armed, 391 [OFr. estoffer.]

sturne, stourne, adj. as sb. strong, brave man, 391, 407, 532, etc.; sterne, adj. 713; steryne, 391T [OE. styrne.]

suget, n. subject, 306 (I subiecte) [OFr. suget.]

suppriset, pp. surprised, overcome, 306 [OFr. suprise.]

surgenes, n.pl. surgeons, 693 [AFr. surgien.]

suwene, pr.pl. pursue, follow, 67 [AFr. suer, OFr. sivre.]

swayne, n. attendant, youth, 398T [ON. sveinn.]

swange, n. flank or groin, 617 [ON. svangi.]

swap, n. cut, stroke, 540 [From next.]

swapped, pt. cut, struck, 514, 617; swapt, 518 (I squappes, pr.) [Probably echoic.]

swathel, n. ? for SWITHELY, 540D; Madden glosses "strong man" with no etymology.

sweyvis, v. sounds, 55L [OE. swēgan.]

swykes, v. deceives, cheats, 540 [OE. swīcan.]

swyre, n. neck, 514 [OE. swīra.]

swithely, adv. intensely, violently, 55, 540, 544L; on the swithe, ?, 514L [OE. swīþlīce.]

swoghes, v. rushes down noisily, 55T (I squoes) [OE. swōgan.]

tablet flure, n. small table or tablet decorated with fleurs-de-lis, 401 [OFr. tablete, floure.]

tade, n. toad, 115T; todes, pl. 121 [OE. tāde.]

taȝt, tauȝte. See TECHE.

tasses, n.pl. a series of plates forming a kilt of armor to protect the thighs, 355; T tasee is an error since the word is always pl. [OFr. tasse.]

teche, v. guide, direct, 34; tauȝte, pt. 35; taghte, 605; taȝt, 656T [OE. tǣcan.]

teldede, pp. ? covered, 386T; ?

an extension of meaning of OE. *teldian,* to pitch a tent.

tend, *v.* pay attention to, 165L [OFr. *atendre.*]

tene, *n.* anger, 282, 512, 605 [OE. *tēona.*]

teneful, *adj.* angry, painful, 605 [OE. *tēonful.*]

tent, *n.* care, heed, 165D, 483L [OFr. *atente.*]

tere, *adj.* hard, tedious, 121; **tore,** 190 (L *tery*) [OE., ON. *tor-;* forms with *e* unexplained.]

thare, *v.* need, 170 [OE. *þearf,* pr. 3 sg. of *þurfan.*]

þike-folde, *adv.* in great numbers, 46 [OE. *þicce* + *-feald.*]

þonked, *pt.* thankcd, 539 [OE. *þoncian.*]

thritty, *adj.* thirty, 218 (L *xxx*) [OE. *þrītig.*]

throli, *adv.* earnestly, 192I [ON. *þraligr.*]

tide, *n.* time, 328I, 460I, 605I [OE. *tīd.*]

tiȝte, *pp.* set, fastened, 355 [Unknown.]

tiȝte, *adv.* ? for *tit,* "quickly," from ON. *títt,* 165D.

tymber, *v.* prepare, devise, 282 (I *tymburt,* pp.) [OE. *timbrian.*]

tynte, *pp.* lost, 282I [ON. *tȳna.*]

tyre, *n.* glory, 151L [OE. *tīr.*]

typing, *n.* message, news, 292; **tidinges,** *pl.* 314 [ON. *tīþendi.*]

todes. See TADE.

tome, *n.* leisure, space, 314 [ON. *tōm.*]

tonge, *n.* tongue, 121, 190 [OE. *tunge.*]

topas, *n.* topaz, 355 [OFr. *topace.*]

tore. See TERE.

tortys, *n.pl.* large candles, 451L [OFr. *tortis.*]

touche, *n.* blow, stroke, 605 [OFr. *touche.*]

toures, *n.pl.* towers, 149 [OFr. *tor, tur.*]

townes, *n.pl.* towns, manors, 149 [OE. *tūn.*]

tracyd, *pp.* ornamented, 354L, 510L [OFr. *tracier.*]

trayfoles, *n.pl.* trefoils, 510T [OFr. *trifoil.*]

trayfoled. See TRIFELED.

tranes, *n.pl.* devices, knots (Madden), 510 [? OFr. *train.*]

tranest, *pp.* ? for TRAUERST, or TRANES, 354I, 510I.

trapped, *pp.adj.* adorned with trappings, 383, 386 [Cf. OE. *betræppan.*]

tras, *n.* track, footsteps, 63, 610 [OFr. *trace.*]

trauayled, *pp.adj.* fatigued, worked, 656 (I *traueling*) [OFr. *travailler.*]

trauerste, *pp.* crossed, 354T; **travercid,** 510L [OFr. *traverser.*]

trentales, *n.pl.* series of thirty Masses, 218 [MedL. *trentale.*]

tresone, *n.* treason, 291 [AFr. *tresun.*]

tresour, *n.* treasure, 149, 664T [OFr. *tresor.*]

in trete, *adv.phr.* in a row, series, 354T [OFr. *trait.*]

trewloues, *n.pl.* true-love knots, 354T; **true-loves,** 510 [OE. *trēowlufu.*]

trifeled, *pp.* ornamented with trefoils, 510 (T *trayfolede*); **trofelyte,** 354T [OFr. *trifoil.*]

trily, ? for TRULY, or TRISE, 386L.

trise, *n*. "Tars?" (Robson), 386I.
tristily, *adv*. sorrowfully, 282L [OFr. *triste* + *-ly*.]
tristres, *n.pl*. hunting-stations, 34, 35; triste, *sg*. 37T; tristre-tre, 37L [OFr. *tristre*.]
troches, *n.pl*. ? for TORCHES, 451I.
trofelyte. See TRIFELED.
trowe, *v*. believe, trust in, 35, 207, 282L (I *troue*) [OE. *trūwian, trēowan, trēowian*.]
trowlt, *pp*. "ornamented with knots" (Robson), 354I, 510I.
true-loves. See TREWLOUES.
turment, *n*. torment, 190, 191; *pl*. 2L [OFr. *tourment*.]
turnaying, *n*. tourneying, 512 [OFr. *to(u)rneier*.]
turne, *v*. reverse course, return, 284, 292 [OE. *turnian*.]

venge, *v*. avenge, vindicate, 500 [OFr. *venger*.]
ventalle, *n*. the movable part of a helmet in front of the mouth, 408; ventaile, 583 [OFr. *ventaille*.]
veres, *n.pl*. cups, 457 [OFr. *verre*.]
vernage, *n*. a white wine, 457 [OFr. *vernage*.]
vesage, *n*. face, visage, 408T [AFr. *visage*.]
viser, *n*. visor, 408 [AFr. *viser*.]
vmbeclipped, *pp*. surrounded, 119 [OE. *ymbe* + *clyppan*.]
vmbyclede, *pp*. wrapped up, 119T [OE. *ymbe* + *clǣþan*.]
vmbyclosut, *pp*. enclosed, 106I, 119I [OE. *ymbe* + OFr. *close*, pp.]

vnclere, *adj*. dark, dim, 119 [*un-* + OFr. *cler*.]
vnclosed, *pt*. opened up, 329 [*un-* + OFr. *close*, pp.]
vncomly, *adv*. unpleasantly, uglily, 106 [*un-* + OE. *cȳmlīc*.]
vncurtays, *adj*. discourteous, 97 [*un-* + OFr. *curteis*.]
vndre, *n*. third hour, late morning, 72; vnder, 219 [OE. *undern*.]
vnfayne, *adj*. reluctant, sorry, 79 [OE. *unfægen*.]
vngayne, *adj*. not plain or direct, 85L [*un-* + ON. *gegn*.]
vnhendely, *adv*. rudely, discourteously, 187 [*un-* + OE. *gehende* + *-ly*.]
vnhides, *v*. clears, reveals, 328 [*un-* + OE. *hȳdan*.]
vn hiȝte, ? for ON HIȝTE, 448I.
vnnethe, *adv*. hardly, 657 (T *unnethes*) [OE. *unēaþe*.]
vnwylles, *n*. displeasure, unwillingness, 424, 425I [OE. *unwilla*.]

waast, *n*. waist, 578 [? OE. **wǣst*.]
wayes. See WEY.
wayment, *pt*. wailed, lamented, 107 [OFr. *waimenter*.]
waymynges, *n.pl*. ? for *waymentynges*, lamentations, 87D [From prec.]
waynes at, *v*. rushes at, makes for, 535, 614 [ON. *vegna*.]
waithe, *n*. hunting, 434 [ON. *veiþr*, OE. *wāþ*.]
wayued (up), *pt*. lifted, opened, 408 [ON. *veifa*.]
wayvid, *pt*. ? for WAYLID, 107L.

wayvis at, *v.* ? for WAYNIS AT, 535L.

wale, *v.* choose, select, 341T [ON. *val,* n.]

wan. See WYNE.

wandrethe, *n.* sorrow, misery, 216T [ON. *vandrǣþi.*]

wane. See WONE.

wantis, *v.* lacks, needs, 319L, 576L; **wanted,** *pt.* 584, **wontut,** 576I [ON. *vanta.*]

warde, *n.* guard, keeping, 487 [OE. *weard.*]

warly, *adv.* warily, 486I [OE. *wærlīce.*]

warry, *v.* curse, 423; **waried,** *pt.* 107; **waret,** *pp.adj.* cursed, 135I [OE. *wiergan.*]

wathely. See WOþELY.

wax. See WEX.

wede, *n.* clothing, garment, armor, 9, 22T, 347, 365D, 658T [OE. *wǣd.*]

wede, *v.* become angry, 558 [OE. *wēdan.*]

weder, *n.* weather, 328, 334 (I, *wederinges,* L pl.) [OE. *weder.*]

wee, *n.* man, knight, 365I, 405, 639; **wy,** 365T; **wees,** *pl.* 692; **wise,** 334; **weys,** 575 [OE. *wiga.*]

wey, *n.* way, road, 315; **wayes,** *pl.* 102T, 136; means, manner, 248; *pl.* 102 [OE. *weg.*]

welde, *v.* rule over, possess, 341T, 365T, 424, 425; control, use, 575; **wolde,** *pt.* 666T [OE. *wealdan, wældan.*]

wele, *n.* wealth, riches, 264I, 341 [OE. *wela.*]

welkene, *n.* sky, heavens, 328 [OE. *wolcen.*]

welle, *n.* spring, 28 [OE. *wella.*]

welle, *v.* well, boil, 186I, 316T [OE. *wellan.*]

welthe, *n.* wealth, riches, 215, 264T, 341I, 425 [OE. *wela, wel,* + *-th.*]

wende, *v.* go, walk, 315T, 561L; **went,** *pt. and pp.* 9, 337, 434, etc. [OE. *wendan.*]

wene, *v.* think, expect, intend, 303, 561, 616I, etc.; **wende,** *pt.* 639, **went,** 584L [OE. *wēnan.*]

went. See WANTIS, WENDE, WENE.

wepenes, *n.pl.* weapons, 575 [OE. *wǣpen.*]

wepus, *v.* weeps, 560; **wepput(te),** *pt.* 559I, 560I [OE. *wēpan.*]

wery, *adj.* weary, 56L, 630 [OE. *wērig.*]

werray, *pr.pl.* wage war on, 56 [OFr. *werreier.*]

werre, *n.* war, fight, 56I, 264, 278, 421; **were,** 427, 502 [ONFr. *werre.*]

wete, *adj.* wet, 87, 102T [OE. *wǣt.*]

wete, *v.* know, learn, 102; **wite,** 197; **wetene,** 237, 246; *pr. 2 sg.* **wost,** 248; *pr. 3sg.* **wote,** 547; *pt. 1sg.* **wotte,** 189I; *pt. 3sg.* **wist,** 206; *imp.* **wete,** 576I [OE. *witan.*]

weting, *n.* knowledge, opinion, 238 [From prec.]

wex, *pt.* waxed, grew, became, 75, 329I, 658; **wax,** 558; **wexun,** 570I [OE. *weaxan.*]

whele, *n.* wheel, 266 [OE. *hwēol.*]

whele-wryghte, *n.* wheelwright, Fortune, 271T [Prec. + OE. *wriht.*]

wheþene, *adv.* whence, 363; qwethun, quethun, 405I, 406I [ON. *hvaþan.*]

wy. See WEE.

wid, *adj.* wide, 328L [OE. *wīd.*]

wyde, *adv.* widely, 9L [OE. *wīde.*]

wight, *adj.* brave, 467L, 560, 575, etc. [ON. *vīgt.*]

wighte, *n.* person, man, 189, 271, 365, etc. [OE. *wiht.*]

wightly, *adv.* bravely, 625L, 703L [ON. *vīgt* + -*ly.*]

wightnesse, *n.* bravery, valor, 264 [ON. *vīgt* + -*nesse.*]

wilde, *n.pl.* wild animals, 56 [OE. **wīld, wildru.*]

wile, *n.* deceit, trick, 421, 425L [? Scand. **wihl-.*]

wilele, *adv.* craftily, 575 [Prec. + -*ly.*]

wyndes, *n.pl.* winds, 328 [OE. *wind.*]

wyne, *v.* win, gain, obtain, 264, 427; wan, *pt.* 421L; won(n)ene, *pp.* 274, 421 [OE. *winnan, wann, (ge)-wunnen.*]

wyne, *n.* wine, 341 [OE. *wīn.*]

wirchippe. See WORSHIPPE.

wirde, *n.* fate, 196I [OE. *wyrd.*]

wirkis. See WORCHE.

wise, *n.* way, manner, 163L [OE. *wīse.*]

wisly, *adv.* wisely, cunningly, prudently, 486, 575L, 625; wisely, 703 [OE. *wīslīce.*]

wysse, *v.* guide, show, direct, 248; wys, 135I [OE. *wissian.*]

wist, wite. See WETE.

wiþ-drow. See DRAWES.

withe þī, *conj.* provided that, 673, 683I [OE. *wiþ þȳ.*]

witis, *v.* goes, dies, 215 [OE. *wītan.*]

witnesse, *n.* testimony, 170T, 273; wittenesse, 165I [OE. *witnes.*]

wlonkes, *n.pl.* nobles, 9I, 87I [OE. *wlonc,* adj.]

wlonkest, *superl. adj.* noblest, most splendid, 9, 347, 696 [OE. *wlonc.*]

wo, *n.* woe, misery, 56, 195, 316, etc.; ways, ? for WA IS, 196I; wofuller, *comp.* 189 [OE. *wā.*]

wode, *adj.* mad, insane, 535 [OE. *wōd.*]

wolde, *n.* possession, control, 666 [OE. *gewāld,* cf. *welde.*]

wone, *n.* dwelling, 159; wane, 316T [Cf. ON. *vān.*]

wonges, *n.pl.* cheeks, 87L [OE. *wang.*]

wonyd, *pt.* lamented, 107L [OE. *wānian.*]

wonyng, *adj.* dwelling, 316; wunnyng, 186I [OE. *wunung.*]

wonnene. See WYNE.

wonte, *pp.adj.* accustomed, 400, 402T [OE. *gewunod.*]

wontut. See WANTIS.

worche, *pr.pl.* work, do, create, cause, 216 (T *wirkis*); worchene, 56 (I *wurchis*), 217 (T *wirkis,* L *work*); wroughte, wroght(e), wroȝte, *pp.* 56L, 189, 217I [OE. *wyrcan, geworht.*]

worþely, *adj.* worthy, noble, rich, 361, 453, 487, etc.; worþily, 159L; always wurliche or wurlok in I; worthilieste, *superl.* 365T [OE. *weorþlic.*]

wost, wote. See WETE.

woþely, *adv.* severely, danger-
ously, 303 (T *wathely*), 692
[ON. *vāþaliga.*]
wrake, *n.* destruction, pain, 216,
217 [OE. *wracu.*]
wrange, *adj.* unjust, 421 [OE.
wrang.]
wrathede, *pt.* angered, 238 (I
wrathes, L *wratthiþ*) [OE.
wrǣþþu, n.]
wrecche, *n.* wretch, miserable
person, 135L [OE. *wrecca.*]

wrechut, *adj.* wretched, miserable, 216I [Prec. + *-ed.*]
wrothely, *adv.* angrily, cruelly,
303L, 692L [OE. *wraþlīce.*]
wroughte, wroght, wroȝte. See
WORCHE.
wunnyng. See WONYNG.
wurchis. See WORCHE.
wurliche, wurlok. See WORþELY.

yete, *n.* gate, 179 (T *ȝate*) [OE.
geat.]

INDEX OF PROPER NAMES